Temple *of* Presence

Temple *of* Presence

The Christological Fulfillment of Ezekiel 40–48
in Revelation 21:1—22:5

Andrea L. Robinson

WIPF *&* STOCK · Eugene, Oregon

TEMPLE OF PRESENCE
The Christological Fulfillment of Ezekiel 40–48 in Revelation 21:1—22:5

Wipf & Stock
An Imprint of Wipf and Stock Publishers
199 W. 8th Ave., Suite 3
Eugene, OR 97401

www.wipfandstock.com

PAPERBACK ISBN: 978-1-5326-6441-0
HARDCOVER ISBN: 978-1-5326-6442-7
EBOOK ISBN: 978-1-5326-6443-4

Manufactured in the U.S.A.   01/10/19

For Wesley, Asher, and Abel

Contents

List of Figures

Acknowledgments

THE CURRENT MONOGRAPH IS a slightly revised form of my PhD dissertation, which was completed at New Orleans Baptist Theological Seminary in 2018. I give effusive thanks to the excellent faculty and staff of NOBTS. In particular, Drs. Dennis Cole, Archie England, Craig Price, Jim Parker, and Rex Butler have overseen my academic development for many years. Your leadership and friendship have helped shape the course of my life. Your example of godly leadership forever will impact the way I minister to others. To my doctoral advisor, Dr. Harold Mosley, your guidance throughout my PhD journey was invaluable. To Dr. Gerald Stevens, your input on my dissertation, from prospectus to finished product to monograph, has made my work immensely better. You never fail to challenge me, and I hope the finished product has made you proud. Thank you for your continuing support and guidance. I am blessed to call you a colleague and friend. To Dr. Gary Manning, your work helped inspire my own, and although not from NOBTS, I am honored that you were willing to serve as a reader. To my fellow Biblical Interpretation cohorts, the quality of your scholarship has challenged me and made me a better scholar. Our friendship continues to bring me joy, and I value each of you.

To Dr. Jeff Griffin and the staff of the John T. Christian Library, thank you for mailing me innumerable books and filling all my special requests without hesitation. I will remember fondly your care and concern to remind me to eat, drink, and sleep in the midst of my marathon library days. I also want to express appreciation to Mrs. Linda Jackson and the staff of Providence House. Your friendly faces made my trips away from home a little less difficult. I will miss my home away from home.

Without the support of beloved family and friends, my research and writing would never have been completed. To my longtime workout partners Doug Sittason and Tom and Lisa Buckle, you always make me laugh and relax for a little while. To my sweet yogis: Carol, Andrea, Sue, Alison, Kathryn, Patti, Sharon, Jan, and Mary Lynn, our morning yoga has kept me sane. Thank you to my church family at Building Church in Madison, Alabama. Your prayers have been a constant source of strength. I want to express gratitude especially to my pastors, Spencer and Ellen Beach, for providing me with the opportunity to pursue my pastoral calling while continuing to engage in academic pursuits.

To my family, you will never know how much I love and appreciate you all. My Pops's constant encouragement was what led me to pursue a PhD. He taught me to work hard and never accept anything less than excellence, but he also taught me that fishing is an important part of life. My Gram taught me to love unconditionally and was my first best friend. I wish you were both here to celebrate this accomplishment with me. I look forward to seeing you again. To my parents, Gary and Debra Kulaw, your adventurous spirit is an inspiration to me. Mama, you taught me strength and perseverance, and that when life brings trials, God will always walk by our side. Gary, I cannot imagine having a better father. I know that God placed you in our lives. To my sisters, Lyndsey and Ginger, you are both strong, accomplished, and beautiful women. Your love and friendship are an encouragement to me. To my adorable nephew and niece, Dylan and Lilly, I look forward to spending more time with you now that I am finished with school! To my aunt and uncle, Ben and Janie Harter, and all my Kentucky family, the trips to visit you are some of the best memories of my childhood. I still love visiting you every summer, and now I will not have to study by the pool (but probably I will anyway)!

Words cannot express the love and appreciation I hold for my husband, Wesley. Even in moments when I doubted my own calling, you never did. Thank you for your encouragement, as well as all the practical ways that you helped me through this process. Even after twenty years together, I am more in love with you than ever. To my two brilliant boys, Asher and Abel, you will never know how much you mean to me. Like your Daddy, you have been a source of endless encouragement. You have sacrificed many of your own wishes so that I could pursue my calling. I hope my accomplishment will inspire you to follow your own dreams. I know God has amazing plans for each of you.

Finally, and most importantly, I want to thank my Lord Jesus. You are the reason I live and breathe. I hope that in some small way my life and ministry will bring honor to you.

Abbreviations

AB Anchor Bible

ABD *The Anchor Bible Dictionary*. 6 vols. Edited by David Noel Freedman. New York: Doubleday, 1992.

ABR Australian Biblical Review

ACNT Augsburg Commentary on the New Testament

AGJU Arbeiten zur Geschichte des antiken Judentums und des Urchristentums

AnBib Analecta Biblica

ANET Ancient Near Eastern Texts Relating to the Old Testament. 3rd ed. Edited by James B. Pritchard. Princeton: Princeton University Press, 1969.

AOAT Alter Orient und Altes Testament

ASTI Annual of the Swedish Theological Institute

AUSS Andrews University Seminary Studies

AUSDDS Andrews University Seminary Doctoral Dissertation Series

BAC Biblioteca de autores cristianos

BASOR Bulletin of the American Schools of Oriental Research

BBR Bulletin for Biblical Research

BDB Brown, Francis, et al. *Enhanced Brown-Driver-Briggs Hebrew and English Lexicon*. Oxford: Clarendon, 1977.

BECNT Baker Exegetical Commentary on the New Testament

BETL Bibliotheca Ephemeridum Theologicarum Lovaniensium

BFCT Beiträge zur Förderung christlicher Theologie

BHT Beiträge zur historischen Theologie

Bib Biblica

BibOr Biblica et Orientalia

BibS(F) Biblische Studien (Freiburg, 1895–)

BJS Brown Judaic Studies

BR Biblical Research

BRS Biblical Resource Series

BSac Bibliotheca Sacra

CBC Cambridge Bible Commentary

CBQ Catholic Biblical Quarterly

CBQMS Catholic Biblical Quarterly Monograph Series

CBR Currents in Biblical Research

CEJL Commentaries on Early Jewish Literature

CRINT Compendia Rerum Iudaicarum ad Novum Testamentum

CTJ Calvin Theological Journal

CTR Criswell Theological Review

DBL Swanson, James. *Dictionary of Biblical Languages with Semantic Domains: Hebrew (Old Testament).* Oak Harbor, WA: Logos Research Systems, 1997.

DJD Discoveries in the Judean Desert

DSD Dead Sea Discoveries

ED Euntes Docete

EJL Early Judaism and Its Literature

EncJud Encyclopedia Judaica. Edited by Fred Skolnik and Michael Berenbaum. 2nd ed. 22 vols. Detroit: Macmillan Reference USA, 2007.

ETL Ephemerides Theologicae Lovanienses

EvQ Evangelical Quarterly

ExpTim Expository Times

FBBS Facet Books, Biblical Series

FOTL Forms of the Old Testament Literature

FT First Things

GKC Gesenius, Wilhelm. *Gesenius' Hebrew Grammar*. Edited by Emil Kautzsch. Translated by A. E. Cowley. Mineola, NY: Dover, 2006.

HALOT Koehler, Ludwig, et al. *The Hebrew and Aramaic Lexicon of the Old Testament*. 4 vols. Leiden: Brill, 1994–2000.

HAT Handbuch zum Alten Testament

HDR Harvard Dissertations in Religion

HNT Handbuch zum Neuen Testament

HSM Harvard Semitic Monographs

HSS Harvard Semitic Studies

HTR Harvard Theological Review

HUCA Hebrew Union College Annual

IBC Interpretation: A Bible Commentary for Teaching and Preaching

IBS Irish Biblical Studies

ICC International Critical Commentary

IDB The Interpreter's Dictionary of the Bible. 4 Vols. Edited by George Arthur Buttrick. Nashville, Abingdon, 1962.

IEJ Israel Exploration Journal

Int Interpretation

IRT Issues in Religion and Theology

JAOS Journal of the American Oriental Society

JBL Journal of Biblical Literature

JE The Jewish Encyclopedia. 12 vols. Edited by Isidore Singer. New York: Funk & Wagnalls, 1925.

JETS Journal of the Evangelical Theological Society

JJS Journal of Jewish Studies

JNES Journal of Near Eastern Studies

JQR Jewish Quarterly Review

JSJ Journal for the Study of Judaism in the Persian, Hellenistic, and Roman Periods

JSJSupp Supplements to the Journal for the Study of Judaism

JSNT Journal for the Study of the New Testament

JSNTSupp Journal for the Study of the New Testament Supplement Series

JSOT Journal for the Study of the Old Testament

JSOTSupp Journal for the Study of the Old Testament Supplement Series

JSP Journal for the Study of the Pseudepigrapha

JSPSupp Journal for the Study of the Pseudepigrapha Supplement Series

JTAK Journal of Theta Alpha Kappa

JTS Journal of Theological Studies

LCL Loeb Classical Library

LHBOTS The Library of Hebrew Bible/Old Testament Studies

L&N Louw, Johannes P., and Eugene Albert Nida. *Greek-English Lexicon of the New Testament: Based on Semantic Domains.* New York: United Bible Societies, 1996.

LNTS The Library of New Testament Studies

LSJ Henry George Liddell, et al. *A Greek-English Lexicon.* 9th ed. Oxford: Clarendon, 1996.

MGWJ Monatsschrift für Geschichte und Wissenschaft des Judentums

MSJ The Master's Seminary Journal

MT Masoretic Text

NAC New American Commentary

Neot Neotestamentica

NICOT New International Commentary on the Old Testament

NIGTC New International Greek Testament Commentary

NovT Novum Testamentum

NTM New Testament Message

NTS New Testament Studies

NTT New Testament Theology

OJRS Ohio Journal of Religious Studies

OTM Old Testament Message

OTPA The Old Testament Pseudepigrapha: Apocalyptic Literature and Testaments. Edited by James H. Charlesworth. Peabody, MA: Hendrickson, 2009.

OTPE The Old Testament Pseudepigrapha: Expansions of the "Old Testament" and Legends, Wisdom and Philosophical Literature, Prayers, Psalms, and Odes, Fragments of Lost Judeo-Hellenistic Works. Edited by James H. Charlesworth. Garden City, NY: Doubleday, 1985.

PRSt Perspectives in Religious Studies

PVTG Pseudepigrapha Veteris Testamenti Graece

RelSRev Religious Studies Review

RevExp Review and Expositor

RivB Rivista biblica italiana

RQ Revue de Qumran

RSMS Religious Studies Monograph Series

SBA Studies in Biblical Archaeology

SBLDS Society of Biblical Literature Dissertation Series

SBLMS Society of Biblical Literature Monograph Series

SBLSP Society of Biblical Literature Seminar Papers

SBT Studies in Biblical Theology

SCS Septuagint and Cognate Studies

SESB Stuttgart Electronic Study Bible

SJLA Studies in Judaism in Late Antiquity

SNT Studien zum Neuen Testament

SNTSMS Society for New Testament Studies Monograph Series

StBibLit Studies in Biblical Literature

STDJ Studies on the Texts on the Desert of Judah

StPB Studia Post-biblica

SVTP Studia in Veteris Testamenti Pseudepigraphica

TDNT Theological Dictionary of the New Testament. 10 vols. Edited by Gerhard Kittel and Gerhard Friedrich. Translated by Geoffrey W. Bromiley. Grand Rapids: Eerdmans, 1964–76.

TGST Tesi Gregoriana, Serie Teologia

THNTC Two Horizons New Testament Commentary

TJ Trinity Journal

TNTC Tyndale New Testament Commentaries

TynBul Tyndale Bulletin

VT Vetus Testamentum

WBC Word Biblical Commentary

WPS Westminster Pelican Commentaries

WS World Spirituality

WTJ Westminster Theological Journal

WUNT Wissenschaftliche Untersuchungen zum Neuen Testament

ZAW Zeitschrift für die alttestamentliche Wissenschaft

ZNW Zeitschrift für die neutestamentliche Wissenschaft und die Kunde der älteren Kirche

Scripture

Old Testament

Gen Genesis

Exod Exodus

Lev Leviticus

Num Numbers

Deut Deuteronomy

Josh Joshua

1–2 Sam 1–2 Samuel

1–2 Kgs 1–2 Kings

1–2 Chr 1–2 Chronicles

Neh Nehemiah

Ps/Pss Psalms

Song Song of Songs

Isa Isaiah

Jer Jeremiah

Lam Lamentations

Ezek Ezekiel

Dan Daniel

Hos Hosea

Obad Obadiah

Mic Micah

Nah Nahum

Hab Habakkuk

Zeph Zephaniah

Hag Haggai

Zech Zechariah

New Testament

Matt Matthew

1–2 Cor 1–2 Corinthians

Gal Galatians

Eph Ephesians

Heb Hebrews

1–2 Pet 1–2 Peter

Rev Revelation

Apocrypha

Tob Tobit

Jdt Judith

Wis Wisdom of Solomon

Sir Sirach

Bar Baruch

1–2 Macc 1–2 Maccabees

Pseudepigrapha

Apoc. Ab. Apocalypse of Abraham

2 Bar. 2 Baruch

3 Bar. 3 Baruch

1 En. 1 Enoch

2 En. 2 Enoch

3 En. 3 Enoch

Jub. Jubilees

LAB Pseudo-Philo

Let. Aris. Letter of Aristeas

Sib. Or. Sibylline Oracles

T. Benj. Testament of Benjamin

T. Dan Testament of Dan

T. Jud. Testament of Judah

T. Levi Testament of Levi

T. Mos. Testament of Moses

Josephus

Ag. Ap. Against Apion

Ant. Jewish Antiquities

J.W. Jewish War

Dead Sea Scrolls

1QH Thanksgiving Hymns

1QM War Scroll

1QS The Community Rule

1QSa The Rule of the Congregation

4QD Damascus Document

4QFlor 4QFlorilegium

4QNJ Description of the New Jerusalem

4QpIsa The Isaiah Pesher

4QShirShabb Songs of the Sabbath Sacrifice

11QT The Temple Scroll

Mishnah and Talmud

b. Babylonian Talmud

Hag. Hagigah

m. Mishnah

Menah. Menahot

Mid. Middoth

Šabb Shabbat

1.

Introduction

PRIOR TO CHRIST, THE Jerusalem Temple was the primary means by which God fulfilled his covenant promise to dwell in the midst of his people.[1] When the First Temple was destroyed, "Both the power of Israel's God and the certainty of Israel's election were called into question."[2] By way of response, the prophets envisioned a new and better temple that could not be destroyed by human means. The inception of an eschatological temple was expected to usher in an age of peace and prosperity. James McCaffrey asserted, "the blessings of salvation reserved for the eschatological age are also inseparably linked with the Jerusalem Temple as the gathering-place of the nations."[3]

However, New Testament (NT) believers view Christ as the fulfillment God's Old Testament (OT) soteriological promises. John[4] himself may have employed a "redemptive-historical" approach as he communicated his eschatological outlook.[5] Throughout the course of the Apocalypse, John reinterpreted OT texts in the light of Christ and his mission. By the time readers reach the latter chapters of Revelation, they are well

---

1. Exod 25:8; 29:45; Lev 26:11–12 (tabernacle); Ezek 37:26–28.

2. Kirschner, "Apocalyptic and Rabbinic Responses," 27. Cf. Zimmer, "Temple of God," 41–46.

3. McCaffrey, *House with Many Rooms*, 60. Cf. Zimmer, "Temple of God," 42.

4. John is used in reference to the authorial designation of Rev 1:4, not as an assertion of apostolic authorship.

5. Beale, *Revelation*, 562, 1091.

prepared to read John's message in close interaction with OT passages that have been anticipated throughout.[6]

In Revelation 21–22, John offered a striking portrayal of a new Jerusalem without a temple, in which he seemed to reference the final chapters of Ezekiel. The puzzling issue for interpreters is why John chose to utilize Ezekiel's *temple* vision if he desired to dispense with the temple. David Mathewson proposed, "by alluding to Ezekiel's vision of a restored temple, John envisions the entire city as the locus of divine glory as the fulfillment of the new covenant promise of God dwelling with his people (cf. Rev 21.3; Ezek 37.26–27)."[7] Further, the new temple of Jesus' body becomes the place where humanity can approach God's presence as Jesus bridges the chasm between heaven and earth.[8]

The purpose of the current research is to evaluate the relationship between Ezekiel's temple (Ezek 40–48) and John's vision of a new heaven and earth (Rev 21:1—22:5). Structural and lexical parallels between the two passages seem to indicate that some type of connection exists. Is Ezekiel's temple consummated in John's eschatological city? If so, why is the city lacking the central feature of Ezekiel's vision—a temple? The guiding thesis is that John presents Jesus Christ as the fulfillment of Ezekiel's temple vision.

Methodology

The following research will consist of a systematic examination of intertextual parallels between Ezekiel 40–48 and Revelation 21:1—22:5. First, an overview of scholarly perspectives on Ezekiel's temple vision will be presented in order to determine the timeless theological core of the vision. Second, a diachronic examination of Second Temple period literature will be performed to determine the tenor of thought in regard to temple and messiah during the period in which Revelation was written. For practical purposes, the sources will be delimited to the following: (1) Works likely predating Revelation include Tobit, 1–2 Enoch, Sibylline Oracle 3, the Testaments of the Twelve Patriarchs, Jubilees, 2 Ezekiel, and the Qumran Sectarian documents. (2) Sources roughly contemporaneous with the

---

6. Bauckham, *Climax of Prophecy*, x–xi; Briggs, *Jewish Temple Imagery*, 104–7; Mathewson, *New Heaven*, 32.

7. Mathewson, *New Heaven*, 111.

8. McCaffrey, *House with Many Rooms*, 252.

time frame in which Revelation was composed include the Similitudes of 1 Enoch, Sibylline Oracles 1–2, 4–5, 4 Ezra (2 Esdras), 1–3 Baruch, the Apocalypse of Abraham, Pseudo-Philo, and the Ezekiel Targum. Although the Mishnah was compiled after the book of Revelation, the volume reflects traditions of the previous four centuries. Additionally, tractate Middoth, in which a temple plan is outlined, was composed soon after the destruction of the Jerusalem Temple, placing the document in the same time frame as Revelation. Therefore, the Mishnah will be included in the analysis. The intent for the diachronic analysis is to determine whether a conceptual framework existed for John to draw upon in his portrayal of Ezekiel's temple in a nonliteral manner.

Third, the relationship between Ezekiel 40–48 and Revelation 21–22 will be examined synchronically, with both micro-level and macro-level analyses. At the macro level, structural and topical parallels will be examined to establish a broad framework for the relationship between the two books. At the micro level, lexical and semantic parallels will be examined.[9] Verses that exhibit close conceptual affinities then will be identified. Finally, the relative certainty and contextual function of each reference will be determined using categories proposed by G. K. Beale.

While schemas for the categorization of intertextual references abound, Beale's classifications are utilized because he has undertaken one of the most comprehensive studies of the use of the OT in Revelation to date. He has provided three "criteria for allusive validity" by which potential intertexts can be organized.[10] First, the *clear allusion* is characterized by language that is nearly identical to an OT passage. The wording is so distinctive that the reference could not have originated elsewhere. Second, the *probable allusion* does not contain phraseology as distinct as the clear allusion, but the probable allusion will contain a word or idea that is uniquely or characteristically linked to an OT referent. A similar structure may indicate a probable allusion as well. Third, the *possible allusion* is characterized by similar language or conceptual affinities.[11] A possible

9. Terminology relevant to the current study was identified for the entirety of Ezekiel and Revelation. Criteria for relevance included (a) the presence of a parallel lexeme, (b) the presence of synonymous lexemes, or (c) temple related terminology. Verses not pertaining to the intertextual relationship between Ezekiel and Revelation were eliminated.

10. Beale noted that the criteria are applicable for OT references as well as extra-biblical sources. Beale, *John's Use*, 62–63.

11. The clear, probable, and possible allusions roughly correspond to Porter's categories of paraphrase, allusion, and echo, respectively. Porter, *Sacred Tradition*, 36–46.

allusion differs from a probable allusion in that the probable allusion is an intentional device used by the author, whereas the possible allusion may be the result of a common conceptual or cultural milieu.[12]

Beale has provided a second set of categories to deal with the nature and function of intertexts. According to Beale, the manner in which John made use of the OT can be classified under seven headings: OT segments as literary prototypes, thematic uses, analogical uses, universalization, possible indirect fulfillment uses, inverted uses, and stylistic use of OT language.[13] For *OT segments as literary prototypes*, Beale explained that John appropriated the OT context and utilized his predecessors as a model for his own composition. John sometimes used OT patterns to predict a future eschatological fulfillment, while in other instances he used the OT context to explain past and present fulfillments. With *thematic uses*, John appropriated OT themes and further developed them. With *analogical uses*, John brought forward key ideas to develop a relationship of continuity with the OT. With *universalization*, John applied Israel imagery to the whole world. *Indirect fulfillment usages* refer to instances in which John informally referred to an OT text "in order to designate present or future fulfillment of OT verbal prophecy."[14] *Inverted uses* are instances where John appeared to contradict the contextual meaning of his OT referent. Finally, *stylistic usages* refer to the solecisms of Revelation. Beale contended that John's hebraic style creates grammatical irregularities, which invoke continuity with the OT.[15]

Delimitations

A few delimitations and definitions are necessary before proceeding. First, I am not proposing that Ezekiel is the sole influence on Revelation 21:1—22:5. The author of Revelation wove a wide variety of OT allusions

12. Beale, *John's Use*, 62–63. Paulien listed five categories. His first three are roughly the same as Beale's, but he added "uncertain allusions" and "nonallusions" (Paulien, "Elusive Allusions," 37–53).

13. Beale, *John's Use*, 75–128.

14. Beale, *Revelation*, 93.

15. Richard Bauckham and C. G. Ozanne also argued that the solecisms of Revelation are an intentional authorial device. The purpose of the current dissertation, however, is not to verify or disprove the theory (Beale, *Revelation*, 35; Bauckham, *Climax of Prophecy*, 286; Ozanne, "Language of the Apocalypse," 3–9).

into a complex tapestry.[16] Second, a comprehensive study of all intertexts between Ezekiel and Revelation will not be undertaken. Only passages deemed relevant to the current study will be examined.

Third, although an analysis of temple imagery in the NT would be fruitful and supportive of the conclusions of the current study, a detailed analysis of NT material is beyond the scope of the research. Many studies on the temple theme in the NT have been published.[17] These studies will be discussed where relevant.

Fourth, the primary text of Ezekiel under consideration will be the LXX version.[18] The text type used by John is a matter of continuing debate. Scholars such as Robert H. Charles, who asserted that John follows the Hebrew text, largely base their conclusion upon John's departure from the LXX in his allusions to the OT.[19] Yet, John also departed from the Hebrew text in his allusions, and even Charles conceded that John was influenced by the LXX and proto-Theodotion.[20] Beale and Moyise proposed that John drew upon Semitic and Greek sources, modifying both as he saw fit.[21] Therefore, in the absence of scholarly consensus, the Greek text provides a straightforward basis of comparison between Ezekiel and Revelation. Where relevant, the Hebrew text of Ezekiel will be considered in addition to the Greek.[22]

Fifth, the contrast between the terms *literal* and *nonliteral* in reference to the prophetic visions should be clarified. The idea exegetes typically intend to convey when referring to the literal fulfillment of Ezekiel's temple is a physical, structural edifice. By way of contrast, Beale regarded Jesus as the literal fulfillment of Ezekiel's temple and largely eschewed the

16. Henry Swete determined that John referred to nearly every book in the Hebrew canon. Swete, *Apocalypse pf St. John*, clii.

17. Beale, *Temple and the Church's Mission*, 169–402; Coloe, *God Dwells with Us*; Lee, *New Jerusalem*, 230–38; Hoskins, *Jesus as the Fulfillment*; Marshall, "Church and Temple," 203–22; McKelvey, *New Temple*.

18. Rahlfs and Hanhart, *Septuaginta*. The Greek text of Revelation under consideration will be from NA28; Aland et al., *Novum Testamentum Graece*, 28th ed.

19. Charles, *Critical and Exegetical Commentary*, lxvi–lxvii. Bauckham, *Climax of Prophecy*, 203; Ozanne, "Language of the Apocalypse," 3–9; Trudinger, "Some Observations Concerning the Text," 82–88.

20. Charles, *Critical and Exegetical Commentary*, lxvii.

21. Beale, *John's Use*, 62; Moyise, *Old Testament in the Book*, 17. Compounding the problem is that the text of both the Hebrew and Greek Scriptures "was rather fluid in the first century A.D" (Hultberg, "Messianic Exegesis in the Apocalypse, 45–47).

22. The Hebrew text referenced will be the *Biblia Hebraica Stuttgartensia*.

literal/nonliteral distinction in his discussion.[23] Nonetheless, for the sake of simplicity, "literal" will carry the nuance of *structural* in the current study. Correspondingly, "nonliteral" will refer to any interpretation that does not propose an exact physical parallel to what has been prophesied.

23. Beale, *Temple and the Church's Mission*, 352.

2.

State of Research

THE FOLLOWING STATE OF research will progress in three stages. First, hermeneutical foundations for the current study will be situated within the broader field of intertextual theory. Second, scholarship on the use of the OT in Revelation, with emphasis on John's use of Ezekiel, will be surveyed. Third, interpretations of Ezekiel 40–48 will be examined with the goal of determining the timeless theological principles of the vision.

Intertextual Foundations

Early forays into intertextuality by biblical scholars often lacked a clear methodology. Samuel Sandmel brought such concerns to light in his 1962 article, "Parallelomania."[1] He opined that historical factors went unnoticed, perceived intertexts were overstated, and as a result, conclusions were dubious. Although the purpose of Sandmel's argument was to point out the shortfalls of intertextual approaches in biblical studies, he did offer a few methodological suggestions, such as giving more attention to the historical setting of individual texts.

Since Sandmel's critique, a plethora of intertextual theories and methodologies have arisen in biblical scholarship. Yet, the notion still lacks precision among biblical scholars.[2] Therefore, the beginnings, pro-

---

1. Sandmel, "Parallelomania," 1–13.

2. In fact, the notion of intertextuality appears to lack precision among all scholars. Graham Allen noted that the "term is in danger of meaning nothing more than whatever each particular critic wishes it to mean." He further contended that any attempt

1

gression, and current state of research in biblical studies will be elucidated in the following section.

Literary Intertextuality

At the most basic level, an intertextual relationship is created when one
text interacts with another. Even more broadly, a *text* is not necessarily
a written work, but any entity that conveys meaning. Intertextuality is
based upon the supposition that the meaning of a text does not proceed
directly from author to reader, but is mediated through the reader's prior
understanding and experience.

One of the first scholars to use the term *intertextuality* was Julia
Kristeva.[3] Her work represents a synthesis of the dialogism of Mikhail
Bakhtin and the semiotics of Ferdinand Saussure. Bakhtin's linguistic and
literary philosophy were based upon the observation that language creates
a dialogue between text and reader. The role of the author is minimized
as many potential meanings are created.[4] Resultantly, Bakhtin's conceptions are more akin to reader-response theory than intertextual theory.[5]
Nonetheless, Bahktin's work is relevant for the influence on Kristeva and
other scholars of intertextuality.

Saussure, whose linguistic philosophy often is termed *structural-
ism*, identified two components of a sign. First, the signifier is the entity
that conveys a message (a text, a word, a sound, an image). Second, the
signified is the concept that is communicated (the mental content of the
sign).[6] Saussure also distinguished between diachronic and synchronic
linguistics. He argued that the synchronic view is the more important,
as "it is the true and only reality to the community of speakers."[7] For

---

to ascertain a fundamental definition for intertextuality would be doomed (Allen,
Intertextuality, 2). Cf. Miller, "Intertextuality in Old Testament Research," 283–309;
Postell, *Adam as Israel*, 43–66; Yoon, "Ideological Inception of Intertextuality," 58–76.

3. Disagreement exists as to whether Kristeva, or her mentor, Roland Barthes, first
introduced the term. See Kristeva, *Desire in Language*; Orr, *Intertextuality*, 20; Yoon,
"Ideological Inception of Intertextuality," 59–60.

4. Bakhtin, *Dialogic Imagination*.

5. Yoon, "Ideological Inception of Intertextuality," 62–63; Allen, *Intertextuality*,
23–24.

6. Saussure, *Course in General Linguistics*, 35; Silva, *Biblical Words and Their
Meaning*.

7. Saussure, *Course in General Linguistics*, 90.

Saussure, therefore, objective meaning could be obtained even if signs were malleable and unfixed.

Both Kristeva and her mentor, Roland Barthes, represent a shift toward poststructuralism. Barthes is known especially for his rejection of authorial intent in relation to the meaning of a text, as explicated in his essay "The Death of the Author."[8] Barthes wrote, "We know now that a text is not a line of words releasing a single 'theological' meaning (the 'message' of the Author-God) but a multi-dimensional space in which a variety of writings, none of them original, blend and clash."[9] Similarly, for Kristeva, a text is inseparable from the surrounding culture. Every text exists as part of a universe of texts, a phenomenon she described as the "intersection of textual surfaces."[10] Therefore, both scholars argued that multiple meanings are created by the interaction between two texts. Further, meaning is not unidirectional, but fluid.[11]

Biblical Intertextuality

Although poststructuralist and reader-response philosophies are alive and well in the field of biblical studies, that which is typically implied by *intertextuality* is the use of the OT in the NT. Possibly the most noteworthy and enduring work in the field of biblical intertextuality is Richard Hays's *Echoes of Scripture in the Letters of Paul*.[12] According to Hays, intertextuality is "the embedding of fragments of an earlier text within a later one."[13] For Hays, meaning is unidirectional and established by the authority and cultural setting of the original author.

While Hays was not the first biblical scholar to examine the use of the OT in the NT, he was one of the first to propose a systematic methodology.[14] Hays outlined seven criteria for identifying the presence of

---

8. Barthes, "Death of the Author," 142–48.

9. Barthes, "Death of the Author," 146.

10. Kristeva, *Desire in Language*, 65.

11. Kristeva, *Desire in Language*, 65–66.

12. Hays, *Echoes of Scripture in the Letters*.

13. Hays, *Echoes of Scripture in the Letters*, 14.

14. Earlier works in which the use of OT in the NT is studied: Dodd, *According to the Scriptures*; Dodd, *Old Testament in the New*; Efird, *Use of the Old Testament in the New*; France, *Jesus and the Old Testament*; Gardiner, *Old and New Testaments*; Gundry, *Use of the Old Testament*.

an intertextual echo.[15] Although he applied his criteria to the Pauline Epistles, part of the enduring value of his method is reproducibility for other passages.[16]

Also noteworthy in the field of biblical intertextuality is Stanley Porter.[17] While Hays designated OT references in the NT as "echoes,"[18] Porter added specificity to the discussion by classifying reference types on a spectrum of relative certainty.[19] Like Hays, Porter contended that meaning is unidirectional and influenced by the historical setting of the original author.[20]

Jon Paulien studied intertextual references specifically in Revelation. He argued that understanding the meaning of a text is predicated upon identifying allusions therein. "The presence of a direct allusion requires the interpreter to trace the material to its source in order to understand the later writing."[21] Further, "to the extent that an interpreter misses an author's allusion to previous literature, that interpreter will misunderstand the author's intention."[22]

Paulien contended that when interpreters casually and nonspecifically identify allusions without methodological vetting, serious misunderstandings of authorial intent can result.[23] Thus, the scholar proposed four criteria for verifying the presence of an allusion in Revelation. The first is external evidence, i.e., the author had access to the source to which

15. The seven criteria are availability, volume, recurrence, thematic coherence, historical plausibility, history of interpretation, and satisfaction (Hays, *Echoes of Scripture in the Letters*, 29–32).

16. Hays applied his methodology to the Gospels in *Echoes of Scripture in the Gospels*.

17. Porter, "Allusions and Echoes," 29–40; Porter, "Further Comments on the Use," 98–110; Porter, *Hearing the Old Testament*; Porter, "Use of the Old Testament," 79–96.

18. Hays used the terms "echo" and "allusion." He designated an echo as a less certain allusion, but often used the terms in a nonspecific manner to denote an intertext.

19. The reference types, in order of decreasing certainty, are formulaic quotation, direct quotation, paraphrase, allusion, and echo; Porter, "Further Comments on the Use," 98–110; Porter, *Sacred Tradition*, 34–47.

20. Numerous other models for identifying instances of biblical intertextuality exist. See, for example, Leonard, "Identifying Inner-Biblical Allusions," 241–65; Manning, *Echoes of a Prophet*, 7–19; Paulien, "Elusive Allusions," 37–53; Postell, *Adam as Israel*, 43–74; Sommer, *Prophet Reads Scripture*, 6–31.

21. Paulien, "Elusive Allusions," 41. Cf. Manning, *Echoes of a Prophet*, 3; Kraft, *Die Offenbarung des Johannes*, 16.

22. Paulien, *Decoding Revelation's Trumpets*, 168.

23. Paulien, "Elusive Allusions," 40.

he purportedly alluded.[24] Second, a verbal correspondence of at least two words is required. Third, thematic parallels or, fourth, structural parallels must be present.[25]

The divergence between the intertextual theories of Hays, Porter, and Paulien and those of the poststructuralists is immediately clear. W. S. Green said of *Echoes of Scripture*, "the book employs a minimalist notion of intertextuality, using it to mean simply the presence of an older text in a newer one. The philosophical and ideological arguments that often accompany discussion of intertextuality, particularly concerning the inherent instability of all texts, are barely mentioned here."[26]

Due to such concerns, along with the original poststructuralist ideology of intertextuality, David Yoon argued that the hyphenated *inter-textuality* should be used to describe the use of the OT in the NT.[27] G. K. Beale, who will be discussed subsequently, likewise preferred the phrases *inner-biblical exegesis* or *inner biblical allusion* to intertextuality.[28] Nonetheless, the current study will retain the use of *intertextuality*, albeit with the distinction that the historical author wrote in such a way that his intended meaning is recognizable by readers.[29]

The Use of the OT in the NT

The nature of the interaction between the two testaments is a matter of continuing debate in the field of biblical studies. In a 1985 article, prior to the major works of both Hays and Porter, Darrell Bock described the use of the OT in the NT as a hotly debated topic that lacked consensus even among evangelicals.[30] In the decades since, a consensus has yet to be reached.

In his two-part article, Bock outlined four evangelical approaches to the use of the OT in the NT.[31] The first category is the "Full Human

24. Authorial access is akin to Hays's criteria of availability (Hays, *Echoes of Scripture in the Letters*, 29–30).

25. Paulien, *Decoding Revelation's Trumpets*, 179–87.

26. Green, "Doing the Text's Work," 59.

27. Yoon, "Ideological Inception of Intertextuality," 74.

28. Beale, *Handbook on the New Testament*, 39–40.

29. Postell, *Adam as Israel*, 64–65.

30. In "Part 1," Bock outlined four approaches (Bock, "Part 1," 209–23).

31. In "Part 2," Bock focused on four "tension points" between the four schools: dual authorship, language-referent, the progress of revelation, and the problem of

Intent School," in which the human communicator is fully cognitive of the message he conveys. Bock wrote of Walter Kaiser, a proponent of the view: "Kaiser rejects *sensus plenior*, dual sense, double fulfillment, or double meaning. He rejects any bifurcation between the divine author's intended meaning and the human author's intended meaning."[32] In regard to biblical prophecy, Kaiser himself explained that the prophets were fully aware of the message they communicated, even those prophecies that may have contained a series of fulfillments. The only aspect of which the prophet was unaware was the time frame.[33]

The second category is the "Divine Intent-Human Words School." Proponents include S. Lewis Johnson, James I. Packer, and Elliott E. Johnson.[34] Such scholars contend that when God speaks through a prophet, the prophet is not fully aware of the message he conveys. Bock explained, "In making the distinction between the human author's intention and God's intention, [proponents] seek to maintain a connection between the human author's words and meaning and God's intention and meaning in order to avoid the appearance of arbitrary fulfillment."[35] Bock himself advocated such a view, explaining that some passages describe patterns rather than specific events, and that God reveals his plan as history progresses.[36]

The third category is the "Historical Progression of Revelation and Jewish Hermeneutical School." Proponents include Earle E. Ellis, Richard Longenecker, and Walter Dunnett.[37] According to such scholars, Jewish exegetical methods of the first century, such as midrash and pesher, influenced New Testament writers. The Christian perspective on salvation history also informed and influenced Christ's followers, who felt the

---

differing texts used in Old Testament citations by their New Testament fulfillment(s) (Bock, "Part 2," 306–19).

32. Bock, "Part 1," 211.

33. See Kaiser, *Uses of the Old Testament in the New*, 61–76; Fitzmyer, "Use of Explicit Old Testament," 297–333.

34. Johnson, *Old Testament in the New*; Packer, "Biblical Authority, Hermeneutics, and Inerrancy," 141–53; Johnson, "Author's Intention and Biblical Interpretation," 409–29.

35. Bock, "Part 1," 213.

36. Bock, "Single Meaning, Multiple Contexts," 105–51.

37. Ellis, "How the New Testament Uses," 199–219; Ellis, *Paul's Use of the Old Testament*; Longenecker, *Biblical Exegesis*; Dunnett, *Interpretation of Scripture*.

freedom to interpret the Scriptures of the day through a christological hermeneutic.

> What the New Testament writers are conscious of is interpreting the Old Testament (1) from a christocentric perspective, (2) in conformity with a Christian tradition, and (3) along Christological lines. And in their exegesis there is the interplay of Jewish presuppositions and practices, on the one hand, with Christian commitments and perspectives, on the other, joined to produce a distinctive interpretation of the Old Testament.[38]

A major weakness of the perspective, however, is how to handle the original meaning of OT prophecies, as will be discussed below.

Finally, the fourth perspective presented by Bock is the "Canonical Approach and New Testament Priority School," advocated by Bruce Waltke. Bock's presentation of the view was brief, and he opined that Waltke's explanation of his own view was vague.[39] Waltke wrote, "By the canonical process approach I mean the recognition that the text's intention became deeper and clearer as the parameters of the canon were expanded. Just as redemption itself has progressive history, so also older texts in the canon underwent a correlative progressive perception of meaning as they became part of a growing canonical literature."[40] Clearly, Waltke's approach is indebted to Brevard Childs, but his explanation leaves unclear whether he believed that the human authors of Scripture fully understood what they wrote.[41]

Although the terminology differs, most theories on the use of the OT in the NT are variations on one or more of Bock's four categories. In a 1982 article, "Analogous Fulfillment," Jack Weir advocated a position that combined elements of Bock's second (Divine Intent/Human Words) and third (Historical Progression/Jewish Hermeneutic) categories. Weir utilized the concept of analogy to argue that each intertext contains subjective and objective elements, such that "the objective anchor in some

---

38. Longenecker, *Biblical Exegesis*, 186. Cf. Moule, *Birth of the New Testament*.

39. Bock, "Part 1," 219.

40. Waltke, "Canonical Approach to the Psalms," 7.

41. The idea of *recontextualization* bears similarities with the historical progression and canonical views. Along such lines, biblical passages are not bound by a single, historically determined meaning. Rather, words or phrases from previous biblical passages are utilized in a new context and given new meaning. See Levenson, "Bible," 24–33; Robbins, *Tapestry of Early Christian Discourse*, 107; Stendahl, "Biblical Theology, Contemporary," 420.

sense must be within the intention or understanding of the prophet."[42] He further explained, "Since every application of a theological symbol, event, or concept to another symbol, event, or concept involves analogy . . . analogy is an accurate model depicting the use of the Old Testament in the New."[43]

According to Weir, his model offers four hermeneutical advantages. First, the hermeneutical methods of the NT writers are implicitly based upon theological analogy.[44] Admittedly, the reasoning is circular, but based upon his preceding explanation the issue Weir may have been getting at is that the NT authors interpreted Scripture in accord with the hermeneutical practices of their day.[45] Second, the analogical model "respects the historical-critical exegesis of both testaments," as differences between the OT and the NT are recognized and expected.[46] Third, the unique message and authority of the OT are retained, while, fourth, Jesus Christ is recognized as the culmination of revelation.[47]

The analogical model draws upon the strengths of the other views while minimizing the weaknesses. While Bock's third view (Historical Progression/Jewish Hermeneutics) is particularly appealing for the current hypothesis, the view does not adequately account for the original meaning of the prophecy. If first-century Christian interpreters had the freedom to completely reinterpret OT prophecies, the original meaning of many prophetic oracles has been distorted and unfulfilled. For example, if the original expectation for Ezekiel's temple was indeed literal, yet later exegetes reinterpreted the vision as something wholly different, was not Ezekiel a false prophet? While such an interpretation may be no problem for secular scholars, evangelicals regard all of Scripture as divinely inspired, including OT prophecies.

The second view (Divine Intent/Human Words) presented by Bock also has much of value. OT prophecies are fulfilled, just not in the manner expected by the one who uttered them. Yet Weir's theory also offers a better way forward in that the true meaning and substance of the original

---

42. Weir, "Analogous Fulfillment," 72.

43. Weir, "Analogous Fulfillment," 73–74.

44. Weir, "Analogous Fulfillment," 74.

45. See also Mickelson, *Interpreting the Bible*, 296; von Rad, *Old Testament Theology*, 97–112.

46. Weir, "Analogous Fulfillment," 74.

47. Hans Walter Wolff regarded the New Testament, and by extension Christ, as the "decisive analogy." See Wolff, "Hermeneutics of the Old Testament," 169–99.

prophecy, which *was* understood by the original prophet, is retained in its NT iteration. Along such lines, Weir's objective anchor is nearly identical to the idea of a timeless theological principle. Therefore, the current research will proceed within the framework of Weir's analogical model and seek to discern the theological core of Ezekiel's vision.

John's Use of the OT and Ezekiel

One of the first scholars to systematically explore the relationship between Revelation and Ezekiel was Albert Vanhoye. The French scholar noted affinities between large sections of both books and demonstrated that the sequence of the Apocalypse roughly parallels the sequence of Ezekiel.[48] A steady stream of research on the relationship between Ezekiel and Revelation continued in the decades that followed.[49] Scholarly contributions can be organized by authors who argue for discontinuity in John's use of the OT, and authors who argue for continuity.

Scholars Advocating Discontinuity

Prominent among scholars who see a large degree of discontinuity in John's use of the OT is Jeffrey M. Vogelgesang. In his unpublished but noteworthy 1985 dissertation, Vogelgesang examined Ezekielian influence on Revelation as a whole. He utilized Revelation 22:1—22:5 as a starting point because the pericope exhibits heavy dependence on Ezekiel, but also departs substantially from the prophet's original message. Vogelgesang postulated that John radically reinterpreted Ezekiel along ten avenues: (1) God's presence extends to all people, not just Israel; (2) the city of Revelation, being situated on a plain, is more accessible than Ezekiel's city, which is situated on a hill; (3) the whole city houses the

48. Vanhoye, "L'utilization du livre d'Ezéchiel," 436–76. Michael Douglas Goulder also proposed that Ezekiel provided the broad structure for Revelation. However, he attributed parallels to the liturgical calendar. See Goulder, "Apocalypse as an Annual Cycle," 342–67. Cf. Comblin, "La liturgie de la Nouvelle," 5–40.

49. Until the last few decades, scholarship on the relationship between Revelation and the OT was scarce. The most noteworthy studies include Gangemi, "L'utilizzazione del Deutero-Isaia nell'," 311–39; Jenkins, *Old Testament in the Book*; Kraft, *Die Offenbarung des Johannes*; Lancellottie, "L'Antico Testmanto nell'Apocallise," 369–84; Schlatter, *Alte Testament in der johanneischen*; Trudinger, "Some Observations Concerning the Text."

glory of God, as opposed to the temple alone; (4) the size of John's city is greater than that of Ezekiel; (5) the walls and gates of the new Jerusalem, rather than excluding the nations, welcomes all people; (6) the jewels of the pagan king of Tyre are transformed and redeemed; (7) no temple exists in the new Jerusalem; (8) the setting of John's vision is urban rather than rural; (9) the massive size of John's city implies that the Hellenistic city model influenced his portrayal of the new Jerusalem; and (10) John's city is portrayed as a redeemed Babylon, an idea that would have been unthinkable for Ezekiel. Vogelgesang concluded that the unifying theme of John's reinterpretation is a universalization of Ezekiel's message.[50]

Around the same time as Vogelgesang, Jean-Pierre Ruiz and Celia Deutsch proposed their own theories on the manner in which the author of Revelation appropriated Ezekielian imagery. In his dissertation, *Ezekiel in the Apocalypse*, Ruiz argued that the author of Revelation creatively reshaped the prophetic tradition. Ruiz contended that John applied a consistent hermeneutic to the book of Ezekiel to portray Rome in terms of Babylon, the enemy of Israel. In doing so, John created a new interpretive matrix for OT themes.[51]

Deutsch proposed a different interpretive matrix for John's use of the OT. In her 1987 article, "Transformation of Symbols," she examined the nature of symbolism and contended that the "trans-temporal nature of myth and symbol allows them to transform themselves to accommodate new experience and shift in community setting."[52] Her discussion focused on four primary categories: Jerusalem as bride, the new Jerusalem and the temple, the new Jerusalem and creation, and membership in the new Jerusalem. She asserted that the symbol of the temple was replaced by the presence. Deutsch concluded that the visions functioned to offer hope to Christians suffering at the hand of Rome.[53]

In more recent articles, several scholars have postulated an even greater rift between John and his OT sources. Robert Royalty examined John's use of wealth in Revelation 1, 4, 17, and 21–22. He hypothesized that "John's free use of biblical texts to construct opulent visions of heaven and the new Jerusalem stands out within Second Temple Jewish

---

50. Vogelgesang, "Interpretation of Ezekiel," 113.

51. Ruiz, *Ezekiel in the Apocalypse*.

52. Deutsch, "Transformation of Symbols," 108.

53. Deutsch, "Transformation of Symbols," 106–26.

literature."[54] Royalty acknowledged the hermeneutical complexity of John's use of the OT but also contended that John felt the freedom to use the OT in whatever manner suited his rhetorical purpose. In regard to Ezekiel's temple, Royalty asserted that John added elements of luxury garnered from Greco-Roman culture.

Paul B. Decock took a postmodern approach and argued that the intertextual relationship between Revelation and John's OT sources continued beyond the author himself. He proposed that John created an intertextual space where meaning can be produced continually by readers. Decock opined that the question of how John used the OT is misleading. John simply viewed the OT as his Scriptures. Decock therefore argued that, "From a hermeneutical point of view the Scriptures were the 'horizon of thinking' of the Christian communities."[55] John's frame of mind was not constrained by what modern readers think of as "original meaning." Rather, in accord with the interpretive milieu of his time, John fully expected that "the old texts would easily bend to the meaning of the new texts."[56]

In the hermeneutical approaches of Ruiz, Deutsch, and Decock, one can see affinities with the dialogism of Bakhtin.[57] The modern champion of such a position is Steve Moyise, who advocated an interactive, or dialogical, model of intertextuality.[58] He contended that interpreters should ponder how two texts interact more so than whether the author respected the original intent of his referent.

In *The Old Testament in the Book of Revelation*, Moyise examined the use of Ezekiel 40–48 in Revelation 21:1—22:5.[59] He argued that the pericope in Revelation draws heavily upon Ezekiel, but also exhibits points of divergence. First, whereas Ezekiel's focus is the temple, John's vision has no temple. Second, John extends the scope of Ezekiel's vision

54. Royalty, *Streets of Heaven*, 79.

55. Decock, "Scriptures in the Book," 406.

56. Decock, "Scriptures in the Book," 406.

57. To an extent, all of the scholars who argue for discontinuity exhibit affinities with Bakhtin. However, Ruiz, Deutsch, and Decock dealt more pointedly with hermeneutical theory.

58. Steve Moyise drew upon the work of Thomas Greene to describe John's use of the OT as "heuristic and dialectical imitation." Moyise, "Intertextuality and the Use of Scripture in the Book of Revelation?" 393; Moyise, *Old Testament in the Book*, 118–21; Greene, *Light in Troy*.

59. Moyise, *Old Testament in the Book*, 64–84.

by extending healing to the nations, who are active participants in the new creation. Moyise wrote, "By firmly making the reader think of Ezekiel's visions and then confronting him or her with drastic changes, the reader is forced to stop and ask what is going on."[60] Ultimately, Moyise did not see Revelation 21–22 as the consummation of Ezekiel's temple vision. Rather, readers are pointed toward the ongoing interaction between the two texts.[61]

Moyise further developed his argument by asserting that John himself would have believed that his visions conveyed the fulfillment of OT prophecy. However, the meaning that John overlaid upon the OT Scriptures would have been totally foreign to the original authors. Resultantly, Moyise proposed a new model for understanding the use of the OT in Revelation in which trajectories of interpretation account for continuities and discontinuities in meaning.[62]

Scholars Advocating Continuity

An early advocate for continuity in John's use of the OT is Mathias Rissi. Rissi examined the manner in which John reinterpreted OT traditions to communicate his message about the new Jerusalem. According to Rissi, John conveyed the final fulfillment of OT prophetic visions, especially those of Ezekiel and Isaiah. Rissi contended that John moved from the particularism of the OT to universalism.[63]

In his 1985 monograph, William J. Dumbrell studied prominent OT themes that find their culmination in Revelation 21–22. Although the scholar dealt only peripherally with Revelation 21–22, his conclusions are relevant here. He contended that Scripture is richly diverse, but is also a unity that grows toward a common purpose. OT themes find partial realization in the NT and complete consummation in the final chapters of Revelation.[64]

---

60. Moyise, *Old Testament in the Book*, 49.

61. Moyise, "Intertextuality and the Book," 295–98; Moyise, *Later New Testament Writings*; Moyise, *Old Testament in the New*.

62. Moyise, "Does the Author of Revelation?," 3–21; Moyise, "Intertextuality and the Use," 391–401.

63. Rissi, *Future of the World*.

64. Dumbrell, *End of the Beginning*.

About a decade later, Jan Fekkes similarly attempted to demonstrate that John utilized OT sources consciously and systematically. Fekkes examined John's use of each intertext and evaluated the level of certainty for each allusion. He classified the references into four categories: visionary experience and language, christological titles and descriptions, eschatological judgment, and eschatological salvation. In regard to Revelation 21:1—22:5, Fekkes contended that John gathered a cluster of OT oracles that revolve around the theme of eschatological salvation. Although Fekkes's primary focus was Isaiah, his conclusions have relevance for intertextual research on other OT sources.[65]

Pilchan Lee offered an extensive study of imagery related to the new Jerusalem and the temple in the OT, NT, and intertestamental period. He contended that the lack of a temple in John's vision would have been a striking and sensational modification from the traditions of the day. Nonetheless, the modification is a "development (rather than a difference) between Revelation and the OT."[66] Lee attributed John's modification of traditional imagery to his christological focus.[67]

Similarly, Robert A. Briggs provided a study of temple imagery in Revelation. He examined the OT as well as Second Temple period Jewish literature for the purpose of determining which texts exercised the greatest influence on Revelation. He concluded that John drew almost exclusively on the OT to present Christ as the fulfillment of Jewish temple expectations.[68]

The following two scholars have undertaken studies that are closest in scope to the current research. First, David Mathewson provided a comprehensive analysis of the use of the OT in Revelation 21:1—22:5. He meticulously worked through Revelation 21:1—22:5 to determine how each allusion or echo functions in the text. Mathewson employed a historical-critical approach as he examined "the original context, meaning and vocabulary" of each OT referent.[69] Additionally, because John's usage of the OT was influenced by his own milieu, Mathewson examined the interpretive history of relevant OT texts in extrabiblical literature.

65. Fekkes, *Isaiah and Prophetic Traditions*.

66. Lee, *New Jerusalem*, 2.

67. In viewing christological fulfillments in Revelation as developments of Old Testament prophecy, Lee followed his mentor, Richard Bauckham. See Bauckham, *Climax of Prophecy*.

68. Briggs, *Jewish Temple Imagery*.

69. Mathewson, *New Heaven*, 21.

The research did not make use of any particular intertextual theory, but Mathewson did propose that "by sustained allusion to a constellation of Old Testament texts the author creates a plurality of semantic effects and associations in articulating his hope of eschatological salvation."[70]

Second, G. K. Beale is well known for his scholarship on Revelation, particularly with regard to the relationship between Revelation and OT prophetic writings. In *John's Use of the Old Testament in Revelation*, Beale refuted the idea that John gave new meaning to the texts upon which he drew. Beale argued for a continuation of *meaning*, although he allowed for variance in *significance* and *application*. Passages where John might seem to diverge from the OT context can be explained by developments in salvation history. Beale contended that John engaged in "interpretive distillation" as he presented the true fulfillment of OT passages.[71]

In *The Temple and the Church's Mission*, Beale examined the symbolism and purpose of temples in the Bible. He explicated the expanding purpose of temples throughout the OT and then examined the spiritualization of the temple in the NT. He highlighted the shift toward understanding Jesus and the church as the temple.

Beale spent an entire chapter on the relationship between Ezekiel's temple and the NT. He postulated that Ezekiel's vision even prior to NT appropriations portrayed a "non-structural end-time temple."[72] The eschatological city of Revelation 21:1—22:5 is therefore the fulfillment of Ezekiel's vision. Beale further argued that Christ himself serves as the consummation of Ezekiel's temple prophecy.

Evaluation

An interesting observation on the theories discussed above is that the interpretations of John's use of Ezekiel in Revelation 21–22 are not strikingly different, even among scholars on opposing ends of the continuity spectrum. The major point of contention seems to be the original meaning of Ezekiel's temple vision. Each scholar's interpretation of Ezekiel seems to be a primary factor in determining whether John has presented his vision in line with Ezekiel's intent. Thus, the need to determine the

---

70. Mathewson, *New Heaven*, 221.

71. Beale, *John's Use*, 78, cf. 75–128; Beale, *Book of Revelation*, 1062.

72. Beale, *Temple and the Church's Mission*, 7.

timeless theological core of Ezekiel's vision again becomes apparent.[73] First, however, the distinctiveness of the current research in relation to previous studies will be elucidated.

Contribution to Scholarship

Beale, Mathewson, and Briggs have proposed that Jesus himself fulfills Ezekiel's eschatological temple vision. Yet, no comprehensive study of the intertextual relationship between Ezekiel 40–48 and Revelation 21–22 has been published to date. Beale comes closest, but his monograph on the temple is broader in scope and does not provide an exhaustive analysis of intertextual links between the two books. Therefore, such a lacuna will be filled by the current dissertation.

Additionally, the analysis of Second Temple period literature will be focused differently than the work of Lee and Briggs. Lee included temple conceptions in his research, but they were not his primary focus. Briggs evaluated temple imagery in Revelation and Second Temple Jewish literature, but gave little attention to Ezekiel. Thus, the current study will focus specifically on temple conceptions as they relate to the visions of Ezekiel and John.

73. Weir, "Analogous Fulfillment," 65–76.

3.

The Temple Vision of Ezekiel

LIKE MODERN EXEGETES, ANCIENT rabbis struggled to interpret Ezekiel, particularly the temple vision of Ezekiel 40–48. "Rabbinical Judaism considered the study of [Ezekiel] dangerous for any but the mature scholar."[1] The authors of the Talmud recounted that Hananiah ben Hezekiah, leader of the Shammai school, burned three hundred jars of oil as he labored over Ezekiel, seeking to resolve the contradictions between the Torah and Ezekiel 40–48. Despite his efforts, the rabbi indicated that the discrepancies will be resolved only when Elijah returns.[2] Nonetheless, scholars continue to seek to understand the message of Israel's most peculiar prophet.

In the current chapter, an investigation of interpretations of Ezekiel's temple vision will be provided. Only the final form of Ezekiel 40–48 will be analyzed. Nonetheless, a brief overview of scholarly perspectives on the redaction history of Ezekiel will lend clarity to the analysis that follows. The (theoretical) process of composition and redaction often influences interpretations of Ezekiel 40–48.

The Unity of Ezekiel

For the most part, until the twentieth century, a consensus existed in regard to the unity of Ezekiel. Rudolf Smend wrote that the structure of the

---

1. Tuell, *Law of the Temple*, 1–2. Cf. Levey, *Targum of Ezekiel*, 2; Sweeney, "Problem of Ezekiel," 11–23.

2. B. Šabb. 13b; b. Ḥag. 13a; b. Menaḥ. 45a.

book would be destroyed entirely if any part were removed.[3] In a more recent monograph, Kalinda Stevenson similarly argued that removing any pieces of Ezekiel's "quilt" would result in a pile of scraps.[4]

On the opposite end of the spectrum, in 1957, Hartmut Gese produced an enduring study of Ezekiel 40–48, in which he argued that the current state of the passage is the result of a long process of accretion and redaction.[5] Walther Zimmerli, drawing upon the work of Gese, likewise contended that as the original words of the prophet were transmitted, expansions and explanations accrued within the text, with chapters 40–48 being the final addition to the book. Nonetheless, he asserted that the final product was not a disparate amalgamation, but "an impressive witness to the painstaking care with which the extant material was arranged into a book."[6] Conversely, Walther Eichrodt asserted that Ezekiel 40–48 was not original to the book at all. The vision was expanded by many different hands with fragments "of widely different origins."[7]

Meanwhile, other scholars continued to maintain that Ezekiel was a unified composition. George Cooke and Carl Howie contended that Ezekiel was the product of a single mind.[8] Moshe Greenberg argued that the visions in the book "cohere and serve a single overriding purpose."[9] Brian Peterson went one step further, asserting that "the book of Ezekiel . . . betrays an overarching mindset and organization second to none."[10]

Other scholars favor a middle ground, advocating an overarching unity while allowing for editing by Ezekiel and/or his followers.[11] Steven Tuell argued for a unified composition, but allowed for the presence of selective expansions in the Persian period. The scholar postulated,

3. Smend, *Der Prophet Ezechiel*, xxi.

4. Stevenson, *Vision of Transformation*, 7. Stevenson's comment was in response to an essay by Steven Tuell, in which he referred to Ezekiel 40–48 as a "crazy-quilt of legislation." Tuell has since changed his view (Tuell, "Temple Vision of Ezekiel," 96–103).

5. Gese, *Der Verfassungsentwurf des Ezechiel*.

6. Zimmerli, *Ezekiel 1*, 74. Cf. Zimmerli, "Message of the Prophet Ezekiel," 131–57; Zimmerli, "Planungen für die Wiederaufbau," 229–55.

7. Eichrodt, *Ezekiel*, 530. Contrary to Eichrodt, Moshe Greenberg pointed out that Ezekiel 37, "which looks forward to the sacrificial cult and which Eichrodt allows to be authentic, contradicts his contention" (Greenberg, "Design and Themes," 182).

8. Cooke, *Critical and Exegetical Commentary*, xvii–xx; Howie, *Date and Composition of Ezekiel*. Cf. Fohrer and Galling, *Ezechiel*; Levenson, *Theology of the Program*.

9. Greenberg, "Design and Themes," 181. Cf. Greenberg, *Ezekiel 1–20*, 376.

10. Peterson, *Ezekiel in Context*, 329.

11. Block, *Book of Ezekiel: Chapters 1–24*, 17–23; Wevers, *Ezekiel*, 26–38, 206–9.

"While the basic vision of the prophet has been expanded, the expansion is purposive and deliberate, and has taken place virtually in one setting."[12] Leslie Allen wrote that although redactional work is apparent, the emendations are in keeping with the original ministry of the prophet Ezekiel.[13]

Interpretations of the Temple Vision

The interpretation of Ezekiel's temple vision is a perennial point of contention among scholars. The analysis which follows here will provide an overview of scholarly perspectives for the purpose of seeking the theological meaning of Ezekiel 40–48.[14] The two primary avenues of interpretation are literal and figurative. The literal view will be surveyed first.

Literal Interpretations

Many Jews and Christians take Ezekiel 40–48 at face value. The dispensationalist view, popularized by the Scofield Reference Bible, is literal and futurist. All prophecies, including Ezekiel 40–48, will be fulfilled in the final days, and Israel's temple will be rebuilt in a glorious future dispensation.[15]

Such a view adheres to a grammatical-historical hermeneutic. Ralph Alexander, favoring the literal approach, argued that the primary alternative, a figurative-spiritual hermeneutic, is impeded by the subjectivity of the interpreter.[16] However, Alexander neglected to acknowledge that variety also exists among literal interpretations.

One major interpretive variation is the sacrificial system outlined in Ezekiel 40–48. Because Christ's atoning death on the cross rendered the OT sacrificial system obsolete (Heb 10:10), a reinstitution of animal sacrifice seems to be a regression in salvation history.[17] Alexander answered

---

12. Tuell, *Law of the Temple*, 13.

13. Allen, *Ezekiel 20–48*, xxv.

14. Because a multitude of interpretations are attested, only the major categories and subcategories will be discussed.

15. Scofield, *Holy Bible*, 888–89n1. Cf. Gaebelein, *Prophet Ezekiel*, 271–73; Gray, *Christian Workers' Commentary*, 265–66; Price, *Temple and Bible Prophecy*, 516–32; Unger, *Great Neglected Bible Prophecies*, 55–95; Unger, "Temple Vision of Ezekiel (1)," 418–32; Walvoord, *Millennial Kingdom*, 310.

16. Alexander, *Ezekiel*, 130–31.

17. Hays, *Temple and the Tabernacle*, 61.

such critiques by comparing the Ezekielian sacrificial ordinances to the rite of communion. Just as temple sacrifices atoned only by pointing forward to Christ's death, the sacrifices of Ezekiel 40–48 point retrospectively to Christ's death.[18]

Mark Rooker is another proponent of the literal futurist view. Yet, even he conceded that the memorial view of sacrifice is weak due to the fact that the text explicitly indicates that the sacrifices are for atonement.[19] Rooker thus favored a symbolic view of the sacrifices mentioned in Ezekiel, despite his otherwise literal hermeneutic.[20] He rationalized the hermeneutical inconsistency by asserting that Christ has fulfilled the purpose of sacrifice. Therefore, Ezekiel's sacrificial prescriptions must refer to general worship practices. Rooker wrote, "The same could not be said of the erection and existence of the Temple, as we are not told in the NT that this promise has been fulfilled."[21] What Rooker failed to note is that Christ is portrayed as the embodiment and fulfillment of the temple in the NT (John 2:19–21; Rev 21:22).

Perhaps the strongest argument in favor of the literal view is the high degree of practical detail in Ezekiel 40–48. Proponents of a literal hermeneutic argue that just as the details of the tabernacle and First Temple were understood as instructions for construction and operation, so should the details of Ezekiel's temple be understood.[22] Lamar Cooper contended that the "extreme attention to detail" in Ezekiel's vision makes sense only if one views the vision as literal.[23] Thus, many believers anticipate the installation of a Third Temple that will be constructed according to the specifications given to Ezekiel. Jewish scholar Chaim Clorfene asserted that "the Messianic Temple will effect a greater revelation of the *Shechina* than was revealed in the Garden of Eden, even greater than was seen at Mount Sinai."[24] Ronald Clements likewise argued that the vision is a blueprint for a restored Israel in the messianic age. The function of the

---

18. Alexander, *Ezekiel*, 133. Cf. Bonar, *Coming and Kingdom*, 222–23; Gaebelein, *Prophet Ezekiel*, 312–13; Walvoord, *Millennial Kingdom*, 311–14; West, *Thousand Years in Both Testaments*, 424–26.

19. Ezek 43:20, 26; 45:15, 17, 20; Rooker, "Evidence from Ezekiel," 119–34.

20. The editor of the Scofield Reference Bible also indicated that the sacrifices are not to be interpreted literally (Scofield, *Scofield Reference Bible*, 888n1).

21. Rooker, "Evidence from Ezekiel," 134.

22. Hitchcock, "Critique of the Preterist View," 219–36; Lee, *New Jerusalem*, 13–14.

23. Cooper, *Ezekiel*, 353. Cf. Wevers, *Ezekiel*, 208.

24. Clorfene, *Messianic Temple*, 5.

temple is to reinstall the presence of God in Jerusalem, which will bring about all the blessings promised to Israel.[25]

A noteworthy proponent of such an argument is Jon Douglas Levenson. The scholar contended, "The highly specific nature of the description of the Temple, its liturgy and community bespeaks a practical program, not a vision of pure grace."[26] Through Ezekiel's legislation, past abuses are remedied, and an ideal society is established. Reforms are not necessarily for the purpose of creating an ideal society from a human perspective, but for creating an ideal society in the view of God.

Greenberg's interpretation of Ezekiel 40–48 is similar to Levenson's. He regarded the vision as the culmination of God's promises to Israel— that God will tabernacle among his people.[27] The details of the architectural and social legislation were designed to preserve God's presence among his people. Greenberg asserted, "Ezekiel first proclaims God's resolve to reestablish his presence again in Israel, then sets out his blueprint for so doing."[28] The former guardians and structures—the temple and priests—which were supposed to ensure God's presence among the Israelites had proven inadequate. Therefore, Ezekiel set forth a program to rectify past abuses and safeguard against future transgressions. Further, through the restoration of Israel, all of humanity would come to recognize the power of God. The repetition of *forever* throughout the vision stresses the permanence and irreversibility of the new dispensation.[29]

John Taylor, although he did not hold to a literalistic interpretation, conceded the strength of such arguments. "In defense of this theory it must be said that as Ezekiel was confidently expecting a literal return from exile, it would not be surprising for him, as a priestly as well as a prophetic figure, to outline the shape of the new temple that would surely need to be rebuilt in Jerusalem."[30]

25. Clements, *God and Temple*, 105–6.

26. Levenson, *Theology of the Program*, 45.

27. Lev 26:11.

28. Greenberg, "Design and Themes," 183. Cf. Bertholet, *Der Verfassungsentwurf des Hesekiel*.

29. According to Greenberg, however, Ezekiel's program ultimately had no effect (Greenberg, "Design and Themes," 182, 200, 208; Greenberg, *Ezekiel 1–20*, 15).

30. Taylor, *Ezekiel*, 251.

Evaluation

Beyond the building of the temple, a complex of ideas can be identified in the literal interpretations of Ezekiel's temple. *First, the fulfillment of God's promises is depicted in Ezekiel 40–48.* The restoration of Israel to the land, along with the rebuilt temple, and God's eternal presence, all fulfill expectations held by Israel. *Second, structures that ensure proper worship are established.* The architectural details and legislative reforms prevent Israel from repeating the same abuses that led to Yahweh's departure in the past. *Third, the eventual fulfillment of the prophetic promises will make the presence of Yahweh available to all people.* The person and power of Yahweh are displayed to the whole world through the restored nation and temple.

Undergirding each strand of thought is the idea of a restored relationship between God and humanity. The rebuilt temple serves as a place where God and his people can meet for fellowship and worship.

Figurative Interpretations

Although the previous scholars contended that a building plan and system of legislation are articulated in Ezekiel 40–48, proponents of literal interpretations fail to take genre into account. Many scholars regard the latter chapters of Ezekiel as apocalyptic or proto-apocalyptic.[31] John Taylor contended that understanding the latter chapters of Ezekiel as apocalyptic, and thus symbolic, yields an interpretation that best represents the literary character and genre of the vision.[32] Even Ralph Alexander acknowledged that Ezekiel 40–48 is apocalyptic, although he did not account for the highly symbolic nature of apocalyptic literature in his interpretation.[33]

---

31. The precise genre of Ezekiel, particularly chs. 38–48, is debated among scholars. Even those who argue against a classification of "apocalyptic" concede that some characteristics of the genre can be found in Ezekiel. Brian Peterson, who regarded Ezekiel as a bridge between prophecy and apocalyptic, provided an excellent survey of the discussion (Peterson, *Ezekiel in Context*, 341–55). Cf. Alexander, *Ezekiel*, 134; Allen, *Ezekiel 20–48*, 212; Coloe, *God Dwells with Us*, 47–48; Hitzig, *Der Prophet Ezechiel*, xiv–xv. To the contrary, Paul Hanson argued that although features of Ezekiel's prophecy were utilized in later apocalyptic writings, the original document was not apocalyptic (Hanson, *Dawn of Apocalyptic*, 228–40).

32. Taylor, *Ezekiel*, 253–54.

33. Alexander, *Ezekiel*, 134.

A figurative understanding is supported by connections between the material in Ezekiel 40–48 and other visionary accounts in Ezekiel. Formulaic phrases link the visions in Ezekiel 1:1–3, 8:1–3, and 40:1, which indicates that Ezekiel 40–48 should be interpreted as a vision, as opposed to a blueprint.[34] The larger units of chapters 1–3, 8–11, and 40–48 are also linked by the movement of God's glory. Moreover, in Ezekiel 43:3, the prophet made explicit the link between the concluding vision, the central visions, and the opening vision, "And it was like the appearance of the vision I had seen, like the vision which I saw when he came to destroy the city; and the visions were like the vision which I had seen by the river Chebar; and I fell on my face."[35] Tuell explained, "We have, then, an interconnected network of three visions which stand as the milestones of Ezekiel's ministry and as key points in the structure of his book. The vision in Ezekiel 40–48 is closely related to the earlier visions, and it demands interpretation of the same terms."[36]

A nonliteral interpretation is further reinforced by the elements that are missing from the vision.[37] Few three-dimensional measurements are given, essential construction information is missing, and the design is highly impractical. Tuell elaborated, "The massive fortified gates of the complex, for example, are out of all proportion to its relatively scant walls."[38]

The presence of mythical elements is further evidence in favor of a figurative interpretation. The high mountain of Ezekiel 40 resembles the cosmic mountain of ancient Near Eastern (ANE) and Greek mythology.[39] The supernatural creatures of gleaming bronze in Ezekiel 1:7 are recalled in Ezekiel 40:3, along with the guide whose appearance is like bronze.[40] Ezekiel 47, where the temple is the source of life and fertility, exhibits

34. (1) A date, (2) the hand of the Lord, and (3) "in visions of God."

35. Unless otherwise noted, all translations are the author's.

36. Tuell, "Ezekiel 40–42," 656. Cf. Gentry, *He Shall Have Dominion*, 365–66; Milgrom and Block, *Ezekiel's Hope*, 64; Parunak, "Literary Architecture," 61–74; Zimmerli, *Ezekiel 2*, 344, 348.

37. Block, *Beyond the River Chebar*, 186; Block, *Book of Ezekiel: Chapters 25–48*, 501–2; Milgrom and Block, *Ezekiel's Hope*, 53; Nogalski, *Interpreting Prophetic Literature*, 107–8; Taylor, *Ezekiel*, 252; Stevenson, *Vision of Transformation*, 5.

38. Tuell, "Ezekiel 40–42," 650.

39. Barker, *On Earth*, 26–30; Blenkinsopp, *Ezekiel*, 197; Block, *Beyond the River Chebar*, 167; Block, *Book of Ezekiel: Chapters 25–48*, 501; Clements, *God and Temple*, 106n3; Coloe, *God Dwells with Us*, 48; Zimmerli, *Ezekiel 2*, 347.

40. Milgrom and Block, *Ezekiel's Hope*, 65; Zimmerli, *Ezekiel 2*, 344, 348.

elements of ANE creation myths. The river that flows from the temple resembles the river that flowed from Eden, and even the act of measuring has cosmogonic undertones.[41]

Susan Niditch argued that the entire closing sequence of Ezekiel reflects the mythological pattern of divine conquest and victory. She drew upon the work of Paul Hanson, who identified the pattern in the Babylonian Enuma Elish and the Ugaritic Baal cycle. Ezekiel's liturgy begins in Ezekiel 38:10–13 with a mythic enemy challenging the Lord. The challenge results in a battle (Ezek 39:1–10), after which the victor establishes order (Ezek 39:11–16). A victory feast (Ezek 39:17–20) and procession (Ezek 39:25–29) then are followed by the establishment of the temple (Ezek 40–48).[42]

Perhaps the most convincing argument against reading Ezekiel 40–48 as a literal blueprint is that Ezekiel never claimed to present a blueprint for construction.[43] Tuell explained, "Nowhere in this text do we find either a decision to build the temple or a divine permission given for its building."[44] Moreover, no evidence can be found that the returning exiles ever attempted to reconstruct their temple or society according to Ezekiel's instructions.[45]

Blenkinsopp suggested that one of the Zion psalms may provide a clue to the ostensibly tedious level of detail in Ezekiel's description of the temple. The psalmist wrote, "Walk about Zion, and go around her; number her towers; incline your heart toward her ramparts; pass through her

41. For further discussion of the primordial river, see Barker, *Gate of Heaven*, 69, 87–79; Coloe, *God Dwells with Us*, 48; Clements, *God and Temple*, 107; Levenson, *Theology of the Program*, 7–36; Patton, "Ezekiel's Blueprint for the Temple," 164–65; Pfisterer Darr, "Wall around Paradise," 271–79. For further discussion of the cosmogonic undertones of measuring, see Hurowitz, *I Have Built You*, 326–27. Cf. Job 38:4–7; *ANET*, 67.

42. Hanson, "Old Testament Apocalyptic Reexamined," 454–79; Hanson, "Zechariah 9 and the Recapitulation," 37–59; Niditch, "Ezekiel 40–48," 208–24.

43. Nonetheless, some scholars have proposed that the structure in Ezekiel 40–48 was based upon the memory of Solomon's Temple, most prominently Zimmerli (*Ezekiel 2*, 356–58). Cf. Allen, *Ezekiel 20–48*, 229–30; Cooke, *Critical and Exegetical Commentary*, 425; Eichrodt, *Ezekiel*, 542; Hanson, *Dawn of Apocalyptic*, 228–40; Howie, "East Gate of Ezekiel's Temple," 13–19. To the contrary, Jacob Milgrom contended that the blueprint was based upon the temple of Apollo at Delphi (Milgrom and Block, *Ezekiel's Hope*, 44–53).

44. Tuell, "Ezekiel 40–42," 652. Cf. Block, *Book of Ezekiel: Chapters 25–48*, 505; Zimmerli, *I Am Yahweh*, 115; Boyle, "'Holiness has a Shape,'" 1–21.

45. Tuell, "Temple Vision of Ezekiel 40–48," 96.

fortified structures, that you may make them known to the next genera-
tion" (Ps 48:12–14). Blenkinsopp thus regarded Ezekiel's description as
a type of shared meditation: "We note also in both the psalm and the
vision the concern not only to see, consider, and meditate but to transmit
to others."[46]

Daniel Block, who provided a more comprehensive discussion of
the elements of the vision, advocated an "ideational" interpretation. He
pointed out that other visions, such as the dry bones vision of chapter
37, are not interpreted literally. Therefore, Ezekiel 40–48 should be interpreted in the same manner—as a representation of theological realities[47]:

> In presenting this theological constitution for the new Israel,
> Yahweh announces the righting of all the old wrongs, and the
> establishment of permanent, healthy deity-nation-land relation-
> ships. Ezekiel's final vision presents a lofty spiritual ideal: Where
> God is, there is Zion. Where God is, there is order and the ful-
> fillment of all his promises. Furthermore, where the presence of
> God is recognized, there is purity and holiness.[48]

Indeed, the layout of the temple complex conveys theological realities. Block averred, "The vertical geography of Ezekiel's temple proclaims
not only the glory and transcendence of God but also his mercy."[49] First,
the temple is placed upon a high hill (Ezek 40:2). Second, the series of
steps and terraces consistently progresses toward the inner court.[50] Third,
a concern for perfection is reflected in the design of the structure. The
steps add up to a combined total of twenty-five, which is "a number that
governs the entire plan."[51] Further, the entire compound is a perfect
square with a perfectly symmetrical inner structure (Ezek 42:15–20). The
symmetry may be intended to convey that nothing about God's design is
"haphazard or coincidental."[52] Fourth, upon the uppermost peak of the

---

46. Blenkinsopp, *Ezekiel*, 198–99.

47. Block, *Beyond the River Chebar*, 172. Cf. Hays, *Temple and the Tabernacle*, 182.

48. Block, *Book of Ezekiel: Chapters 25–48*, 506.

49. Block, Block, *Beyond the River Chebar*, 189. Cf. Barker, *Gate of Heaven*, 12, 25.

50. Ezek 40:6, 22, 26, 31, 34, 37, 49.

51. Block, *Beyond the River Chebar*, 187. Cf. Michael Chyutin, who pointed out
that ideal city plans often utilized "number mysticism, which was part of the arithme-
tic and geometry of the ancient world" (Chyutin, "New Jerusalem," 94). Cf. Chyutin,
New Jerusalem Scroll from Qumran, 12–13.

52. Block, *Beyond the River Chebar*, 188. Cf. Boyle, "Holiness has a Shape," 5–6, 13;
Stevenson, *Vision of Transformation*, 42, 47.

complex sat the central altar of the temple (Ezek 43:17), which represents the point of contact between God and sinful people. One would expect the divine throne room, the holy of holies, to be the center of the complex, but instead the altar is at the center. Block explained, "Although ancient temples were perceived primarily as the residence of the deity, from this design the worshipper is reminded that access to the deity presupposes correctly administered sacrifices. The altar represents the key to communion between worshipper and deity."[53]

Fifth, the compound intentionally seems constructed to correct past abuses. In Ezekiel 44:6–8, the prophet indicated that Levites previously had failed to guard the sanctity of the temple, and kings had encroached personally upon the sacred space. In the new temple, the outer wall is six cubits high and six cubits thick, a sizable and imposing barrier (Ezek 40:5), and interior spaces are demarcated in such a way that "access to them is regulated."[54] Therefore, one might conclude that even the architectural details of the complex bear theological significance.[55]

Tuell also contended that theological realities are conveyed by the vision. He postulated that an original vision was purposefully redacted during the Persian period to create a new law code for the returning exiles.[56] The original nonredacted material, however, was intended to convey theological truths rather than architectural details. Tuell asserted that only selected measurements were provided and that "any attempt to represent Ezekiel's temple graphically involves a considerable amount of speculation."[57] The original purpose of the vision was to reassure God's people of his presence.[58]

Tuell drew upon the informative study of Victor Hurowitz to support his conclusion that the temple description was not intended as an actual blueprint. Hurowitz outlined the typical pattern of building accounts in Semitic and Mesopotamian writings:

1. The circumstances of the project and decision to build

53. Block, *Beyond the River Chebar*, 189.

54. Block, *Beyond the River Chebar*, 189.

55. Nogalski, *Interpreting Prophetic Literature*, 107–8.

56. The redacted legislation in Ezekiel 40–48 became the religious polity of Judea in the Persian period. Ezekiel's "original concern for the divine Presence has been preserved," but "the function of the text has been redirected" (Tuell, *Law of the Temple*, 75).

57. Tuell, *Ezekiel*, 285.

58. Tuell, *Ezekiel*, 287, 295–96.

2. Preparations, such as drafting workmen, gathering materials

3. Description of the building

4. The dedication rites and festivities

5. Blessing and/or prayer of the king, etc.

6. Blessings and curses of future generations[59]

Hurowitz's pattern holds for biblical temple building, but numerous elements are missing in Ezekiel's vision. Tuell explained, "Ezekiel's temple plan is hybrid, combining different sorts of structures into a wholly unique form."[60]

Another genre proposed by Hurowitz is the descriptive account, where detailed measurements of existing structures are provided. Such accounts are not found elsewhere in the Bible, but numerous examples can be found in Mesopotamian literature.[61] Hurowitz, therefore, proposed that Ezekiel's temple should be viewed through the lens of ANE temple *description* accounts rather than *building* accounts. Hurowitz also pointed to "an independent Israelite or Judean tradition of describing buildings, which is continued most notably in the Qumran *Temple Scroll* and the Mishnah's tractate *Middoth*."[62]

Tuell further posited that Ezekiel's temple vision is a description of the heavenly temple. He contended that the prophet was given a tour through "the heavenly archetype, the *real* temple, of which the temple of Jerusalem was but a shadow."[63] Ezekiel's temple is, thus, "an architectonic manifestation of Yahweh's glory," as the divine presence is mediated through verbal iconography.[64] "The detailed description serves to give us an overwhelming sense of the symmetry and order in the temple's design. It also enables us to share in Ezekiel's experience, to see in our mind's eye what he sees. But we cannot even begin to construct Ezekiel's temple on the basis of these measurements."[65]

---

59. Hurowitz, *I Have Built You*, 64.

60. Tuell, "Ezekiel 40–42," 651.

61. Hurowitz, *I Have Built You*, 224–59. Cf. Tuell, "Ezekiel 40–42," 653–54.

62. Hurowitz, *I Have Built You*, 247–48 (emphasis his). Cf. Block, *Beyond the River Chebar*, 184–85.

63. Tuell, "Ezekiel 40–42," 657 (emphasis his). Cf. Joyce, "Ezekiel 40–42," 17–41; Levey, "Targum to Ezekiel," 139–58.

64. Tuell, "Temple Vision of Ezekiel 40–48," 101.

65. Tuell, "Ezekiel 40–42," 652. Cf. Tuell, *Ezekiel*, 295–96.

Both Hanna Liss and Stephen Cook likewise argued that the literary aspect of the vision is central to interpretation. Liss wrote that the illusory nature of the vision protects the sanctity of the temple. The holiness of the sanctuary cannot be encroached upon because no one from the real world occupies the complex. Priestly and princely duties are described, but no one other than God resides in the precincts.[66]

In addition to preserving the sanctity of the temple, the literary nature of the vision also renders the structure more accessible, as anyone can enter "simply by reading."[67] Ezekiel enters the model world of the temple for the purpose of bringing the sanctuary back and making the holy precinct accessible to his audience.[68] Further, the "literary construct aims to train Israel in patterning its life in such a way as to interconnect with the holiness of God and thus grow in sanctification. Growth in sanctification over time will amount to progress towards the reign of God."[69] The literary iconography, thus, becomes a medium for the divine presence. Through the literary reality, readers can experience the presence of God as they share Ezekiel's transcendent vision. By means of lexical and syntactical complexity, worshippers can form complex images in their minds, such that they can visualize what Ezekiel saw even in his absence.[70] Similarly, Corrine Patton asserted that the textualized temple "became a source for spiritual contemplation and eschatological vision, because then it did exist and function, not as building, but as hope."[71]

Susan Niditch also proposed that Ezekiel 40–48 served a devotional function for the exilic community. Niditch drew parallels between Ezekiel's vision and Buddhist mandalas, which are created in reflection of the real mandala in the sacred realm. Through ritual activity and meditation, proselytes experience the sacred:

> Closest to the [sacred] realm itself are the three-dimensional buildings, palaces of the deities, built with real materials . . . Exceedingly detailed instructions for the building of mandalas exist in largely untranslated Tantric literature, written in a difficult-to-understand shorthand employed by those initiated

66. Liss, "Describe the Temple," 122–43.

67. Liss, "Describe the Temple," 135. Cf. Cook, "Ezekiel's God Incarnate!," 132–49; Tuell, "Divine Presence and Absence," 97–116.

68. Cook, "Ezekiel's God Incarnate!," 147.

69. Cook, "Ezekiel's God Incarnate!," 149.

70. Tuell, "Ezekiel 40–42," 649, 662.

71. Patton, "Ezekiel's Blueprint for the Temple," 189–90.

into the special science of the sacred spaces. These texts, with detailed information on design, lay-out, size, structure, and building materials, must make one think of Ezekiel 40–48.[72]

Niditch labeled Ezekiel's vision as cosmogonic due to the defining and differentiating of reality. She asserted that Ezekiel's detailed hierarchy of people, places, and boundaries creates a "map of reality."[73] She continued, "What has been described and demarcated is not merely a city and a land, but the whole world, self-contained, self-sufficient, and in that wholeness, holy."[74]

Yet, Ezekiel's was not a spatial creation but a moral and relational one.[75] Bennett Simon suggested that the carefully designed spaces of the new temple may reflect the condition of the new heart promised in Ezekiel 36:36. "The emphasis on geometry and measurement serves as an attempt to calm the disturbances caused by persistent moral and theological problems that are recalcitrant to definitive solution."[76] Such conceptions do not stray far from ANE beliefs, in which building a temple transforms chaos into orderly cosmos.[77] Perhaps Ezekiel took the common teleological framework of temple building and applied the formulaic details to the moral realm.

Indeed, in Ezekiel 43:10–11, the prophet expressly articulated that the design of the temple should create an awareness of sin among the people. Zimmerli wrote that the architectural plan of the temple became "the basic document of a penitential sermon."[78] Block even suggested that Ezekiel 43:10–11 may provide the key to interpreting the entire vision. The people's recognition of their shame in light of the temple's perfection will lead them to an understanding of the magnitude of God's grace.[79]

Perfection may function as the basis of the phrase "measure the plan," וּמָדְדוּ אֶת־תָּכְנִית (Ezek 43:10). The rare term תָּכְנִית is used only in Ezekiel 28:12 and 43:10, both times in reference to perfection. The verbal

---

72. Niditch, "Ezekiel 40–48," 212.

73. Niditch, "Ezekiel 40–48," 217.

74. Niditch, "Ezekiel 40–48," 218.

75. Simon, "Ezekiel's Geometric Vision," 411–38. Cf. Nielsen, "Ezekiel's Visionary Call as Prologue," 99–114.

76. Simon, "Ezekiel's Geometric Vision," 412.

77. Lundquist, "Temple, Covenant, and Law," 293–305; Walton, *Lost World of Genesis One*, 71–76. Cf. *ANET* 68–69.

78. Zimmerli, *I Am Yahweh*, 117.

79. Block, *Beyond the River Chebar*, 186; Tuell, *Ezekiel*, 301.

root may yield clarification as well. The term תכן can be used of physical or moral evaluation.[80] Joseph Breuer suggested that the phrase implies weighing individual entities to determine their relationship to one another.[81] Therefore, to "measure the plan" may indicate that when the people see or hear the plan they evaluate the temple as perfect and, by comparison, recognize their own inadequacy. Simon wrote, "We thus see a confluence of proper proportion in the moral and architectural realms."[82]

The thesis of Ellen Davis accords well with the literary theories of Tuell, Liss, Cook, Niditch, and Simon. Davis contended that Ezekiel represented a new form of prophecy, in which the figure of the prophet was replaced by the text, as the medium of prophecy is not verbal, but textual. Indeed, in Ezekiel 43:11, the prophet's angelic guide may have indicated that Ezekiel should make the plan known *by* writing the vision for the people: הוֹדַע אוֹתָם וּכְתֹב.[83] Davis contended that the written medium rendered the message independent of the prophetic figure and the response of the people, so that the information could come straight from God. The unidirectional communication allowed Ezekiel to create a new world in response to the failures of the past and the fall of Jerusalem. Thus, the direct communication from the Lord became an authoritative message of hope by providing a teleological framework for the future.[84]

Regardless of interpretive variations, scholars of a figurative bent tend to agree that the details of Ezekiel 40–48 serve to ensure that the holiness of God cannot be profaned. Stevenson argued that the primary purpose of Ezekiel's vision is to define gradations of holiness—to separate holy and common.[85] Both the priestly hierarchy and the spatial dimensions reflect gradations of holiness. "Like the hierarchy of sacerdotal roles, this detailed spatial hierarchy guards the temple's sanctity, and it

---

80. BDB 1067.

81. Breuer, *Book of Yechzkel*, 251.

82. Simon, "Ezekiel's Geometric Vision," 431.

83. Menahem Haran suggested that the conjunction should be viewed as a *vav explicativum*, whereby the *vav* is used to explain a corresponding phrase. Haran, "Law-Code of Ezekiel XL–XLVIII," 45–71. Cf. GKC, 484n1b.

84. Davis, *Swallowing the Scroll*, 118.

85. Stevenson, *Vision of Transformation*, 19, 117. Cf. Ganzel and Holtz, "Ezekiel's Temple in Babylonian Context," 211–26; Greenberg, "Design and Themes," 193; Liss, "Describe the Temple," 133–37; Milgrom and Block, *Ezekiel's Hope*, 43; Tuell, *Law of the Temple*, 59; Tuell, *Ezekiel*, 301.

allows the Israelite congregation a safe, tempered exposure to the burning, sanctifying power of God."[86]

Jonathan Klawans proposed that Ezekiel especially criticized sins
that defile the land and sanctuary, which resulted in the departure of
God's glory and the people's exile from the land.[87] Further, Ezekiel viewed
the First Temple as "vastly inadequate—structurally and otherwise—to
the task of maintaining the requisite holiness of God's residence. Ezekiel's
is not just a vision of what will be but equally a vision of what should
have been. The vision of the future contains within it a critique of the
past."[88] Thus, both Klawans and Stevenson described the vision as one of
transformation rather than restoration. Ezekiel never hoped to return his
people to the past, but a new and better future.[89]

As indicated by the foregoing analysis, numerous scholars contend
that through the vision in chapters 40–48, Ezekiel intended to inspire
hope and transformation among the exiles. Certainly his vision was relevant for the original hearers, but believers throughout history have also
appropriated the message. Through familiar, recognizable forms, Ezekiel
communicated timeless truths about God himself and God's relationship
with his people.[90]

The utility of the vision in inspiring past and present hearers does
not preclude an element of future fulfillment. Beale viewed Jesus Christ
as the fulfillment of Ezekiel's temple vision. Daniel Hayes likewise saw
Christ in Ezekiel's prophecy. He proposed that the vision in 40–48 points

> figuratively and representatively to realities brought about by
> Jesus Christ in the New Testament and probably realized in the
> new Jerusalem described in Revelation 21–22, which contains
> numerous similarities. What Ezekiel is shown is a vision of hope
> for the future in which the presence of God and true worship of
> God are restored, events that are fulfilled by the incarnation of
> Christ and the final new heavens and new earth of Revelation
> 21–22.[91]

86. Cook and Patton, "Introduction," 14.

87. Ezek 5:11; 8:9–18; 11:6–7; 22:10; 36:17.

88. Klawans, *Purity, Sacrifice, and the Temple*, 95–96. Cf. Hays, *Temple and the
Tabernacle*, 63–103.

89. Klawans, *Purity, Sacrifice, and the Temple*, 95; Stevenson, *Vision of Transformation*, 149.

90. Taylor, *Ezekiel*, 253.

91. Hays, *Temple and the Tabernacle*, 182.

Upon the advent of Christ, the theological realities of the temple are transformed dramatically. Jesus' sacrifice renders the need for animal sacrifice obsolete, and the Spirit becomes the medium through which God dwells among his people.

Evaluation

Several points can be distilled from the discussion of figurative inter-pretations. *First, the perfection of God's plan is expressed symbolically through highly ordered legislation and architecture.* Verbal iconography allows readers to process complex images and anticipate a new, better reality. *Second, the holiness of God is emphasized through the design and symmetry of the temple and surrounding precincts.* The hierarchies of the temple, land, and people ensure that the holiness of God never again can be profaned. *Third, all elements work together to safeguard the perpetual presence of God with his people.* Proper boundaries ensure the presence of God within the restored paradise, as the preceding chaos is transformed into a new cosmos. Additionally, the sacrifices and rituals point to the centrality of worship in the new reality.[92] True worship can take place be-cause the perfection of the temple creates an inviolable penitence in the people. The renewed individuals are free to commune with God absent any of the former barriers to fellowship.

The foundational emphases of the figurative interpretations do not differ greatly from those of the literal interpretations. Regardless of the hermeneutical standpoints of individual interpreters, the presence of God with his people is of central importance to Ezekiel's message. The timeless theological principle, therefore, is God dwelling with his people in perfect communion.

92. Taylor, *Ezekiel*, 253.

4.

Temple and Messiah in Literature Predating Revelation

THE TEMPLE WAS A favorite topic of Jewish writings. Klawans explained, "As is widely recognized, the temple was the fulcrum of ancient Jewish religion. The centrality of the temple as a social institution can hardly be denied."[1] Thus, the destruction of the temple in 586 BCE and 70 CE impacted the Jewish people in a profound way. The struggle to redefine identity in the face of such loss is illustrated in the literature of the time.[2]

Ezekiel's prophecy of a glorious future was iterated within the context most familiar to him—a hierocratic Jewish framework. For Ezekiel and the people to whom he prophesied, a restored Israel was inconceivable without a restored temple.[3] Beale explained, "It is unlikely that the prophet could have imagined that the fulfillment of that prophecy would be in a non literal structure and would be only in the Messiah and in God's presence with his people in the new creation."[4]

John was influenced by a similar Jewish ideology as Ezekiel. Yet, as he drew upon Ezekiel and other OT texts, John creatively reshaped traditions in the light of his Christian ideology. Such Jewish and Christian

1. Klawans, *Purity, Sacrifice, and the Temple*, 104.

2. Knibb, "Temple and Cult," 401–16; Vogelgesang, "Interpretation of Ezekiel," 134–35.

3. Bauckham, *Climax of Prophecy*, 450; Bullock, *Introduction to the Old Testament*, 303; Block, *Book of Ezekiel: Chapters 25–48*, 505; Köstenberger, "John," 415–512; Spatafora, *From the "Temple of God,"* 46.

4. Beale, *Book of Revelation*, 1098.

traditions will be examined in the current and following chapter in order to determine the tenor of thought in regard to the temple and the messiah in John's contemporary setting. Although the mind-set of the audience is not a determining factor in how John utilized Ezekiel's vision, the attestation of similar interpretations increases the likelihood that John was intentional as he reframed Ezekiel 40–48.[5] James Charlesworth explained that Christology, in particular, "did not evolve, with unexpected jumps and mutations, but it developed out of pregnant elements ready for maturation."[6]

Correspondingly, the meaning of an apocalyptic text is best sought by comparison with similar works.[7] Adela Yarbro Collins suggested, "An apocalyptic work reflects elements of the religious tradition with which its author primarily identified. At the same time, however, those traditional elements have often been modified through the author's experience of the world-thoughts of other ethnic or cultural groups in his environment."[8] The "network of intertextuality" is especially important for apocalyptic texts due to the elusive nature of the genre.[9] Thus, extrabiblical documents are important in identifying the ideological and theological matrices of early Christianity, particularly those of Revelation.[10] However, determining whether John was familiar with any particular document is exceedingly difficult. The intent for a diachronic analysis is, therefore, to determine whether a general matrix of thought existed for John and

5. For an evaluation of the "audience-oriented approach," see Porter, *Sacred Tradition*, 3–25.

6. Charlesworth, *Old Testament Pseudepigrapha*, 81. Cf. Kirschner, "Apocalyptic and Rabbinic Responses," 31; Rowland, "Temple in the New Testament," 469–83.

7. Vorster, "'Genre' and the Revelation," 103–23.

8. Collins, "History-of-Religions Approach to Apocalypticism," 380. Cf. Bauckham, *Climax of Prophecy*, xi–xii, 38–91; Vogelgesang, "Interpretation of Ezekiel," 80, 93–95.

9. Vorster, "'Genre' and the Revelation," 110. Cf. Aune, "Apocalypse of John and the Problem," 65–96; Collins, *Apocalypse*; Koch, "What Is Apocalyptic?" 16–36; Hanson, "Old Testament Apocalyptic Reexamined," 454–79; Mathewson, "Revelation in Recent Genre Criticism"; Vogelgesang, "Interpretation of Ezekiel," 134.

10. Although Revelation is categorized as apocalyptic, a number of differences can be identified between Revelation and other apocalyptic works, most noticeably the lack of pseudonymity. For discussions of the differences, see Morris, *Book of Revelation*, 25–27; Mounce, *Book of Revelation*, 23–24.

his readers to draw upon in their understanding of Ezekiel's temple in a nonliteral manner.[11]

For practical purposes, the sources examined will be delimited. Sources likely predating Revelation will be covered in the current chapter. These include Tobit, Baruch, 1–2 Enoch, Sibylline Oracle 3, the Testaments of the Twelve Patriarchs, Jubilees, 2 Ezekiel, and the Qumran Sectarian documents.

Two further delimitations will be helpful before proceeding. First, a detailed exegesis of each work will not be provided. Instead, only salient passages will be addressed, particularly those relevant to Ezekiel and Revelation. Second, the purpose of the analysis is not to establish direct lines of influence, but rather the manner in which the works contributed to the general theological and literary milieu of Second Temple period Judeo-Christian thought.

Tobit

The pseudepigraphic book of Tobit can be dated with some confidence to 225–175 BCE.[12] Tobit, a pious Jew, is the subject of the book that bears his name. Tobit's faithfulness is demonstrated by his regular tithes and visits to the Jerusalem Temple for holy days, that is, prior to his deportation to Assyria.

The destruction of the temple is reported in Tobit 13:9–17. Demolition is portrayed as a precursor to rebuilding, as the author anticipated the restoration of Jerusalem. Tobit prays that the glory of God will shine on all nations, and that the city will last forever: "For Jerusalem will be built as a city for His dwelling for eternity . . . And the gates of Jerusalem

11. The term *temple* carries a wide breadth of mythological and theological associations. John M. Lundquist provided a taxonomy of temple conceptions in which common elements include: a cosmic mountain, primordial waters, cosmological orientation, liminal space, sacral meals, and sacrifice (Lundquist, "What Is a Temple?" 205–19). Cf. Lundquist, "Common Temple Ideology," 53–76. However, in the following analysis, the designation of *temple* will require that structural or architectural elements be present.

12. Carey Moore explained, "The book's *terminus ad quem* is unquestionably pre-Maccabean, for it evidences none of the ethnic and religious hatred of that period (167–135 B. C. E.)" (Moore, *Tobit*, 42). Cf. Craghan, *Esther, Judith, Tobit, Jonah, Ruth*, 134–35; Fitzmyer, *Tobit*, 51; Gross, *Tobit, Judit*, 9; Lee, *New Jerusalem*, 82; Oesterley, *Introduction to the Books*,168–69.

will be constructed in sapphire and emerald, and all your walls in precious stone; the towers of Jerusalem will be constructed in gold, and the ramparts in pure gold; the streets of Jerusalem will be paved with garnet and the stone of Ophir" (Tob 13:16).[13] Although the city is restored, a new temple never is mentioned. Nonetheless, the imagery implies the presence of a temple, as towers are a common symbol for temples.[14]

The restoration ostensibly points toward the Second Temple, since the one that is destroyed in the passage is Solomon's. Yet, the vivid description implies that more is in view than a typical city. Although precious stones and costly materials are a common feature of the heavenly Jerusalem, the book of Tobit exhibits little fantastical imagery that typically accompanies the heavenly realm. Further, the narrative leads the reader to anticipate a literal restoration of Jerusalem. The description of the restored Jerusalem, thus, most likely portrays the eschatological state. Jerusalem is understood as the ideal dwelling for the Lord, and as such "it must be rebuilt with splendor."[15] Further, "Tobit depicts Jerusalem as a person, place, and symbol; it is sinful and righteous, destroyed and rebuilt, temporal and eternal."[16] Thus, the analysis can conclude with a high level of confidence that Tobit envisions a renewed Jerusalem and temple in the eschaton.

Baruch

Baruch is a composite document that was completed between 200 and 60 BCE.[17] Like Tobit, Baruch exhibits a diaspora perspective. Both authors anticipated a return to the land as well as a literal restoration of Jerusalem in the eschatological age.[18]

In the early chapters of Baruch, the existence of both the heavenly temple and the earthly one are implied. The heavenly temple is mentioned only in passing: "O Lord look down from your holy dwelling place

13. Tob 13:17 (13:16 NRSV) is translated from the text family Sinaiticus.

14. Barker, *Gate of Heaven*, 128–30. Cf. Gen 11:1–9; 1 En. 87:3; 89:50, 73; Sib. Or. 5:423–25.

15. Fitzmyer, *Tobit*, 316. Cf. Lee, *New Jerusalem*, 84; Moore, *Tobit*, 282–85.

16. Griffin, "Theology and Function of Prayer," 345.

17. Helyer, *Exploring Jewish Literature*, 74–75; Metzger, *Introduction to the Apocrypha*, 89–90; Oesterley, *Introduction to the Books*, 263–65; Tov, *Septuagint Translation of Jeremiah*, 111–33.

18. Moore, *Tobit*, 208–85, 293–95.

and think of us" (Bar 2:16). Then in Baruch 2:26, the destruction of the Jerusalem Temple is referenced obliquely: "And the house that is called by your name, you have made as it is today on account of the wickedness of the house of Israel and the house of Judah."[19]

The sins of the people are portrayed as the cause of Jerusalem's destruction. By placing blame on the people, the author is able to maintain the sanctity of Jerusalem and explain why the city has fallen.[20] Correspondingly, hope for restoration is at the heart of the book.[21]

A poem describing the restoration of Zion is found in Baruch 4:5—5:9. The hope expressed in the psalm is an earthly one as the author provided a vision of the people returning to the homeland.[22] The book concludes with the following lines:

> For God has ordered that every high mountain and the eternal hills be made low, and the valleys filled into level ground, so that Israel should walk securely in the glory of God. And the woods and every fragrant tree have shaded Israel at the command of God. For God will lead Israel with joy, in the light of His glory with mercy and righteousness, which are from himself. (Bar 5:7–9)

As with Tobit, the vividness of the restoration is a depiction of the blessings of the eschatological age.[23] No mention is made of a restored temple, but in context, such an omission is not surprising. The book gives little attention to the temple, restored or otherwise. The absence does not imply that no temple is present in the eschaton, only that the author did not feel a need to discuss the sanctuary.

The Testaments of the Twelve Patriarchs

The composition history of the Testaments of the Twelve Patriarchs is a controversial issue among scholars of the pseudepigrapha.[24] According

19. Cf. Bar 3:2–8; 4:7–8, 12–13.

20. Lee, *New Jerusalem*, 141–43.

21. Bar 2:27–35; 4:5–6, 18, 21–37; 5:1–9; Cf. Helyer, *Exploring Jewish Literature*, 174.

22. Pfeiffer, *History of New Testament Times*, 425.

23. Lee, *New Jerusalem*, 142–43; Moore, *Tobit*, 293–95.

24. Briggs, *Jewish Temple Imagery*, 126–27; Collins, *Apocalyptic Imagination*, 133–34; Kee, "Testaments of the Twelve Patriarchs," 775–828; Slingerland, *Testaments*

to Howard Kee, the testaments were composed in the Maccabean period between 150 and 100 BCE, and the Jewish documents bear evidence of Christian interpolations from the early second century CE.[25] Conversely, Marinus de Jonge asserted that the testaments were originally Christian, but with Jewish interpolations.[26] Regardless of whether the original work was Jewish or Christian, the documents seem to reflect an openness to several strands of Judaism during the Second Temple period.[27]

Only the testaments of Levi, Dan, and Benjamin contain material that is relevant to the current study. The analysis will begin with the Testament of Levi.

The Testament of Levi

The primary purpose of the Testament of Levi (T. Levi) is to legitimize Levi and his successors as priests. The ascent of a priestly figure to the heavenly temple is described in chapters 1–5, which John Collins referred to as a "full-blown apocalypse."[28] The opening is vaguely reminiscent of Ezekiel 40:1–4[29]: "Then a sleep fell upon me, and I beheld a high mountain . . . And behold the heavens were opened, and an angel of God said to me: Levi, enter" (T. Levi 2:5–6).[30] The continuing narrative describes an ascent from a high mountain and a journey through seven heavens. The top three heavens are holy, with the highest heaven housing God's throne. Margaret Barker noted that the three levels correspond to the temple precincts: the courtyard, *hekal* (holy place), and *debir* (holy of holies). Therefore, seeing God's presence in the most holy place is the climax of the vision.[31]

---

of the Twelve Patriarchs.

25. Kee, "Testaments of the Twelve Patriarchs," 777–78.

26. de Jonge, *Testaments of the Twelve Patriarchs.* However, in a more recent work, de Jonge and Hollander conceded that the Testaments in their current state could represent a reworking and appropriation of an originally Jewish text (Hollander and de Jonge, *Testaments of the Twelve Patriarchs,* 82–85).

27. Kee, "Testaments of the Twelve Patriarchs," 778.

28. Collins, *Apocalyptic Imagination,* 137–38.

29. Manning, *Echoes of a Prophet,* 80.

30. Translations of the testaments of the twelve patriarchs are reproduced from Hollander and de Jonge, *Testaments of the Twelve Patriarchs.*

31. Barker, *Gate of Heaven,* 162; Hollander and de Jonge, *Testaments of the Twelve Patriarchs,* 144.

The latter chapters of the testament are relevant as well. In Testament of Levi 15 and 16, the author discussed the destruction of the Jerusalem Temple (T. Levi 15:1; 16:4), and in Testament of Levi 17:10, he described restoration. Yet, sinful priests still officiate in the restored house, as the reconstruction appears to precede further punishment on evil priests. The sinfulness of the priests (T. Levi 17:11) will provoke the vengeance of the Lord (T. Levi 18:1), who will raise up a "new priest," the messiah (T. Levi 18:1–3). The messiah will restore the earth to an edenic state, providing light, peace, and knowledge (T. Levi 18:10–11). Such eschatological blessings are brought about by the opening of heaven and the heavenly temple, from which holiness and glory come to rest upon the messiah (T. Levi 18:5–6).

Of interest to the current study is that no temple is rebuilt. Klawans contended that the absence of a physical temple in the Testament of Levi should not be overemphasized, as the testament is set prior to the time in which a physical temple existed.[32] However, attention to the temple earlier in the narrative creates the expectation for a restored temple in the eschaton. The presence on an eternal priesthood with no mention of the temple or sacrificial service is a glaring and noticeable incongruence.

Instead, the author of the Testament of Levi emphasized that a temple is not required because the messiah "will open the gates of paradise" (T. Levi 18:10). The "temple of glory" is mentioned in Testament of Levi 18:6, but the author gave no indication that the heavenly temple comes down to earth, as the sanctuary sometimes does in apocalyptic literature.[33] Therefore, the Testament of Levi provides an example of a paradisal earth in which the eschatological blessings are brought about by the messiah, who reigns forever in the absence of a physical temple (T. Levi 18:8).

The Testament of Dan

The author of the Testament of Dan (T. Dan) also anticipated a messianic figure from the tribe of Levi. Moreover, two messiahs may be envisioned—one royal and one priestly.[34] In chapter 5, the author indicated

32. Klawans, *Purity, Sacrifice, and the Temple*, 133.

33. To the contrary, Beale interpreted T. Levi 18:6 and T. Benj. 9:2 as depicting a literal eschatological temple (Beale, *Book of Revelation*, 1092).

34. The idea of two messiahs is expressed also in T. Judah, although the term *messiah* never is used (T. Jud. 21:2–4). The Qumran sectarians likewise anticipated both a priestly and a royal messiah (4QD VII, 18–21; XII, 23–XIII, 1; 1QS IX, 9–11; 1QSa

that salvation will come from the tribes of Levi *and* Judah (T. Dan 5:9). Nonetheless, the passage proceeds with singular pronouns, indicating that the messianic figure will defeat Beliar and grant eternal peace. As in the Testament of Levi, the saints rest in an edenic setting. Yet, where the author of the Testament of Levi made no explicit mention of the new Jerusalem, the parallelism of Testament of Dan 5:12 indicates that Eden and new Jerusalem are the same entity: "And the saints will rest in Eden; and the righteous will rejoice in the new Jerusalem, which will be to the glory of God forever."

The author also indicated that when Israel repents, the Lord will bring his people back to his holy place. The verses read, "And so when you return to the Lord, you will obtain mercy, and he will bring you into his sanctuary, proclaiming peace to you" (T. Dan 5:9). At first glance, the verse appears to refer to the temple. However, context indicates that the sanctuary should be interpreted as the Lord himself, as in Exodus 11:16 and Testament of Benjamin 10:11. If the Lord is the sanctuary to which the author referred, then no mention is made of a temple in the new Jerusalem. The eternal paradise prospers for eternity "because the Lord will be in the midst of it living together with men" (T. Dan 5:13).[35]

The Testament of Benjamin

The author of the Testament of Benjamin (T. Benj.) also spoke of salvation through a messianic figure in chapters 9–10. Israel and the gentiles will gather in the new Jerusalem for the coming of the messiah[36]:

> But the temple of God will be in your portion, and the last will be more glorious than the first; and there the twelve tribes and all the Gentiles will be gathered together, until the Most High will send forth his salvation in the visitation of an only-begotten prophet. [And he will enter into the first temple, and there the Lord will be outraged and set at nought and lifted upon a tree. And the veil of the temple will be rent, and the spirit of God will pass on to the Gentiles, as a fire that is poured out. And he will rise from Hades and ascend from earth unto heaven. And I knew how humble he will be on earth and how glorious in heaven]. (T. Benj. 9:2–3)

II, 11–21).

35. Hollander and de Jonge, *Testaments of the Twelve Patriarchs*, 286.

36. Hollander and de Jonge, *Testaments of the Twelve Patriarchs*, 435–36.

In Testament of Benjamin chapter 9, the author anticipated salvation from an "only-begotten prophet" (T. Benj. 9:2). The lines in brackets are almost certainly a Christian interpolation indicating that the preceding lines were understood to refer to Christ, as least by some exegetes.[37] Additionally, the author of the Testament of Benjamin professed belief in the appearance of God on earth as a man[38]:

> Then we also will rise, each one over our tribe, worshipping the king of heaven who appeared on earth in the form of a man of humility; and as many as believed in him on earth, will rejoice with him. Then also all men will rise, some unto glory and some unto shame. And the Lord will judge Israel first for unrighteousness done to him, because they did not believe that God appeared in the flesh as a deliverer. (T. Benj. 10:7–8)

The "king of heaven" and "man of humility" in the passage is the Lord, and also likely the same figure as the "only-begotten prophet" from the previous chapter.

The author also mentioned a former temple and a latter temple in chapter 9. The glory of the final temple finds expression in the unification of Israel and the nations as well as the "(second) advent of Jesus Christ in Jerusalem at the end of times."[39] The former temple appears to refer to all iterations of the early Jewish temple, since the "last" seems to be the temple of the eschatological age.

Determining whether the latter temple is literal or figurative is difficult. The identification of the last temple as a gathering place for Jews and gentiles appears to indicate that the temple is a physical structure. However, an edenic eschaton without a temple is envisioned in both the Testament of Levi and the Testament of Dan. As the testaments present a generally unified perspective on the future of Israel, the latter temple will be identified as a metaphorical reference to the same messiah that figures in the Testament of Levi and the Testament of Dan.[40]

---

37. Hollander and de Jonge, *Testaments of the Twelve Patriarchs*, 37, 436; Kee, "Testaments of the Twelve Patriarchs," 827.

38. de Jonge, *Jewish Eschatology*, 167.

39. Hollander and de Jonge, *Testaments of the Twelve Patriarchs*, 435.

40. de Jonge, *Jewish Eschatology*, 166.

1 Enoch

The oldest of the Enochian literature, 1 Enoch is a composite work. The document commonly is divided as follows:

1. The Book of Watchers (1–36)
2. The Similitudes (37–71)
3. The Book of Astronomical Writings (72–82)
4. The Book of Dreams (83–90)
5. The Epistle of Enoch (91–107)

The majority of the book can be dated to the second century BCE. However, the Similitudes were composed possibly as late as the first century CE.[41] For the current study, only the Book of the Watchers, the Similitudes, and the Book of Dreams will be discussed. Due to the later dating, the Similitudes will be discussed in the next chapter.

The Book of Watchers

The Book of Watchers, 1 Enoch 1–36, is composite.[42] Chapters 1–5 consist of a judgment oracle. Chapters 6–11 are comprised of a revolt by "heavenly watchers," concomitant earthly evil, and God's judgment by means of the flood. Chapters 12–16 are a commentary on the previous material, along with an account of Enoch's heavenly commissioning. Chapters 17–19 and 20–36, finally, are parallel descriptions of Enoch's cosmic journeys.[43]

The first relevant passage is 1 Enoch 10:16—11:2. Following a recapitulation of the flood narrative, the restoration of creation commences as God commands the angel Michael to renovate the earth. In verse 21, the author may have hinted at a messianic figure, as the Lord says, "All nations shall worship and bless me; and they will all prostrate themselves

41. Black, *Book of Enoch*, 1–7; Collins, *Apocalyptic Imagination*, 44; Isaac, "1 (Ethiopic Apocalypse of) Enoch," 5–89; Knibb, *Essays on the Book*, 143–60; Nickelsburg, *1 Enoch 1*, 14.

42. The final form likely took shape by the mid-third century BCE, although some sections may predate the Hellenistic period (Nickelsburg, *1 Enoch 1*, 7).

43. Nickelsburg, *1 Enoch 1*, 7; VanderKam, "Biblical Interpretation in 1 Enoch," 96–125.

to me."[44] Hanson viewed the person being worshipped as a messianic figure who makes the restoration possible. Nations come to worship the new king as the earth is cleansed from defilement and suffering forever.[45] Lee associated such proceeding with the eschatological temple, which is described as the site of God's glorification and the place where all nations will come to worship. Lee further contended that the glorification of the Lord in 1 Enoch 10:16–22 indicates that the eschatological temple is an essential component of the new creation.[46] Contrary to Lee's assertion, however, the temple is mentioned nowhere or even hinted at in these verses. God, or the messianic figure proposed by Hanson, is glorified in a creation *without* the temple.

The next relevant chapter is 1 Enoch 14, which comprises the earliest heavenly ascent narrative in Jewish literature, with the possible exception of Ezekiel 40–48. The heavenly sanctuary had become a topic of curiosity and a source of hope following the destruction of Solomon's Temple. Martha Himmelfarb explained, "This process can be traced back to Ezekiel, who takes the throne of cherubim out of the holy of holies of the Jerusalem temple and turns it into a vehicle that can carry the glory of God from the defiled temple (chs. 1, 8–11)."[47]

In 1 Enoch 14, the seer proceeds through heaven, which is portrayed as a temple. Nowhere does the author state outright that the tour takes place in a temple. However, several features indicate that the heavenly temple is in view. First, the palace of a deity is by definition a temple. Second, in 1 Enoch 14:9–11, the location is described as a "great house" with walls, floors, and a ceiling. Third, the description of the angels approaching God suggests that at least some of them were regarded as priests. Fourth, the author of Testament of Levi 2–5 drew upon Enoch's vision in an explicit account of the heavenly temple.[48]

Numerous similarities can be identified between the temple visions of Enoch and Ezekiel: being transported by God, visionary language (cloud, wind, water, fire), cherubim, God's throne, and the absence of

---

44. Translations of 1 Enoch are reproduced from Isaac, "1 (Ethiopic Apocalypse of) Enoch."

45. Hanson, "Rebellion in Heaven," 195–233.

46. Lee, *New Jerusalem*, 56, 71.

47. Himmelfarb, "Apocalyptic Ascent," 211. Cf. Himmelfarb, "From Prophecy to Apocalypse, 145–65; Joyce, "Ezekiel 40–42," 17.

48. Himmelfarb, "Apocalyptic Ascent," 211; Nickelsburg, *1 Enoch 1*, 256.

people.[49] Additionally, "In form and content [1 En. 14:8—16:4] corresponds closely to the call scenes of biblical prophets, especially that of Ezekiel."[50] In biblical call narratives, the prophet is typically passive, while Enoch, like Ezekiel, is actively involved in his vision. Thus, Ezekiel 8–11 and 40–48 seem to have served, at least in part, as a model for 1 Enoch 14.[51] Himmelfarb wrote, "For Jews of the Second Temple period and later, Ezekiel is a most suitable source for the description of [heavenly ascents]."[52] That Ezekiel's visions were used as a pattern for later ascent narratives may indicate that at least some authors or groups interpreted Ezekiel's vision as a heavenly ascent.

Like Ezekiel, Enoch proceeds from the outer to the inner sanctum. The progression can be divided into three sections—the description of the first house of the temple (1 En. 14:8-14), the description of the second house of the temple (1 En. 14:15-17), and the description of the throne in the second house (1 En. 14:18-20). However, unlike Ezekiel's more mundane journey, Enoch's trek becomes increasingly fantastical, with hailstones, fire, snow, lightning, and astrological phenomena. Also, unlike Ezekiel's vision, Enoch's journey becomes increasingly hazardous until he eventually collapses in terror (1 En. 14:13-14, 24). The author of the vision portrayed God as dangerously unapproachable, yet paradoxically, Enoch is able to approach the throne. Such dissonance highlights a major point of theology, which is that God's presence is accessible to only a few who are exceptionally righteous (1 En. 14:21).[53]

Also in contrast to Ezekiel's vision, the author of the Book of Watchers emphasized the preexistence of the heavenly temple as opposed to the eschatological manifestation of the structure. In chapter 14, the author gave no indication that the heavenly temple ever replaces the earthly one. The chariot-throne is fixed in heaven, completely separate from the realm

49. Nickelsburg provided a detailed list of parallels (Nickelsburg, *1 Enoch 1*, 254–56). Cf. Briggs, *Jewish Temple Imagery*, 118–19; Himmelfarb, "From Prophecy to Apocalypse," 149; Klawans, *Purity, Sacrifice, and the Temple*, 130.

50. Nickelsburg, *1 Enoch 1*, 254.

51. Nickelsburg, "Enoch, Levi, and Peter," 575–600.

52. Himmelfarb, "From Prophecy to Apocalypse," 153. However, both Nickelsburg and Himmelfarb noted that a significant difference can be found between the two visions. That is, Ezekiel does not ascend to heaven (Nickelsburg, "Enoch, Levi, and Peter," 580–81).

53. Nickelsburg, *1 Enoch 1*, 260.

of the earth.[54] In later chapters, the author implied that the heavenly temple is connected in some way to the earth, but the heavenly temple never is explicitly said to come down and replace the earthly one.

In 1 Enoch 18:6–10, the presence of God rests upon a mountain throne made of various jewels. Although no mention of a temple occurs, precious stones are often a feature of heavenly and eschatological temples. Therefore, Lee contended that in chapter 18, God's throne is portrayed in the heavenly and earthly temples simultaneously.[55] Further, the presence of God generates an edenic landscape.

The edenic setting is revisited in 1 Enoch 24:1—25:6.[56] The passage is connected to 1 Enoch 18 by the mountains upon which the throne sits. In chapters 24–25, the mountain of God exhibits precious stones and bears a fragrant tree. Michael, still Enoch's guide, explains that the high mountain is the throne of God, "where the Great Holy One, the Lord of glory, the King of eternity, will sit, when he descends to visit the earth" (1 En. 25:3).[57] At the time of judgment, the elect will eat of the tree, enter the sanctuary, and live a long life on the earth (1 En. 25:6).[58]

Unlike the vision in chapter 14, little explicit temple imagery is present. While the mountain bears a throne and precious jewels, no mention is made of temple architecture or implements. The closest the passage comes to temple imagery is 1 Enoch 25:5, where the tree (of life) will be planted near the "house of the Lord," and 1 Enoch 25:6, where righteous enter into the "sanctuary" (1 En. 25:6). *House* and *sanctuary* are common terms for the temple, but here refer to the edenic state and God's presence.[59] Moreover, the "chapters can be read as a rather accurate description of the geographical surroundings of Jerusalem."[60]

---

54. Nickelsburg, *1 Enoch 1*, 260.

55. Lee, *New Jerusalem*, 71.

56. Józef Milik regarded chs. 21–25 as a reworking of chs. 17–19 (Milik, *Books of Enoch*, 25). Eibert Tigchelaar felt that the sections are more likely parallel accounts of a common tradition (Tigchelaar, *Prophets of Old*, 158–60).

57. The verb "to visit," ἐπισκέπτομαι, is used in the sense of judgment here. The Greek term never is used to indicate merely a "visit" in the English sense, but rather some type of concern for a person or situation (Beyer, "ἐπισκέπτομαι, ἐπισκοπέω, ἐπισκοπή, ἐπίσκοπος, ἀλλοτριεπίσκοπος," 604; Nickelsburg, *1 Enoch 1*, 312).

58. Numerous parallels with Revelation 21–22 can be identified in 1 Enoch 24–26, but most of the affinities "are somewhat generic" (Briggs, *Jewish Temple Imagery*, 119n53).

59. As in Exodus 11:16 and Testament of Benjamin 10:11.

60. Tigchelaar, *Prophets of Old*, 160–61. Cf. Bautch, *Study of the Geography*; Milik,

The author seemed to be combining the ANE tradition of the divine mountain with temple traditions.[61] The presence of God makes the place holy, and his throne is the source of life. Indeed, the water that typically flows from the temple flows from the mountain upon which the throne is situated (1 En. 26:1–3). Therefore, although the scene exhibits several features of a temple—the presence of a divinity, the throne, the primordial waters, the tree of life, and a high mountain—no architectural structure is present.[62] The fantastical imagery represents features of the eschatological landscape rather than elements of a structural temple.

The Book of Dreams

The Book of Dreams, 1 Enoch 83–90, can be divided into two parts. A vision of the flood (chapters 83–84) will not be discussed. Only the second vision (chapters 85–90) is relevant for the current study. These chapters contain the Animal Apocalypse, in which the history of humanity is allegorized through animals.[63]

Most relevant here are chapters 89–90, which refer to a fallen house that was rebuilt (1 En. 89:72–73; 90:28–29). The return of the exiles and rebuilding of the temple seem to be in view here.[64] Yet, the rebuilt temple is rejected: "And they began again to build as before and they raised up that tower, but all the bread on it was polluted and not pure. And besides all these things, the eyes of the sheep were blind, and they did not see, and their shepherds likewise" (1 En. 89:73).[65]

In 1 Enoch 90:20–29, the old polluted tower is removed as a new house is constructed by the Lord (of the sheep) in the same location as the previous house. While *temple* never is mentioned, some scholars identify the new "house" with the heavenly temple.[66] Others assert that

---

Books of Enoch, 36–37; VanderKam, *Enoch and the Growth*, 137.

61. Bautch, *Study of the Geography*, 279; Nickelsburg, *1 Enoch 1*, 282–83.

62. Lundquist, "What Is a Temple?" In 1 Enoch 24–26, no walls, floors, ceilings, doors, gates, or temple implements are present.

63. The Animal Apocalypse likely was written in response to events surrounding the Maccabean revolt (Charles, *Apocrypha and Pseudepigrapha*, 2:182; Manning, *Echoes of a Prophet*, 90).

64. Black, *Book of Enoch*, 273; Nickelsburg, *1 Enoch 1*, 394; Tiller, *Commentary on the Animal Apocalyse*, 337.

65. Nickelsburg, *1 Enoch 1*, 387.

66. Black, *Book of Enoch*, 278; Hamerton-Kelly, "Temple and the Origins," 1–15.

neither the earthly nor the heavenly temple is in view. James Vanderkam explained, "There is no warrant in the AA for interpreting this house as the temple in Jerusalem. In the apocalypse the word for temple is always *tower*."[67]

Alternately, the house may be identified as the new Jerusalem. George Nickelsburg wrote, "The new Jerusalem is brought by the Lord of the sheep, presumably from heaven. It is both greater and higher than the old house (v. 29) and thus possesses the characteristics of both the city and the temple (cf. 89:50: the house is broad and large and the tower is high)."[68] Patrick Tiller likewise argued that the renewed house is a city. The old temple never is renewed or renovated, but replaced completely by a city.[69] "The author speaks only of a new city and not of a new temple. The author has given consistent and clear attention to the temple, and it is inconceivable that it is here merely assumed. Neither do the pillars, beams, and ornaments imply a temple since they can belong to a city as well as to a temple."[70] Therefore, in agreement with Nickelsburg and Tiller, understanding the house as the entire new Jerusalem appears most in keeping with the terminology used in the Animal Apocalypse.

Another detail relevant to the current research can be found in the occupants of the city. In 1 Enoch 90:29, the author stated that "all the sheep were within it."[71] Tiller noted that some manuscripts read "the owner of the sheep was in the midst of it."[72] Tiller found either reading possible, but he did observe that the variant reading would explain why no tower was in the house. "The owner now apparently dwells in the

67. See 1 Enoch 89:50, 54, 56, 66, 67, 73; Vanderkam interpreted the "house" as the Davidic kingdom (VanderKam, *Enoch and the Growth*, 168–69). Cf. Briggs, *Jewish Temple Imagery*, 121–22.

68. Nickelsburg, *1 Enoch 1*, 404. Lee identified the tower as the heavenly temple and the house as the new Jerusalem (Lee, *New Jerusalem*, 67–69). Vogelgesang contended that the house can be identified as the temple and the eschatological Jerusalem simultaneously (Vogelgesang, "Interpretation of Ezekiel," 143).

69. Tiller, *Commentary on the Animal Apocalypse*, 375. Cf. Spatafora, *From the "Temple of God,"* 64.

70. Tiller, *Commentary on the Animal Apocalypse*, 376. To the contrary, Briggs argued that if the author of the Animal Apocalypse intended to describe a new Jerusalem without a temple, "he almost certainly would have done so plainly, as John did in Revelation" (Briggs, *Jewish Temple Imagery*, 124). Cf. Beale, *Book of Revelation*, 1092. Knibb argued that whether a temple is included in expectations here is inconclusive (Knibb, "Temple and Cult," 407).

71. Isaac, "1 (Ethiopic Apocalypse of) Enoch," 71.

72. Tiller, *Commentary on the Animal Apocalypse*, 376.

house with the sheep and no longer in a tower above them."[73] Matthew Black went further, preferring the variant reading due to "the biblical promises that God would dwell in the midst of Israel."[74] Therefore, the variant reading provides a fitting parallel to the idea of a new Jerusalem that needs no temple because the Lord dwells within the city.

Several relevant conclusions can be drawn from the Animal Apocalypse. First, the author anticipated an eschatological Jerusalem that would replace the current, imperfect establishment (1 En. 90:28–29). Second, the new Jerusalem will be the center of redeemed humanity (1 En. 90:30–36). Third, a possible messianic figure, a white bull, effects the purification and unification of all people (1 En. 90:37–38). Fourth, the messianic figure takes the place of the temple, at least in some manuscripts.

2 Enoch

The date and provenance of 2 Enoch are uncertain. Francis Andersen suggested that composition may have taken place in the late first century CE, but he also noted that "in every respect 2 Enoch remains an enigma."[75] Accordingly, scholars also debate whether the work is of Jewish or Christian origin, although consensus appears to lean toward a Jewish core.[76]

As for subject matter, the author of 2 Enoch described a journey through ten heavens. The heavenly temple is mentioned in the third, seventh, and tenth heaven but no reference is made to an earthly sanctuary.

In chapters 8–9, an account of the third heaven, the author described an edenic paradise with a tree of life and streams of milk, honey, and oil. The tree of life also serves as "the place where the Lord takes a rest when he goes into paradise."[77] The attending angels inform Enoch

73. Tiller, *Commentary on the Animal Apocalypse*, 376.

74. See, for example, Isaiah 8:18; Ezekiel 43:9; Zephaniah 3:17; Black, *Book of Enoch*, 279.

75. Andersen, "2 (Slavonic Apocalypse of) Enoch," 97. Annie S. D. Maunder, an Irish astronomer, proposed that 2 Enoch was a medieval composition (Maunder, "Date and Place of Writing," 309–16). Her proposal received little support, and Robert Charles refuted her argument in "Date and Place of Writing," 161–64. For more conventional discussions of dating see Andersen, "2 (Slavonic Apocalypse of) Enoch," 91–221; Collins, *Apocalyptic Imagination*, 197; Nickelsburg, *Jewish Literature*, 221–25.

76. Andersen, "2 (Slavonic Apocalypse of) Enoch," 95–96; Charlesworth, *Pseudepigrapha and Modern Research*, 104; Lee, *New Jerusalem*, 74; Himmelfarb, *Ascent to Heaven*, 38; Sacchi, *Jewish Apocalyptic and Its History*, 241–42.

77. Translations are reproduced from Andersen, "2 (Slavonic Apocalypse of)

that the edenic setting has been prepared for the righteous as an eternal inheritance (2 En. 9:1).

Lee suggested that the cultic activity (i.e., worship) of the angels implies a priestly function (2 En. 8:8). Resultantly, "it may be possible to say that the Heavenly Paradise is part of God's throne or Temple."[78] Indeed, the idea of a *prepared place* resonates with cultic imagery.[79] Therefore, evidence leans toward an identification of the locale as part of the heavenly temple.

In the seventh and tenth heavens, Enoch is allowed to see God upon his throne.[80] Features of the seventh and tenth heavens more overtly reflect aspects of the heavenly temple. From the seventh heaven, Enoch sees into the tenth heaven where cherubim, seraphim, and other creatures worship around the throne. When Enoch enters the tenth heaven, he is anointed and given new garments in a ceremony reminiscent of "priestly investiture" (2 En. 22:8–10).[81]

In chapters 39–66, Enoch provides admonitions to his sons based upon his journeys. Enoch informs his children that soon he will ascend to the highest heaven, and he exhorts them to live righteously in order that they may receive the eternal inheritance (ch. 55). Correspondingly, Enoch explains that when creation ends, all people will be judged by the Lord. The righteous will enter the age of eternity and immortality (ch. 65).

The nature of the eternal state is difficult to discern. For the purpose of discussion, both the longer and shorter recensions of 2 Enoch 65:10 will be reproduced:

> But they will have a great light, a great indestructible light, and paradise, great and incorruptible. For everything corruptible will pass away, and the incorruptible will come into being, and will be the shelter of eternal residences. (2 En. 65:10J; longer recension)

Enoch."

78. Lee, *New Jerusalem*, 76.

79. Prepared place as promised land: Exod 23:20; Deut 1:29–33; Ezek 20:6; as ark of the covenant: 1 Chr 15:1–3; 12:2; 2 Chr 1:4; as rooms within the temple: 2 Chr 3:1; 31:11; as the temple: Exod 15:17; Sir 47:13; 49:12; Wis 9:8; 2 Chr 8:16. Cf. Coloe, "Temple Imagery in John," 368–81; McCaffrey, *House with Many Rooms*, 88–89.

80. In 2 Enoch 20:3 and 21:1, Enoch sees the throne from the edge of the seventh heaven. In 2 Enoch 22:2, he has entered the tenth heaven, where the throne rests.

81. Himmelfarb, *Ascent to Heaven*, 40. Cf. Lee, *New Jerusalem*, 77.

> But they will have a great light for eternity, (and) an indestructible wall, and they will have a great paradise, the shelter of an eternal residence. (2 En. 65:10A; shorter recension)

Lee interpreted the description of the eternal state as the new Jerusalem/temple. He noted that recension A exhibits a structure in which the great light parallels the indestructible wall, and the great paradise parallels the eternal residence. Therefore, the light emitting from the wall comes from the gemstones, a characteristic feature of the new Jerusalem. The wall, thus, may "be seen as indicating the main structure of the eschatological New Temple/Jerusalem."[82] To the contrary, in 2 Enoch 66:11A and 66:7J, the faces of the righteous shine like the sun. The context clearly identifies the source of the light as the faces of the righteous rather than the wall.[83]

Andrei Orlov noted the importance of face imagery throughout the book of 2 Enoch. In chapter 1, Enoch is awakened to frightening angelic faces (2 En. 1:5), and his own face contorts with fear (2 En. 1:7–8). Enoch's face transforms once more when he beholds the glorious face of the Lord in 2 Enoch 22:1–10. Orlov asserted that "such symbolism often establishes an important theophanic nexus," in which facial imagery is linked to the presence of fear in the narrative.[84] "This juxtaposition of the danger motif with the tradition of the divine Face found in the biblical accounts of Moses would prove to be very important for the authors of 2 Enoch, wherein the motif of the frightening luminosity of the divine visage occupied an important conceptual place."[85] If Orlov is correct, perhaps the great light, indestructible wall, and shining faces all represent the absence of fear and security of the eternal state. Just as Enoch's face was transfigured in chapter 22, all of the righteous are transformed in chapter 65.

Contrary to Lee's assertion, the transformation of the righteous is emphasized rather than building imagery. Furthermore, the wall never is mentioned in the longer recension. If the wall were a critical element in the passage, one would expect the structure to be present in both versions. Instead, the point seems to be that believers are made ready for their new dwelling, the heavenly temple. Nothing in the passage indicates that the heavenly temple is established on the earth. In fact, the author of 2 Enoch

---

82. Lee, *New Jerusalem*, 79.

83. As with Moses, in Exodus 34:29–35.

84. Orlov, "Glorification through Fear," 172–73.

85. Orlov, "Glorification through Fear," 174.

indicates that the earth is destroyed: "And when the whole of creation, visible add invisible, which the Lord has created, shall come to an end, then each person will go to the Lord's great judgment" (2 En. 65:6).

Jubilees

Jubilees is a pseudepigraphic work, likely composed between 160 and 140 BCE.[86] Jubilees bears affinities with apocalyptic literature, but unlike typical apocalypses the text is missing key elements such as otherworldly journeys and symbolic language.[87] Although the direction of influence is difficult to ascertain, the work may have been influenced by earlier portions of Enoch.[88]

Often designated as "rewritten Scripture," the author of Jubilees narrated Moses's encounter with God on Mt. Sinai.[89] The revelation includes the history of humanity and the history of Israel. The book concludes with a collection of legal statutes on Passover, Jubilee years, and Sabbath.

As Jubilees features a retelling of the Pentateuch, references to the tabernacle and temple are grounded in the history of Israel. However, subtle references to the heavenly temple can be found throughout. In Jubilees 1:17, God promises to build a sanctuary in the midst of his people and dwell with them. On the surface, the author expressed an expectation for the historical temple and tabernacle.[90] In the larger context of Jubilees, however, the author may have been hinting at the heavenly temple that would appear in the eschaton.[91] Collins wrote that "*Jubilees* 1:23–29 anticipates a time when the Jews will turn to God and he will live among them for all eternity."[92] Heaven and earth will be renewed in a new era of healing, peace, and blessing.

---

86. Endres, "Watchers Traditions," 121–35; Nickelsburg, *Jewish Literature*, 73–74; Wintermute, "Jubilees," 35–142; VanderKam, *Book of Jubilees*, 17–21; VanderKam, *Textual and Historical Studies*, 283.

87. Charles, *Apocrypha and Pseudepigrapha*, v; Hamerton-Kelly, "Temple and the Origins," 1; Wintermute, "Jubilees," 37.

88. Likewise, later portions of Enoch—the Similitudes—may have been influenced by Jubilees (Endres, "Watchers Traditions," 121–35; Wintermute, "Jubilees," 49).

89. Briggs, *Jewish Temple Imagery*, 134; VanderKam, *Jubilees*, 117.

90. Charles interpreted the temple here as the Second Temple (Charles, *Book of Jubilees*, 5).

91. Hamerton-Kelly, "Temple and the Origins," 1; Knibb, "Temple and Cult," 410.

92. Collins, *Apocalyptic Imagination*, 82.

The welfare of the temple is linked directly to the obedience of the people, as the author of Jubilees stressed the importance of *halakha*.[93] In Jubilees 23:16–31, the holy of holies is polluted due to covenant infidelity. Resultantly, the people are given over "to judgment and to captivity and pillage and destruction" (Jub. 23:22–23). When the people finally begin to "search the law" and "return to the way of righteousness," they are blessed with peace and prosperity (Jub. 23:26–31).[94] The author, however, made no reference to a restored temple.

The heavenly temple is mentioned on several occasions. References to the "house of the Lord" and "gate of heaven" (Jub. 27:25) are likely subtle references to the God-made heavenly temple.[95] An even clearer reference to the heavenly temple is provided in the blessing over Levi: "May the Lord give you and your seed very great honor. May he draw you and your seed near to him from all flesh to serve in his sanctuary as the angels of the presence and the holy ones" (Jub. 31:14). Thus, the author highlights angelic service that is happening presently in the heavenly temple.[96]

Through the various temple references in Jubilees, the author juxtaposed the idea of the heavenly temple with the idea of God dwelling on earth. Therefore the book may anticipate a union of the heavenly and earthly sanctuaries in the eschaton.

Sibylline Oracle 3

Sibylline Oracle 3 (Sib. Or. 3) began taking shape in the mid-second century BCE among Egyptian Jewry. The work consists of a "conglomeration of oracles from various sources."[97] A few Christian redactions can be identified, but otherwise the document seems to have been completed by 45 BCE. General consensus exists as to the Jewish origin of Sibylline Oracle 3, but ironically the book has been preserved only in Christian documents.[98]

93. Briggs, *Jewish Temple Imagery*, 134.

94. Translations of Jubilees are reproduced from Wintermute, "Jubilees."

95. Lee, *New Jerusalem*, 95.

96. Hamerton-Kelly, "Temple and the Origins," 1–2.

97. Collins, *Sibylline Oracles of Egyptian Judaism*, 21. Cf. Buitenwerf, *Book III*, 124–34.

98. Christian interpolations are likely 93–96, 371–72, and 776, although only 776 is certain (Buitenwerf, *Book III*, 124–26).

The author of Sibylline Oracle 3 emphasized the establishment of an ideal king and kingdom. Salvation is envisaged in political and earthly terms as the king subdues earthly enemies. Resultantly, the earth is transformed and the temple is exalted.

Lines 295–488 consist of a loose collection of oracles, most of which are *ex eventu*, along with actual predictions of the future that reflect the concerns of the author.[99] Relevant lines are as follows.

First, the destruction of the temple by the Babylonians and their subsequent punishment are described in Sibylline Oracle 3:300–13. Second, the defeat of Gog and Magog by Libya is described in lines 319–23. "It is not clear why Gog and Magog are mentioned here . . . Gog, sometimes in combination with Magog, functions as an eschatological enemy, but there are no indications that the author of Sib. Or. III viewed them in this way."[100] Third, in lines 324–36, violent actions against the temple are committed. The violence is perpetrated by "daughters of the west," likely a reference to Rome.[101] After Rome is punished, the earth returns to an edenic state (lines 367–80).[102]

Next, lines 489–829 are a collection of future predictions, many of which emphasize proper worship. The oracle against Greece in lines 545–72 predicts that Greece will be spared punishment if she will bring offerings to the temple. In lines 545–72, the rejection of idolatry is concomitant with offering sacrifices in the temple:

> The future ideal is the restoration of pious men who not only keep the law but fully honor the temple of the great God with all kinds of sacrifices (vs. 575). In the final utopian state the Jews will live peacefully around the temple, and the Gentiles will be moved to "send to the temple" and ponder the law of God (vs. 702–31). The Jerusalem temple is of vital importance

99. Buitenwerf, *Book III*, 219.

100. Oddly, lines 265–87 describe the same event, although the destruction is attributed to the Assyrians. Buitenwerf suggested that the author of Sib. Or. 3 did not make a distinction between the Assyrians and Babylonians (Buitenwerf, *Book III*, 215, 218).

101. Buitenwerf, *Book III*, 219.

102. The sibyllist used language that evokes the creation narrative of Genesis 1–2: "Serene peace will return to the Asian land, and Europe will then be blessed. The air will be good for pasture for many years, bracing, free from storms and hail, producing everything, including *birds and creeping beasts of the earth*" (Sib. Or. 3:367–70, italics added). Translations of all Sibylline Oracle passages are reproduced from Collins, "The Sibylline Oracles," (1984), 357–82.

for the true religion and should become a place of worship for all nations.[103]

Therefore, the temple appears to be literal and material, although the structure also is eternal.

The sibyllist upheld the Jewish people as a model of piety. The Jews are portrayed as pious men who devote themselves to the Lord and honor his temple.[104] The reward for the Jews' righteousness is to live blissfully upon the land and "be exalted as prophets" (lines 550–52). Moreover, all nations share in the eschatological blessings and bring gifts to the temple of God (lines 767–808).

A messianic king also plays a role in the eschatological blessings, although his role is ambiguous. The messiah can be identified in three sections: lines 286–87, lines 611–15, and lines 652–56. In the first passage, a "king from heaven" will judge all men with fire and blood (lines 286–87). When he arrives in Egypt he will bring an army and "chop up everything," "fill everything with misery," and "overthrow the royalty of Egypt" (lines 611–15). Finally, in lines 652–56, the king will inaugurate peace on earth through a combination of war and diplomacy.

In the first and third passages, the action of the king is followed by a restoration of the temple. Rieuwerd Buitenwerf and Collins both argued that in lines 286–87, the author referred to Cyrus rather than an eschatological figure, as the temple that is restored comes after the exile.[105] John Nolland, however, contended that the oracle refers to a messianic figure. Nolland noted that the description of blood and smoke "does not seem entirely fitting for Cyrus," but the phrase does resemble the eschatological expectations of Joel 3:3 and Joel 4:2.[106]

Nonetheless, at least one and likely all three of the passages refer to a messianic king who will restore a physical temple. "We must conclude that the temple occupied a central place in the thought of the sibyllist even as did the savior king."[107] Therefore, the author of Sibylline Oracle 3 straightforwardly anticipated a material temple from which a messiah would rule in the eschaton.

103. Collins, *Apocalyptic Imagination*, 123.
104. Buitenwerf, *Book III*, 240.
105. Buitenwerf, *Book III*, 207; Collins, *Sibylline Oracles of Egyptian Judaism*, 38.
106. Nolland, "*Sib. Or.* III," 160.
107. Collins, *Sibylline Oracles of Egyptian Judaism*, 45.

Summary and Evaluation

A survey of the salient points discussed thus far will be offered before the
next group of texts is analyzed. First, the authors of both Tobit and Sibylline Oracle 3 anticipated a literal eschatological temple. Additionally,
the author of Sibylline Oracle 3 was explicit in expecting a messiah who
would rule from the temple. The author of Tobit mentioned no messianic
figure, but through the fantastical details of the temple-city, he implied
that the dwelling would be fit for divinity. Second, the author of Baruch
anticipated the restoration of Jerusalem, but was silent on the fate of the
temple and expressed no messianic hopes. Third, of the works surveyed
thus far, 2 Enoch is unique in the expectation that the righteous ascend to
the heavenly temple in the eternal state. Fourth, the author of Jubilees reinterpreted Scripture to anticipate the union of the heavenly and earthly
temples in the eschaton. Similarly, in portions of the Book of Watchers
(1 En. 14–26), the author may have implied that God's heavenly dwelling
place will come to the earth in the eschaton, but no structural edifice is
present.

Fifth, several passages provide parallels to John's portrait of an
eschatological city in which the messiah replaces the temple. In the
Testaments of Levi, Dan, and Benjamin, a messiah brings about an eschatological age. In the Testament of Levi, the author seemed to anticipate
a restored temple, but one never materializes. Moreover, the author of
the Testament of Dan and the Testament of Benjamin implied that the
messiah takes the place of the temple. Likewise, in portions of 1 Enoch,
a messiah rules from the midst of an eschatological creation without an
architectural temple. In the Book of Watchers (1 En. 1–36), all nations
come to worship a divine messiah at the center of a renewed earth (1
En. 10–11). In the Animal Apocalypse (1 En. 85–90), a messianic figure
purifies creation and then dwells in the midst of his people, at least in
some manuscripts.

A comment should be made on the relation of the foregoing texts to
Ezekiel as well. The attestation of parallels between the heavenly journeys
of Enoch (1 En. 14) and Levi (T. Levi 1–5) with Ezekiel's temple vision
indicates that Ezekiel 40–48 was used as an inspiration for heavenly ascent narratives. Such usage may imply that Ezekiel's temple vision was
understood, at least by some authors, as a heavenly ascent. Further investigation will be undertaken later in the chapter.

Qumran Sectarian Literature

The Qumran community existed from the Maccabean period until the first century CE when the sect was destroyed by Rome in the Jewish revolt of 66–70 CE.[108] The literature of the sectarians is saturated with eschatological imagery, such that the community is regarded by some scholars as an apocalyptic sect.[109]

The group was founded upon the presumption that the Jerusalem Temple was defiled irreparably.[110] The sectarians may have seen in their own situation a repeat of the exile of Ezekiel's time.[111] The literature of the sect, therefore, illustrates the struggle of the sectarians to devise a solution to worship God in the absence of a temple. Three proposed solutions are attested in the sectarian documents: (1) the community as a temple, (2) the heavenly temple, and (3) and the eschatological temple.[112]

The Community Rule (1QS)

In many documents from Qumran, the *yahad* is described in terms typically reserved for the temple. In the Community Rule, the council of the community is described as "an Everlasting Plantation, a House of

108. Allegro, *Dead Sea Scrolls*, 94–100; LaSor, *Dead Sea Scrolls*, 45–47; Nickelsburg, *Jewish Literature*, 119–22; Stegemann, *Library of Qumran*, 58–64; VanderKam, *Dead Sea Scrolls Today*, 99–108.

109. Cross, *Ancient Library of Qumran*, 76–78. The initial designation of the community as apocalyptic by Cross has come under scrutiny. Collins noted that no original apocalyptic works have been found at Qumran, although he did not entirely disagree with Cross (Collins, "Was the Dead Sea Sect?" 25–51; Collins, "Apocalypticism and Literary Genre," 2:403–30). Davies regarded the entire discussion as illegitimate, as defining a social group with a literary descriptor is problematic (Davies, "Qumran and Apocalyptic," 127–34). Conversely, Rowland defined apocalyptic as more of a mindset than a literary genre (Rowland, *Open Heaven*, 9–11).

110. Baumgarten, "Sacrifice and Worship," 141–59; Schiffman, *Qumran and Jerusalem*, 81.

111. Manning detected a subtle reference to Ezekiel in the time frame of 390 years between the fall of Jerusalem and the founding of the community (4QD I, 5–6; Ezek 4:4–5). As such, the "*Damascus Document* appropriately treats the account of the Exile in Ezekiel 39 as history rather than prophecy, but it views God's prior abandonment of the Temple as a paradigm, or a type, of the present abandonment. In the community's eyes, God had also abandoned the Second Temple, and its destruction was imminent" (Manning, *Echoes of a Prophet*, 27).

112. Lee, *New Jerusalem*, 86.

Holiness for Israel, an assembly of Supreme Holiness for Aaron . . . a Most Holy Dwelling for Aaron . . . a House of Perfection and Truth" (1QS VIII, 5–10).[113] Correspondingly, the Jerusalem Temple never is mentioned.[114]

The community also performs many of the functions of the temple: "They shall atone for guilty rebellion and for sins of unfaithfulness, that they may obtain loving-kindness for the Land without the flesh of holocausts and the fat of sacrifice. And prayer rightly offered shall be an acceptable fragrance of righteousness, and perfection of way as a delectable free-will offering."[115] Elizabeth Schüssler Fiorenza explained, "Since the community has taken over the holiness of the temple, the only means for maintaining the holiness of Israel and for achieving atonement of sins is life in the Qumran community in perfect obedience to Torah."[116] Thus, the prayers and righteous living of the sect effect atonement for the land.

Additionally, just as the temple and the land are bounded by concentric rings of holiness, members of the *yahad* are ranked according to levels of sanctity.[117] The community consists of an inner council within the larger community. The inner council is referred to as a cornerstone and a rampart, based on Isaiah 28:16 (1QS VIII, 7). The Isaiah pesher likewise describes the inner council as the foundation of the temple: "*And I will lay your foundation with sapphires* (liv, 11c). Interpreted, this concerns the Priests and the people who laid the foundations of the Council of the Community . . . The congregation of His elect (shall sparkle) like a sapphire among stones."[118] Additionally, the chief priests are identified as pinnacles of agate and the chiefs of the tribes as gates.

Corresponding to the strict hierarchy, new members are excluded from the communal meal for at least a year. Even full members can be excluded if they become ritually impure (1QS VI, 13–24). Additionally, any member who transgresses a rule has to begin anew the initiation process (1QS VII, 17–21). According to Klawans, the reason for such extreme purity and atonement regulations in the community is because

113. Unless otherwise noted, translations are reproduced from Vermes, *Complete Dead Sea Scrolls.*

114. Baumgarten, "Sacrifice and Worship," 150.

115. 1QS IX, 3–6; cf. 4QS VI, 5–7.

116. Schüssler Fiorenza, "Cultic Language," 166. Cf. Allegro, *Dead Sea Scrolls*, 98, 112; Gärtner, *Temple and the Community*, 21, 53; Nickelsburg, *Jewish Literature*, 142.

117. See m. Kelim 1:6–9.

118. 4Q164 I, 2–3; cf. 1QS III, 2; 1QSa I, 26–28. Cf. Mathewson, "Note on the Foundation Stones," 487–98.

their measures were less efficacious than those performed at the temple.[119] Rules were necessarily strict in order to "fulfill the requirement of the level of purity as a Temple."[120]

Some scholars argue against the idea that the sectarians regarded themselves as a replacement temple. Robert Briggs contended, "If this radical tenant had in truth been concocted and espoused, one would expect to find it set down in no uncertain terms (accompanied by copious elaboration and apologetic) among the writers of a 'priestly' sect so zealous for the Torah. But no such evidence is yet in hand."[121] While Briggs is correct that the Qumran corpus provides no direct exposition of the community-as-temple idea, numerous documents indicate that the function and identity of the *yahad* were linked closely to those of the temple.

Allan McNicol offered a mediating position and argued that the community-as-temple passages in 1QS were the initial reaction of the community to religiopolitical tensions of the time rather than an overarching tenet of the community's ideology.[122] McNicol is correct that the covenanters viewed their community temple as a temporary substitute until a restored Jerusalem temple could be established. Such an expectation for a future material temple will be discussed in the following sections.

The Temple Scroll (11QT)

Similar to Ezekiel 40–48, the author of Temple Scroll outlined a physical temple and corresponding legislation. Also as with Ezekiel 40–48, scholars are divided on whether the author of the Temple Scroll described a conceptual ideal or a structure to be built in the future. Thus, a few comments should be made on the relation between the Temple Scroll and Ezekiel before interpretations of the Temple Scroll are examined.

119. Klawans, *Purity, Sacrifice, and the Temple*, 147.

120. Lee, *New Jerusalem*, 100. Cf. Klawans, *Purity, Sacrifice, and the Temple*, 147; Schiffman, *Sectarian Law*, 199; Yadin, *Temple Scroll*, 1:186.

121. Briggs, *Jewish Temple Imagery*, 189. Cf. Davies, "Ideology of the Temple," 287–301; Marshall, "Church and Temple," 217.

122. McNicol, "Eschatological Temple," 133–41. To the contrary, Gärtner argued that the Qumran community envisioned themselves as a fully spiritualized temple with no expectation for a restored Jerusalem temple in the future (Gärtner, *Temple and the Community*, 21). However, Gärtner's monograph was published prior to the release of the Temple Scroll.

First, neither the author of the Temple Scroll nor the author of
Ezekiel 40–48 described an actual historical temple. As such, both documents were composed possibly as critiques of existing temples.[123] The
literary temples represented an ideal that the past and current temples
never attained.

Second, the differences between the Temple Scroll and Ezekiel 40–
48 far outweigh the similarities. Although both temples have predomi-
nantly square shapes, possibly reflecting an ideal design, the author of the
Temple Scroll did not follow the plan of Ezekiel.[124] Yigael Yadin suggested
that the author of the scroll understood Ezekiel's temple as the eschatological one that God would build, and the temple of the scroll as one
the sectarians would build in the near future. Yadin also proposed that
Ezekiel's temple may have been mentioned at some point in the Temple
Scroll, as columns XXIX and XXX, which describe the eschatological
temple, are badly damaged.[125]

The temples of the Temple Scroll are described as follows: "And I
will consecrate my [t]emple by my glory, (the temple) on which I will
settle my glory, until the day of blessing on which I will create my temple
and establish it for myself for all times, according to the covenant which
I have made with Jacob at Bethel" (11QT XXIX, 8–10).[126] The "temple
of glory" appears to be the material temple outlined in the scroll. "The
author of the scroll is quite explicit that he is discussing the Temple to
be built one day by the Children of Israel, and not the eschatological
Temple."[127] Then, on "the day of blessing" the temple described by the
author of the Temple Scroll will be replaced by the temple of God.[128]

123. Patton, "Ezekiel's Blueprint for the Temple," 155; Wise, "4QFlorilegium and
the Temple," 103–32.

124. Milgrom, "New Temple Festivals," 125–34; Patton, "Ezekiel's Blueprint for the
Temple," 155; Yadin, Temple Scroll, 1:191.

125. Yadin, Temple Scroll, 1:191, 2:125.

126. Yadin, Temple Scroll, 1:183, 2:128–29.

127. Yadin, Temple Scroll, 1:183. Cf. Klawans, Purity, Sacrifice, and the Temple, 159;
Lee, New Jerusalem, 91–96; Milgrom, "New Temple Festivals," 132; Schiffman, "Temple Scroll between the Bible," 19; Schiffman, "Theology of the Temple Scroll," 109–23.

128. Briggs, Jewish Temple Imagery, 162–63; Milgrom, "New Temple Festivals,"
132; Yadin, Temple Scroll, 1:182–200, 2:129. Not all scholars agree that two temples are
in view. See Wacholder, Dawn of Qumran, 21–28. Identifying a single temple in the
passage depends upon translating "until (עד) the day of blessing" as "during the day of
blessing," which is an atypical usage of עד.

The author of the Temple Scroll indicated that the community desired a return to a reality centered around a material temple. Although authors of other sectarian documents seemed to give the impression that the covenanters rejected the temple, Klawans urged caution in labeling the sectarians as "rejectionist."[129] The author of the Temple Scroll envisioned replacing the temple of the Maccabean period "with a gargantuan temple that would have covered virtually all the existing city of Jerusalem . . . So we can say essentially that the temple plan presented here was a reformist plan for a structure that was never actually built."[130]

Further insight into the temples of the Temple Scroll may be gained by an examination of 4QFlorilegium and the Damascus Document. Therefore, these two documents will be surveyed in tandem with the Temple Scroll.

4QFlorilegium (4QFlor)

The brief text 4QFlorilegium is an interpretation of 2 Samuel 7:10–14. While the author termed his work a midrash, elements of pesher interpretation are prevalent as well.[131] Depending upon one's interpretation, the author described one, two, or three temples:

> This is the House which [He will build for them in the] last days, as it is written in the book of Moses, *In the sanctuary which Thy hands have established, O Lord, the Lord shall reign for ever and ever* (Exod. xv, 17–18). This is the house into which [the unclean shall] never [enter, nor the uncircumcised] . . . And strangers shall lay it waste no more, as they formerly laid waste the Sanctuary of Israel because of its sin. He has commanded that a Sanctuary of men be built for himself, that they may send up, like the smoke of incense, the works of the Law. (4QFlor I, 3–6; italics denote biblical quotation)

Virtually all scholars agree that the "house" of the last days is the future temple that will be built by the Lord. Most exegetes also agree that

129. Klawans, *Purity, Sacrifice, and the Temple*, 147.

130. Schiffman, "Temple Scroll between the Bible," 18.

131. Gärtner, *Temple and the Community*, 31; Schwartz, "Three Temples of 4QFlorilegium," 83–91; Wise, "4QFlorilegium and thr Temple," 106. The title "Florilegium," or anthology, was a provisional descriptor given to the text by Allegro. Although inaccurate, the moniker has endured (Allegro, "Further Messianic References," 174–87; Allegro, "Fragments of a Qumran Scroll," 50–54.

the "Sanctuary of Israel" is the First and/or Second Temple. The "Sanctuary of Men," however, is a matter of dispute. The *miqdash adam* may be (1) the same entity as the historical temple, (2) a future temple that will be built by the Lord, or (3) the community of the faithful (i.e., the *yahad*).[132]

Michael Wise identified only two temples in 4QFlorilegium. In addition to the historical "Sanctuary of Israel," Wise argued for one further temple with two iterations. The scholar interpreted the temple of the Temple Scroll and 4QFlorilegium as a binomial eschatological temple. The first phase consists of the temple Israel is commanded to build in the Temple Scroll, and the second phase is the edenic temple that God will create himself. Wise found no community-as-temple ideology in the Temple Scroll or 4QFlorilegium.[133]

Conversely, numerous scholars interpret the *miqdash adam* as a community temple. Geza Vermes contended that 4QFlorilegium is one of the primary texts that "serves to present the sectarian doctrine identifying the Community with the Temple."[134] According to Devorah Dimant, "The activity of the community in recreating the sacred realm of the temple is, in fact, what is intended by the term 'Temple of Man' (מקדש אדם) in both *4QFlorilegium* (=4Q174) and 4QD."[135] Further, promises made to Israel are applied to the Qumranites,

> thus reflecting the understanding that the community is the true heir of Israel's biblical heritage, to the exclusion of other segments of contemporary Judaism. Combined with the sacral reality of the community as temple, such a restrictive understanding implies that the temple sacral sphere and its cult are transposed from the concrete, physical and contemporary temple into the reality of a well-defined small group, perceived as the elect and righteous.[136]

132. Wise provided a detailed chart and discussion of various scholars and their identification of each temple. Wise, "4QFlorilegium," 108. Cf. Briggs, *Jewish Temple Imagery*, 150–54; Dimant, "4QFlorilegium and the Idea," 165–89; Gärtner, *Temple and the Community*, 30–42; McNicol, "Eschatological Temple," 133–41; Schwartz, "Three Temples of 4QFlorilegium," 83–84; Yadin, *Temple Scroll*, 1:182–87; 2:129.

133. Wise, "*4QFlorilegium* and the Temple," 131.

134. Vermes, *Complete Dead Sea Scrolls*, 493. Cf. Gärtner, *Temple and the Community*, 34–35; Lee, *New Jerusalem*, 121.

135. Dimant, "Apocalyptic Interpretation of Ezekiel," 38.

136. Dimant, "Apocalyptic Interpretation of Ezekiel," 38.

Thus, the community temple is not an interim substitute for the eschatological temple or defiled Jerusalem temple, "but a foretaste and guarantee of the eschatological Temple" wherein some of the blessings of the eschatological age are experienced.[137]

The Damascus Document (4QD)

Although the Damascus Document does not appear to have been written by the sectarians, it was well attested at Qumran and likely reflects sectarian ideology.[138] In particular, the pesher on Ezekiel 44:15 in the Damascus Document yields insight into the community's understanding of the temple:

> And He built for them a sure house in Israel whose like has never existed from former times until now. Those who hold fast to it are destined to live for ever and all the glory of Adam shall be theirs. As God ordained by the hand of the Prophet Ezekiel, saying, *The Priests, the Levites, and the sons of Zadok who kept the charge of my sanctuary when the children of Israel strayed from me, they shall offer me fat and blood (Ezek. xliv, 15).* The *Priests* are the converts of Israel who departed from the land of Judah, and (the *Levites* are) those who joined them. The sons of Zadok are the elect of Israel, the men called by name who shall stand at the end of days. (4QD III, 19–IV, 5; italics denote biblical quotation)

Wise argued that the author of the Damascus Document presented the idea of a twofold eschaton, as in the Temple Scroll and 4QFlorilegium. In the first phase, the laws and temple of the Damascus Document would function. In the second, the temple made by God would supplant the previous one.[139] The scholar contended that Ezekiel 40–48 was understood to refer to the first phase of the eschatological temple. Therefore, the community interpreted Ezekiel 44:15, in the Damascus Document, as a reference to themselves serving in a future eschatological temple.[140]

To the contrary, Dimant and F. García Martinez argued that the author of the Damascus Document advocated the community-as-temple

---

137. Lee, *New Jerusalem*, 122.

138. Wise, "*4QFlorilegium* and the Temple," 113–14.

139. Wise, "*4QFlorilegium* and the Temple," 114–15; Wise, "Temple Scroll," 195–271.

140. Wise, "*4QFlorilegium* and the Temple," 126.

interpretation. The explicit interpretation of Ezekiel 44:15 in 4QD III, 19–IV, 5 identifies the officiates in the temple as the community of the last days (i.e., the sectarians themselves).[141] Dimant further explained that regarding the Levites as officiates in the temple makes sense only when one understands the community to be the temple.[142]

The possible allusion to 1 Samuel 2:35 in 4QD III, 19–IV, 1 reinforces such a reading. The verse in 1 Samuel consists of a prophecy about a faithful priest for whom the Lord would build an enduring "house," in the genealogical sense of the word. The author of the Damascus Document linked 1 Samuel 2:35 to Ezekiel 44:15, understanding both to refer to the same house. Accordingly, the "sure house" is understood as the temple and the community at the same time. The usage of present and past tense supports the idea that the house is not a future temple but the current community of the righteous.[143]

Worthy of note is that another passage from Ezekiel is referenced in the Damascus Document. The author cited Ezekiel 9:4 in 4QD XXIX, 11–13 to describe the destruction of Jerusalem by the Babylonians in a literal fashion. "It clearly shows that the CD's author was also familiar with a simple, literal mode of interpretation, and had recourse to it when it suited his purpose."[144]

In agreement with Dimant, the clear identification of community members as priestly officiates in the "house" of God implies that the sectarians viewed themselves as a replacement, albeit temporary, temple. Thus, the authors of both the Damascus Document and 4QFlorilegium seem to promulgate the community-as-temple ideology.

Although 4QFlorilegium and the Damascus Document refer to the community as a temple, Wise's proposal of a twofold eschatological temple still bears merit. The author of the Temple Scroll appears to describe a temple that will be built one day in place of the defiled Temple of Jerusalem: "Solomon's sanctuary as God originally intended it to be erected."[145] In other sectarian documents, which will be discussed shortly, a restored temple is anticipated but with eschatological nuances. Thus, the author of

---

141. Dimant, "Apocalyptic Interpretation of Ezekiel," 37–40; Martínez, "Apocalyptic Interpretation of Ezekiel," 163–76.

142. Dimant, "Apocalyptic Interpretation of Ezekiel," 37.

143. Dimant, "Apocalyptic Interpretation of Ezekiel," 37.

144. Dimant, "Apocalyptic Interpretation of Ezekiel," 40.

145. Briggs, *Jewish Temple Imagery*, 164. Cf. Mansoor, *Dead Sea Scrolls*, 200.

the Temple Scroll described a first-stage eschatological temple that will be followed by a temple constructed by the Lord himself.

The War Scroll (1QM)

The author of the War Scroll envisioned an impending war between the sons of light and the sons of darkness.[146] The sons of light are the sectarians and their attending angels. The sons of darkness are identified as the "Kittim" and the "army of Belial" (1QM I, 1). The evil forces also are referred to as "Gog and all his assembly" (1QM XI, 15), indicating that the battle is of an eschatological nature.[147] The eschatological age is reflected in the description of the post-victory state: "The dominion of the Kittim shall come to an end and iniquity shall be vanquished . . . The sons of righteousness shall shine over all the ends of the earth . . . And at the season appointed by God, His exalted greatness shall shine eternally to the peace, blessing, glory, joy, and long life of all the sons of light" (1QM I, 6–9).

In addition to the mention of Gog in XI, 15, other parallels with Ezekiel can be identified. First, in both the War Scroll and Ezekiel, the purpose of Gog's defeat is making God known to the nations (1QM XI, 15; Ezek 38:23).[148] Second, in both Ezekiel and the War Scroll, Gog is destroyed by the Lord (1QM XI, 15; Ezek 38:22). Third, of the biblical temple accounts, only in Ezekiel 40–48 is a particular station assigned to the ruler.[149] The author of the War Scroll may expand upon such an idea, as the chiefs of the tribes "attend daily at the gates of the Sanctuary" (1QM II, 2–4). Fourth, a messianic figure likely is mentioned in both Ezekiel and the War Scroll. The author of the War Scroll referenced a star from David and

---

146. Bauckham described Revelation as a Christian War Scroll, in which victory takes place through martyrdom. "Revelation makes lavish use of holy war *language* while transferring its *meaning* to non-military means of triumph over evil." Further, John took up the apocalyptic militancy of Old Testament prophecy and reinterpreted war in the light of Christian values (Bauckham, *Climax of Prophecy*, 210–37 [233], emphasis his]).

147. The author of 4Q285 fr. 4, likely a fragment of the War Scroll, quoted directly from Ezekiel 39:3, in which Ezekiel described the defeat of Gog to describe the defeat of the Kittim.

148. Manning, *Echoes of a Prophet*, 36.

149. The prince of Israel sits in the gate to eat bread before the Lord (Ezek 44:1–3).

a scepter from Israel (1QM XI, 1–7).[150] The author of Ezekiel was more subtle, but the installation of a Davidic ruler just prior to the battle with Gog indicates that the messiah is present in Ezekiel as well.[151]

That God himself destroys the enemies has led some scholars to contend that no messiah figure is present in the War Scroll.[152] Jim Parker proposed, however, that the authors of the War Scroll and Ezekiel anticipated a *divine* messiah.[153] Michael Knibb took a mediating position, arguing that messianic ideas are present but muted in the War Scroll.[154]

Especially relevant to the current study is the temple in which worship takes place after the battle. Although the temple is mentioned only obliquely (1QM II, 3), the author's attention to priestly service indicates a literal interpretation is appropriate. Sacrifices are to be offered daily at the site of the battle (1QM II, 2–5), and a return to Jerusalem after the battle is anticipated (1QM III, 11; VII, 4).[155] Thus, the temple of the War Scroll appears to be the first-stage eschatological temple.

The contribution of the War Scroll to the current study is minimal. Although a messiah seems to be present, his relationship to the future temple is ambiguous. Nonetheless, the War Scroll reinforces the idea that the sectarians anticipated a return to a literal temple in Jerusalem at some point in the future.

The Thanksgiving Hymns (1QH)

The Hodayot is a sectarian hymnbook similar to the biblical book of Psalms.[156] Further evidence of the community-as-temple ideology can be found in the hymns, as well as belief in a heavenly temple. The heavenly

---

150. The phrase may reflect the expectation for two messiahs. Cf. 4QD VII, 18–21; XII, 23–XIII, 1; 1QS IX, 9–11; 1QSa II, 11–21. Cf. T. Dan 5:9 and T. Jud. 21:2–4.

151. Manning, *Echoes of a Prophet*, 35. Cf. Davies, *1QM, the War Scroll*, 85, 100, 115–16.

152. Sanders, *Judaism*, 296; Stegemann, "Some Remarks," 479–505; Steudel, "Eternal Reign," 507–25.

153. Parker, *War Scroll*, 29–33 (Other possible attestations of a divine messiah include T. Benj. 10:7–8; 1 En. 10:16–11:2; and 4 Ezra 13:32–36).

154. Knibb, "Eschatology and Messianism," 379–402.

155. Briggs, *Jewish Temple Imagery*, 178; Manning, *Echoes of a Prophet*, 41; McKelvey, *New Temple*, 53; Yadin, *Scroll of the War*, 199.

156. Vermes, *Complete Dead Sea Scrolls*, 243.

temple is interconnected closely with the community temple through the worship and lifestyle of the sectarians.

The temple never is mentioned explicitly, but implicit references can be found in numerous passages. In 4Q427 7 I, 13–15, community members join with the heavenly assembly in worship: "Sing, O beloved ones, sing to the king of [glory, rejoice in the assem]bly of God, ring forth joy in the tents of salvation, give praise in the [holy] habitation, [ex]tol together among the eternal hosts, ascribe greatness to our God and glory to our king."[157]

In column II, further indication of joint worship between the heavenly and earthly communities is provided. The sectarians are rewarded for their righteousness by being lifted up into the heavenly temple (4Q427 7 II, 8–11). The dominance of the present tense reinforces "the fact that the blessings are already being experienced."[158] Rewards typically reserved for the eschatological age are experienced in the present for the community—light, peace, and joy replace wickedness, sickness, and oppression.

In column XIV of the Thanksgiving Hymns, the sectarians are linked to the angelic community: "For Thou wilt bring Thy glorious [salvation] to all the men of Thy Council, to those who share a common lot with the Angels of the Face" (1QH XIV, 13). Thus, the members of the *yahad* currently experience the same blessings and serve in the same capacity as the angels who dwell in the presence of the Lord. Further, as priestly officiates in the temple, members mediate eschatological blessings to the world (1QH XIV, 14–19).

The meaning of 1QH XIV, 24–31, which is replete with building imagery, is less clear:

> But I shall be as one who enters a fortified city, as one who seeks refuge behind a high wall until deliverance (comes); I will [lean on] Thy truth, O my God. For Thou wilt set the foundation on rock and the framework by the measuring-cord of justice; and the tried stones [Thou wilt lay] by the plumb-line [of truth], to [build] a mighty [wall] which shall not sway; and no man entering there shall stagger. For no enemy shall ever invade [it since its doors shall be] doors of protection through which no man shall pass. (1QH XIV, 24–27)

157. Schuller, "Hymn from a Cave," 610.
158. Lee, *New Jerusalem*, 112.

Two possibilities exist for the city here. First, the city could be the literal new Jerusalem, as described in the Temple Scroll and War Scroll. Second, the fortified city could symbolize the community of the righteous, as in the Community Rule.[159] The latter is more likely, as context indicates that the lines are intended symbolically. Indeed, the immediately preceding lines identify the author as a "sailor in a ship amid furious seas" (1 QH XIV, 22). Therefore, the building imagery should be understood likewise as symbolic.[160]

Further, many of the architectural elements of 1QH XIV closely parallel those of 1QS VIII. First, the high wall with a secure foundation is mentioned in both documents. Second, the framework of the city in 1QH XIV is laid with "the measuring-cord of *justice*" (italics added). Although the measuring cord is not mentioned in 1QS, the "house" is a mediator of justice to the world (1QS VIII, 9). Third, the group described in 1QS VIII is not the entire community but the inner council. Similarly, in 1QH XIV, the architectural elements represent the core of the city:

> Just as foundation, battlement, and gates are the core parts of the New Jerusalem/Temple building, the inner group is the core part of the whole Community. Just as the three architectural elements are not separated from the rest of the building but are connected with and represent the whole building, so the inner group represents the whole Community.[161]

Also of interest to the current study is column XVI of 1QH. With the imagery of trees and fountains that nourish creation, the author seems to have drawn upon Ezekiel 47.[162] As in previous passages, the community is identified with the blessings of the eschatological age.

The hymn begins as the author rests by a stream in the desert. The community is described with edenic imagery:

> [For Thou didst set] a plantation of cypress, pine, and cedar for Thy glory, trees of life beside a mysterious fountain hidden among the trees by the water, and they put out a shoot of the everlasting Plant. But before they did so they took root and sent out their roots to the watercourse that its stem might be

---

159. See 1QS VIII, 5–10.

160. Lee, *New Jerusalem*, 115.

161. Lee, *New Jerusalem*, 117.

162. Hughes, *Scriptural Allusions and Exegesis*, 158–59.

open to the living waters and be one with the everlasting spring.
(XVI, 5–7)

Additionally, the Plant "was hidden and was not esteemed," and no one
may drink of the water who "has not believed in the fountain of life"
(XVI, 10–14).

Several items of interest can be identified. First, parallels can be recognized with the terminology in 1QS VIII, as the community is described
as an "everlasting plantation." Here, the imagery is developed further to
describe the community as a grove of trees. Second, the roots are nourished by living waters and an everlasting spring. Third, the Plant not only
is nourished by the stream but is one with the water. Fourth, the stream is
said to proceed directly from the mouth of the gardener (1QH XVI, 16).

The imagery is complex, as the sectarians appear to be identified
with both trees and water, yet the community is doubtless in view. The
community leader is the gardener who digs the trench for the river
and weeds the banks (i.e., establishes and maintains the community)
(XVI, 21–26). The water that shelters and nourishes the *yahad* is his
teaching.[163] Moreover, by alluding to Ezekiel 47, the author is casting the
leader of the community, from whom the life-giving waters originate, in
the role of the temple.

The hymn concludes with the gardener becoming ill. He is unable
to perform his function and lead the community (XVI, 26–36). The
impending death of the leader is relevant for the implication that the
gardener of the hymn is not the messiah.[164] Indeed, Menahem Monsoor
argued that, as a whole, the Thanksgiving Hymns exhibit little messianic
expectation, with no clear references to a messiah at all.[165]

Thus, the analysis of the Thanksgiving Hymns contributes the following to the discussion. First, the community already participates in
the heavenly temple through prayer and worship. Second, interpreters
should be cautious of making a stark distinction between the community
temple and the heavenly temple, as the heavenly temple and corresponding blessings are actualized in the community.[166] Third, as an extension
of the heavenly temple, the community serves the function of the temple

---

163. Manning, *Echoes of a Prophet*, 58, 197.

164. Manning, *Echoes of a Prophet*, 58.

165. Mansoor, *Thanksgiving Hymns*, 91.

166. Lee, *New Jerusalem*, 109–18.

both now and in the eschatological age in mediating blessing and justice to the world.

Fourth, the portrayal of the community leader as a temple yields an informative parallel for the current study. The leader serves as the foundation of the temple as the person around whom the community is constructed. Similarly, the NT portrays Jesus Christ as the cornerstone of the temple, while the community of his followers are described as a temple as well.[167]

Songs of the Sabbath Sacrifice (4QShirShabb)

Even more so than the Hodayot hymns, the Songs of the Sabbath Sacrifice (Shirot) depict the simultaneity of heavenly and earthly worship.[168] The time of the whole offering on the Sabbath was regarded as a period in which heaven was especially permeable and therefore a propitious time for joining in the heavenly liturgy.[169] The purpose of the Shirot is, thus, to "direct the worshiper who hears the songs recited toward a particular kind of religious experience, a sense of being in the heavenly sanctuary and in the presence of the angelic priests and worshippers."[170]

The Shirot do not translate worshippers to heaven but create a heavenly experience for worshippers in the earthly domain.[171] "Where the other Qumran documents merely allude to the experience of communion with the angels, the Sabbath Shirot provide a primary vehicle."[172] Additionally, the heavenly temple is not a metaphorical structure or literary device, but an actualized reality in which the covenanters participated.[173] As such, recitation of the Shirot reaffirmed the sectarian identity as a priestly community.[174]

---

167. Christ: John 2:19–22; Eph 2:20; Christ's followers: Gal 2:9; Eph 2:20; 1 Cor 3:16–17; 2 Cor 6:16; 1 Pet 2:5.

168. Barker, *Gate of Heaven*, 45; Briggs, *Jewish Temple Imagery*, 170–78; Vermes, *Complete Dead Sea Scrolls*, 321.

169. Jdt 9:1; Luke 1:10; Josephus, *Ag. Ap.* 2:23; Newsom, *Songs of the Sabbath Sacrifice*, 20.

170. Newsom, *Songs of the Sabbath Sacrifice*, 17.

171. Newsom, "Merkabah Exegesis in the Qumran," 11–30.

172. Newsom, *Songs of the Sabbath Sacrifice*, 64.

173. Lee, *New Jerusalem*, 109.

174. Newsom, "Merkabah Exegesis in the Qumran," 13; Lee, *New Jerusalem*, 105.

Carol Newsom asserted that the authors of the Shirot used Ezekiel's temple as a pattern for the heavenly temple and the worship conducted there, particularly in the final five songs.[175] In an analysis of the Hebrew text, she determined that much of the language used to describe the heavenly temple can be traced to Ezekiel 40–48.

> The Sabbath Shirot are in no sense simply a commentary on Ezekiel 40–48. Many of the interests of the Shirot do not coincide with those of Ezekiel. The Shirot are not, for instance, concerned with the dimensions of the heavenly temple, with a complete account of all its chambers, or with the details of the legal material found in Ezekiel 40–48. What does concern the Sabbath Shirot is a description of the angels and their praise in the heavenly temple; and it appears that the author has selected and expanded those materials in Ezekiel which lend themselves to such an account. While the broken condition of the Sabbath songs make it difficult to specify just how closely Ezekiel 40–48 served as a structural outline for the Sabbath songs nine through thirteen, there is enough evidence to indicate its crucial role.[176]

For example, in the final five songs the author systematically described the structure and features of the heavenly sanctuary in the manner of a temple tour. Just as in Ezekiel, the tour progresses from the outer courts to the inner sanctum of the heavenly temple.

In the twelfth and thirteenth songs, the author appeared to draw upon the return of Yahweh to Ezekiel's temple (Ezek 43:1–12)[177]:

> The Cherubim bless the image of the chariot-throne that appears above the firmament, [then] they joyously acclaim the [splend]or of the luminous firmament that spreads beneath his glorious seat. As the wheel-beings advance, holy angels come and go. Between his chariot-throne's glorious [w]heels appears something like an utterly holy spiritual fire . . . The spirits of the living [go]dlike beings move to and fro perpetually, following

---

175. Newsom, "Merkabah Exegesis in the Qumran," 15; Newsom, *Songs of the Sabbath Sacrifice*, 53–58. Cf. Manning, *Echoes of a Prophet*, 43–48; Martínez, "Apocalyptic Interpretation of Ezekiel," 176; Wise et al., *Dead Sea Scrolls*, 365.

176. Newsom also suggested that, to a lesser extent, the author of the songs also drew upon the *merkabah* visions in Ezekiel 1 and 10 (Newsom, *Songs of the Sabbath Sacrifice*, 52).

177. Manning, *Echoes of a Prophet*, 43–45; Newsom, *Songs of the Sabbath Sacrifice*, 57.

the glory of the [wo]ndrous chariots. (4Q405 frag. 20 col 2 + frags. 21–22)[178]

The author thus combined various passages from Ezekiel 1, 10, and 40–48 to create the setting of heavenly Sabbath worship.[179] Newsom even argued that the vision of God's glory in the twelfth and thirteenth songs was an intentional exegesis of Ezekiel.[180] In contrast, Dimant argued that the Songs do not show a preference for Ezekiel over other biblical sources. The author of the Shirot drew upon "an intricate mosaic of biblical allusions."[181] Indeed, hierocratic and hekhalotic details are described in other temple tour accounts besides Ezekiel's.[182] However, Newsom did not claim that Ezekiel was the only inspiration for the Shirot, only that his visions were the primary influence.[183]

Even if the author of the Shirot drew upon Ezekiel 40–48 only in part, the usage may reflect an understanding of Ezekiel's temple as the heavenly one.[184] Further, the presence of the manuscript at Masada indicates that the work enjoyed broader circulation than Qumran alone.[185] Therefore, the wider circulation of the Shirot is further evidence that Ezekiel's temple was understood commonly as the heavenly one, as already observed in such texts as 1 Enoch and the Testament of Levi.

In regard to broader temple understandings, the description of the temple in the Shirot substantiates the idea that the earthly sanctuary reflects the basic plan of a heavenly counterpart.[186] Indeed, the sectarians did not view the heavenly temple as a distinct entity from the earthly

178. Wise et al., *Dead Sea Scrolls*, 375.

179. Newsom also detected an allusion to Psalms 68:17–19; Newsom, *Songs of the Sabbath Sacrifice*, 57, 319.

180. Newsom, "Merkabah Exegesis in the Qumran," 16.

181. Dimant, "Apocalyptic Interpretation of Ezekiel," 41–42.

182. See 1 En. 14; 11QT XXIX–XXX; m. Mid.; T. Levi 1–5, 15–18.

183. Newsom, *Songs of the Sabbath Sacrifice*, 53–54.

184. The eschatology of the Shirot is consistent with that of Ezekiel as well. God's presence could not dwell in the defiled Jerusalem Temple, so he dwelt among the righteous exiles and would return one day to a restored temple in Jerusalem (Manning, *Echoes of a Prophet*, 46–48).

185. Newsom and Yadin, "Masada Fragment," 77–88; Wise et al., *Dead Sea Scrolls*, 366.

186. Dimant, "Apocalyptic Interpretation of Ezekiel," 43.

one.[187] The covenanters understood themselves as simultaneously serving in the heavenly temple and the earthly (community) temple.

Description of the New Jerusalem (4QNJ)

The Description of the New Jerusalem scroll likely was not composed at Qumran, as the document lacks distinctive elements of sectarian ideology. However, the large number of copies found indicates that the document was read and studied by the group.[188] The author of the document did not actually use the name of Jerusalem for the city described.[189] Yet, the scroll has not been preserved in entirety, so the omission should not be overemphasized.[190]

Like the Shirot, the Description of the New Jerusalem scroll appears to be modeled after the tour of the temple in Ezekiel 40–48.[191] The scroll contains a detailed description of a city, a temple, and rituals conducted therein. Unlike in Ezekiel, emphasis is placed upon the city, as opposed to the temple.[192] However, the author of the Description of the New Jerusalem scroll does not depict a heavenly city. The city and temple are the eschatological temple and eschatological Jerusalem.[193]

As in Ezekiel, the visionary author is taken on a tour by an angelic guide.[194] Further parallels emerge as the account unfolds. First, the angelic guide measures the features of the city-temple. Second, the gates are the same dimensions as in Ezekiel 40–48. Third, the temple-cities of both the Description of the New Jerusalem scroll and Ezekiel are intended as places of worship for all nations.[195] However, most of the details that are

187. Manning, *Echoes of a Prophet*, 48.

188. Chyutin, *New Jerusalem Scroll from Qumran*, 9; Dimant, "Apocalyptic Interpretation of Ezekiel," 45–46.

189. Neither did Ezekiel refer to his temple-city as Jerusalem in Ezekiel 40–48.

190. Chyutin, *New Jerusalem Scroll from Qumran*, 110.

191. Dimant, "Apocalyptic Interpretation of Ezekiel," 46; Manning, *Echoes of a Prophet*, 41.

192. Mathewson, *New Heaven*, 120.

193. Briggs, *Jewish Temple Imagery*, 168; Martínez, "Apocalyptic Interpretation of Ezekiel," 176; Vermes, *Complete Dead Sea Scrolls*, 568.

194. Opposite Ezekiel's vision, the tour in 4QNJ proceeds from the inner sanctum to the outer courts.

195. Chyutin, *New Jerusalem Scroll from Qumran*, 12–13, 111–12; Vermes, *Complete Dead Sea Scrolls*, 568.

provided concern the city rather than the temple. Such use of Ezekielian temple imagery to describe the city is highly reminiscent of the manner in which John drew upon Ezekiel 40–48 in Revelation.[196]

The author's use of not only Ezekiel, but Isaiah, indicates that the city-temple described in the scroll may have been seen as the fulfillment of prophetic texts.[197] The city in the Description of the New Jerusalem scroll has a golden wall (11Q18 23–24), bejeweled streets (5Q15 I, 6–7) and a sapphire door (2Q24 3), reminiscent of Isaiah 54:11–12 and Tobit 13:16. In Tobit, the structure appears to be literal, while in Isaiah the nature of the description is uncertain.[198] In the Isaiah Pesher (4Q164), the author seemed to indicate that the community is the fulfillment of Isaiah 54:11–12. However, in the Description of the New Jerusalem scroll, the author seemed to portray the temple in a literal fashion. "One is struck by the extreme concreteness of the description in the *New Jerusalem* as compared with the symbolic-allegorical interpretation found in the community's writings. Not once does the author hint at a symbolic, or even a figurative understanding."[199] Lee observed that the sectarians had no problem with understanding Isaiah 54 in two ways: "This double fulfillment of Isa. 54:11–12 demonstrates that the Community Temple and the eschatological New Temple are equally significant to the sectarians."[200] Further, since Ezekiel's temple vision had not yet been fulfilled, the sectarians believed that the prophecy "would be fulfilled in and through them."[201] Gary Manning explained that the sectarians may have desired to "fill in the details of the priests' duties and living spaces, since the hope of the community was that they would dwell in the restored city. Just as Ezekiel's Temple measurements had the rhetorical effect of concretizing the hopes of the Exiles, *New Jerusalem's* housing measurements concretized the hopes of the Qumran community."[202]

---

196. The similarities between 4QNJ and Revelation are so pronounced that Vogelgesang proposed John might have been influenced by 4QNJ (Vogelgesang, "Interpretation of Ezekiel," 152–55).

197. Lee, *New Jerusalem*, 127.

198. Dimant, "Apocalyptic Interpretation of Ezekiel," 47.

199. Dimant, "Apocalyptic Interpretation of Ezekiel," 48.

200. Lee, *New Jerusalem*, 127.

201. Manning, *Echoes of a Prophet*, 42.

202. Manning, *Echoes of a Prophet*, 41–42.

Second Ezekiel (4Q385–391)

Second Ezekiel, or Pseudo-Ezekiel, is a mid-first-century-CE Jewish text excavated from Qumran.[203] Like the Description of the New Jerusalem scroll, the document lacks distinctive elements of sectarian ideology and likely was not composed at Qumran. However, the presence of the scroll indicates that 2 Ezekiel was read and studied by the group.[204]

The author of 2 Ezekiel provided commentary upon the prophecies of Ezekiel pseudepigraphically through the words of the prophet himself. An exegesis of (First) Ezekiel is provided in a manner similar to the Qumran pesharim, presenting a "reworking of the pertinent Biblical texts in an apocalyptic context."[205] Thus, the subject matter is based on the biblical prophecies of Ezekiel, but Ezekiel's visions are interpreted in the symbolic manner of apocalypses. The work also includes historical surveys, which are a common feature of apocalyptic literature. Therefore, 2 Ezekiel combines apocalyptic tendencies with the literary forms common to the sectarian community.[206]

In particular, 2 Ezekiel exhibits a large degree of similarity to 2 Baruch and 4 Ezra. All three works provide a dialogue between God and prophet in regard to the final destiny of Israel. The primary difference is that Baruch and Ezra are guided by an angelic mediator, while Ezekiel speaks directly with God. John Strugnell and Dimant thus proposed that 2 Ezekiel is a "very close forerunner" of 2 Baruch and 4 Ezra.[207]

Most unfortunate for the current research, no reference to Ezekiel 40–48 appears in the work; commentary is offered only on chapters 1–39.[208] Nonetheless, the presence of 2 Ezekiel at Qumran provides another example "of the far-reaching influence exercised by the prophecies

---

203. Vermes, *Complete Dead Sea Scrolls*, 571. For a discussion of scholarship on 2 Ezekiel, see Mueller, *Five Fragments of the Apocryphon*, 26–77.

204. Josephus mentioned an apocryphal work of Ezekiel, but whether Pseudo-Ezekiel is the same document is unknown (*Ant.* 10:79). Cf. Dimant, "Apocalyptic Interpretation of Ezekiel," 45–46; Dimant and Strugnell, "Merkabah Vision in *Second Ezekiel*," 331–48; Mueller, *Five Fragments of the Apocryphon*, 16–17; Stone, "Ancient *Testimonia* to the Existence," 7–9; Strugnell and Dimant, "4Q Second Ezekiel," 45–58.

205. Strugnell and Dimant, "4Q Second Ezekiel," 47.

206. Strugnell and Dimant, "4Q Second Ezekiel," 47.

207. Strugnell and Dimant, "4Q Second Ezekiel," 48, 56–57.

208. Manning noted that the author of frag. 65 seemed to begin a description of the new Jerusalem, as in Ezekiel 40–48 (Manning, *Echoes of a Prophet*, 72).

of Ezekiel on contemporary authors."[209] Furthermore, the author's use of (First) Ezekiel affords an example of Ezekiel's prophecies being understood in an apocalyptic and symbolic fashion.[210]

Summary and Evaluation

A distinct doctrine of the Qumran community was the sectarian understanding of themselves as a temple of righteous individuals. The documents in which the community-as-temple ideology can be found are the Community Rule, 4QFlorilegium, the Damascus Document, and the Thanksgiving Hymns. Several indications of the ideology can be identified. First, through designations such as "Everlasting Plantation," "House of Holiness," and "House of Perfection and Truth," temple-related terminology is applied to the community. Second, the *yahad* served many of the functions that traditionally were ascribed to the temple, such as atoning for the land and mediating eschatological blessings. Third, strict hierarchal and purity requirements were imposed in order to achieve requisite standards of holiness. Fourth, the depiction of community members as priests indicates that they viewed themselves as officiates in a temple.

The temple-less situation of the community was viewed as a temporary condition that would be rectified after the reigning evil powers were defeated by the righteous remnant. Klawans explained, "Most likely, the sectarians saw their temple-free existence as a *provisional* response to an undesired circumstance."[211]

> While the community takes on certain characteristics of the temple, the texts do not assert that the community is better than or even as good as a temple would be. Indeed, compared to the temple that they themselves envision in the *Temple Scroll*, the community offers limited access to the divine presence and relatively inadequate means of achieving atonement.[212]

---

209. Dimant and Strugnell, "Merkabah Vision in *Second Ezekiel*," 348. Cf. Dimant, "Apocalyptic Interpretation of Ezekiel," 50.

210. Second Ezekiel is not fully apocalyptic. As with canonical Ezekiel, many of the characteristic features of apocalyptic literature are missing (Manning, *Echoes of a Prophet*, 73).

211. Klawans, *Purity, Sacrifice, and the Temple*, 163.

212. Klawans, *Purity, Sacrifice, and the Temple*, 168.

Therefore, in addition to their self-understanding as a community temple, the sectarians also anticipated a material temple that one day would replace the defiled Jerusalem Temple. The author of the Temple Scroll, much like the author of Ezekiel 40–48, provided detailed architectural guidelines for a restored Jerusalem and temple.

The temple of the Temple Scroll is not a heavenly one, but a preliminary eschatological one that would be built in the future and replace the irreparably tainted Jerusalem Temple. Likewise, the author of the Description of the New Jerusalem scroll described a resplendent temple and city. Although the descriptions in the Description of the New Jerusalem scroll diverge in detail from those in the Temple Scroll, the temple and city appear to be the eschatological version, rather than the heavenly temple established by God. Likewise, the author of the War Scroll appeared to reference the first-stage eschatological temple.

In distinction from the future eschatological temple, the heavenly temple was a real and vibrant reality for the community. Members believed that they actively participated in heavenly worship with the angels. The clearest descriptions of communion with heaven can be found in the Thanksgiving Hymns and Sabbath Songs. The authors of both documents described the participation of the covenanters in heavenly worship. Through such communion, members would experience eschatological rewards in the present and mediate blessings to the world. Further, as indicated by the authors of the Temple Scroll, 4QFlorilegium, and the Damascus Document, the heavenly temple would replace the man-made temple in the eschaton.

Although attempts have been made to provide a straightforward description of the three temples of Qumran, the temple ideology of the sectarian documents is complex. Determining whether any given temple is the heavenly temple, eschatological temple, or community temple is difficult. The three sanctuaries overlap throughout the scrolls.[213] Moreover, the same imagery is used often to describe different concepts, and Scripture is used freely to suit the needs of various authors. In other words, the difficulty in clearly delineating the temples of the scrolls is a direct reflection of the ambiguity in the texts. The sectarians themselves drew no stark distinctions between their various conceptions of the temple.

Several implications for the interpretation of Ezekiel's temple vision can be identified. First, like other scriptural texts, Ezekiel 40–48

213. Lee, *New Jerusalem*, 86.

was malleable for the authors of the scrolls. Similar to Ezekiel 40–48, the author of the Temple Scroll provided architectural details for the new Jerusalem and temple. That Ezekiel's temple was not used as a model may indicate that the author viewed Ezekiel's temple as the heavenly one that would replace the earthly temple described in the scroll. Likewise, the author of the Songs of the Sabbath Sacrifice drew on Ezekiel 40–48 as inspiration for a portrayal of the heavenly temple. Thus, as in 1 Enoch 14 and Testament of Levi 1–5, Ezekiel 40–48 seems to be a frequent referent for portrayals of the heavenly temple.

Conversely, the Description of the New Jerusalem scroll, also modeled after Ezekiel 40–48, appears to portray the first-stage eschatological temple and city. The document may thus represent an intermediate stage between Ezekiel and Revelation in which the city, rather than the temple, is of central focus. "While it is unlikely that John was familiar with *DNJ*, it is likely that both belong to a similar tradition of adapting and expanding Ezek. 40–48 to suit their purposes."[214]

Second, Ezekiel was used metaphorically in the scrolls. The author of 1QH 16 alluded to Ezekiel 47 to cast the community leader in the role of the temple, and the author of the Damascus Document cited Ezekiel 44 to describe the community as a temple.

Third, the author of 2 Ezekiel provided an example of the canonical Ezekiel being understood in a symbolic and apocalyptic fashion. Further, because 2 Ezekiel does not seem to have been written by sectarian authors, the document may evidence "a more widespread tendency in the Judaism of the second century BCE to interpret Ezekiel 'apocalyptically.'"[215]

Thus, the visions of Ezekiel, particularly chapters 40–48, permeated the thought of the sectarians. The book of Ezekiel not only helped shape the thought of the Qumran community, but served as a conduit for sectarian ideology. Martinez wrote that the text "was profoundly reinterpreted and re-used as a channel for new ideas. In other words, the community did not hesitate to use Ezekiel's words, giving them a new meaning in order to express its own apocalyptic worldview."[216] Conversely, Manning asserted that the sectarian authors remained faithful to the message of Ezekiel:

214. Mathewson, *New Heaven*, 120.

215. Martínez, "Apocalyptic Interpretation of Ezekiel," 176.

216. Martínez, "Apocalyptic Interpretation of Ezekiel," 176.

In the majority of the allusions to Ezekiel, Qumran authors exhibited a great sensitivity to the message of Ezekiel. Even brief allusions were usually derived from passages in Ezekiel that contributed to the author's point or resonated with the same theological themes. Of course, Scripture references were always applied to the community or used to advance a position peculiar to Qumran. Ezekiel was appropriated for use within Qumran, but often without violence to the sense of Ezekiel.[217]

Perhaps the assertions of Martinez and Manning can be harmonized somewhat. The authors of the scrolls did indeed give the words of Ezekiel new significance as they appropriated the prophecies for themselves, but at the same time remained faithful to the original sense of the prophet's words. Further, the sectarians used Ezekiel and other Scriptures to define their identity, bolster their legitimacy, and articulate their beliefs. The hypothesis that Christian authors, such as John, might have used Ezekiel's visions to communicate their own distinctive ideologies is, thus, thoroughly plausible.

217. Manning, *Echoes of a Prophet*, 74.

5.

Temple and Messiah in Literature Contemporaneous with Revelation

THE TIME PERIOD IN which Revelation was composed—the latter part of the first century CE—was a tumultuous time for the Jewish people. The destruction of the Jerusalem Temple in 70 CE elicited a strong response from both Jews and Christians. Many of the resulting works are relevant for the current study.[1] The writings examined here include the Similitudes of 1 Enoch, Sibylline Oracles 1–2 and 4–5, 4 Ezra (2 Esdras), 1–3 Baruch, the Apocalypse of Abraham, Pseudo-Philo, and the Ezekiel Targum. Although the Mishnah was compiled after the book of Revelation, the volume reflects traditions of the previous four centuries. Additionally, tractate Middoth, in which a temple plan is outlined, was composed soon after the destruction of the Jerusalem Temple, placing the document in the same time frame as Revelation. Therefore, the Mishnah will be included in the analysis.

Although many passages in the NT are relevant, they will not be explicated. The idea of Jesus as a replacement for the temple is relatively common in the NT.[2] Further, although most of the NT documents were composed by the time Revelation was written, "it is difficult to prove that

---

1. The Similitudes of 1 Enoch is the only document in the current section that was not written after the fall of Jerusalem.

2. Coloe, *God Dwells with Us*; Beale, *Temple and the Church's Mission*, 169–402; Hoskins, *Jesus as the Fulfillment*; Lee, *New Jerusalem*, 230–38; Marshall, "Church and Temple," 203–22; McKelvey, *New Temple*.

the author of Revelation had direct access to any one of them."[3] Moreover, Revelation as an apocalypse is unique in the NT. Extrabiblical literature must be examined to find works of a parallel genre.

The Similitudes of Enoch

The dating of the Similitudes is a contentious issue. Early in the history of scholarship on the Similitudes, Charles argued for a date in the late Maccabean period (ca. 94–79 or 70–64 BCE).[4] On the opposite end of the spectrum, Józef Milik argued for a date in the third century CE (ca. 270 CE).[5] Most scholars now favor a date of composition somewhere between the mid-first century BCE and the mid-first century CE.[6] Collins, for example, argued for a date of 60–70 CE. That no fragments of the Similitudes were found at Qumran supports the later dating.[7]

Despite the absence of the document at Qumran, parallels between the Similitudes and other Second Temple period works are extensive. Gabriele Boccaccini wrote, "There is virtually no element in the document that cannot be found elsewhere in Second Temple Jewish and early Christian and rabbinic literature."[8] He continued, "The document as a whole therefore testifies to a stage in which the encounter and merging of the Sapiential, Messianic, and Apocalyptic paradigms were still at their inception—a stage that parallels the earliest origins of the Jesus movement and is the logical premise for the theological developments in Paul and the later Christian tradition."[9]

A messianic figure, the "son of man," plays a major role in the Similitudes. The messianism is so similar to that of the Gospels that some scholars have proposed that the work is Christian, or at least features Christian interpolations.[10] However, general consensus leans toward the

3. Paulien, "Elusive Allusions," 45.

4. Charles, *Book of Enoch*, 263–64.

5. Milik, *Books of Enoch*, 91–96.

6. Boccaccini, *Enoch and the Messiah*, 415–96; Briggs, *Jewish Temple Imagery*, 120; Knibb, *Essays on the Book*, 143–60; Nickelsburg and VanderKam, *1 Enoch 2*, 58–66; Suter, *Tradition and Composition*, 23–32.

7. Collins, *Apocalyptic Imagination*, 177–78.

8. Boccaccini, "Finding a Place," 265.

9. Boccaccini, "Finding a Place," 268.

10. Campbell, "Origin and Meaning," 145–55; Milik, *Books of Enoch*, 96–98. Although Leslie Walck did not contend that the Similitudes is a Christian document, he

Similitudes being a Jewish work, as no traces of vicarious sacrifice or resurrection are present.[11]

Although the phrase "son of man" carries with it "the eschatological associations of Daniel 7," the identity of the figure does not depend entirely on Daniel.[12] Unlike the figure in Daniel, the Enochian son of man sits upon a throne to execute judgment.[13] Further, the son of man is associated with "the righteous" and "the holy," which can refer to either angelic or human beings. Therefore, the author implied that the elect human community lives in close relationship with the angelic world. The son of man figure represents the union of the heavenly and earthly communities both in "present hiddenness and future manifestation."[14]

The Similitudes consists of three interrelated parables: chapters 38–44, 45–57, and 58–71. The messianic figure appears in all three, referred to variously as the "chosen one" (1 En. 45:3–6), the "righteous one" (1 En. 53:6), and the "anointed one" (1 En. 48:10; 52:4). In the first parable, the "righteous one" appears to judge sinners and usher in the eschaton.

In the second parable, the author emphasized that the ministry of the "chosen one" makes life in the new heavens and earth possible. In 1 Enoch 45:3–5, the messiah is enthroned, after which he dwells among the elect in the new world:[15] "On that day, I shall make my Chosen One dwell among them, and I shall transform heaven and make it a blessing and a light forever; and I shall transform earth and make it a blessing. And my chosen ones I shall make to dwell on it, but those who commit sin and error will not set foot on it."[16]

In the final parable, the "anointed one" is seated upon the throne of glory.[17] Surprisingly, Enoch himself is identified as the "son of man"

---

did argue that the book exercised heavy influence on the Gospel of Matthew (Walck, "Son of Man," 299–337.

11. Nonetheless, the community that produced the Similitudes may have arisen from the same milieu as the early Christian writers (Nickelsburg and VanderKam, *1 Enoch 2*, 66). Cf. Collins, *Apocalyptic Imagination*, 177–78; Helyer, *Exploring Jewish Literature*, 388; Suter, "Weighed in the Balance," 217–21.

12. Collins, *Apocalyptic Imagination*, 184–85. Cf. Helyer, *Exploring Jewish Literature*, 388.

13. Kvanig, "Son of Man," 179–215.

14. Collins, *Apocalyptic Imagination*, 187.

15. Lee, *New Jerusalem*, 63; Nickelsburg and VanderKam, *1 Enoch 2*, 119.

16. Translations of the Similitudes are reproduced from Isaac, "1 (Ethiopic Apocalypse of) Enoch."

17. 1 En. 61:8; 62:1–2; 69:27.

(1 En. 71:14). Helge Kvanig noted that the attribution of the "son of man" to an individual (i.e., Enoch) is paralleled in the designation of Christ as the "son of man."[18] Most relevant for the current study, however, is that Enoch as the "son of man" is regarded as an eternal dwelling for the righteous (1 En. 71:16).

Several relevant conclusions can be drawn from the Similitudes. First, the author of the Similitudes articulated an expectation for a messianic figure who would usher in the eschaton. Second, the advent of the messiah effects the transformation of the heavens and the earth. Third, although the messiah is enthroned, no indication is given that he reigns from a temple. The heavenly temple featured in the Similitudes is nowhere said to be manifested on the earth.[19] The "congregation of the righteous" appears on earth, presumably from heaven, but the temple does not (1 En. 38:1). Fourth, the "son of man" is described in terms usually reserved for the temple, "an eternal dwelling."

4 Ezra

Fourth Ezra is a late-first-century Palestinian text written in response to the fall of the Jerusalem Temple.[20] The events of 70 CE are the impetus for questions on theodicy, which is the primary concern of 4 Ezra. However, the ostensible occasion for the text is the destruction of Jerusalem in 586 BCE.[21] Chapters 2–14 appear to be the original Jewish body of the work, while chapters 1 and 15 are later Christian additions.[22] Although the messiah is not the focus of the work, the figure plays a substantial role in the eschatological scheme. Additionally, the traditional expectation of

18. Kvanig, "Son of Man," 213–14.

19. See 1 En. 71.

20. Collins, *Apocalyptic Imagination*, 196; Kirschner, "Apocalyptic and Rabbinic Responses," 28; Metzger, "Fourth Book of Ezra," 517–59; Nickelsburg, *Jewish Literature*, 270; Oesterley, *Introduction to the Books*, 146–56; Stone, *Features of the Eschatology*, 1–11; Stone, *Fourth Ezra*, 9–10.

21. Collins, *Apocalyptic Imagination*, 200; Kirschner, "Apocalyptic and Rabbinic Responses," 29–30.

22. Metzger, "Fourth Book of Ezra," 517. Lee asserted that chs. 3–13 are the original Jewish body of the work, while chs. 1–2 and 14–15 are Christian additions (Lee, *New Jerusalem*, 129).

a messianic kingdom is present, but is overshadowed by a concern to understand the conditions of the afterlife.[23]

In 4 Ezra 7:3–14, the author described a city "full of all good things" with a narrow entrance that is difficult to access (vv. 6–8).[24] Here, the city represents the inheritance of Israel, which can be obtained only by persevering through great trial (vv. 10–14). The city also symbolizes all the blessings of the Lord, including immortality. The author did not explicitly say so, but the blessings appear to be eschatological rewards.[25]

The reference to the city in 4 Ezra 7:26–44 is more specific. The "unseen city" and "hidden land" most likely refer to the heavenly Jerusalem.[26] Moreover, the eschatological tone of the chapter indicates that the city of verses 26–44 is the same as that of verses 3–13. The identification of the city as the heavenly one is strengthened by 4 Ezra 8:52 and 13:36, in which the city is described as preexistent.[27] Surprisingly, Ezra's city has no temple, only the "splendor of the glory of the Most High," which provides light (4 Ezra 7:42).

In eschatological texts, the "glory of God" is closely akin to the judgment of God. Because the heavenly luminaries cease to shine, the glory of God is the only source of illumination. Accordingly, the truth is revealed and reward or punishment is dispensed. "Glory" is also a theophanic term for the one who sits upon the *merkabah* in connection "with the appearance of God on earth."[28] Thus, the possibility exists that the divine light emanates from a messianic figure.

In chapter 13, further support for such an interpretation is provided. The author indicated that God will send his son to deliver creation (4 Ezra 13:32), after which the son will stand upon Mt. Zion in victory (4 Ezra 13:33–36). At such a time "Zion will come and be made manifest to all people, prepared and built, as you saw the mountain carved out without hands" (4 Ezra 13:36). With such imagery, the author seemed to portray the union of the earthly and heavenly Jerusalem. Michael Stone

---

23. Metzger, "Fourth Book of Ezra," 521.

24. Translations of 4 Ezra are reproduced from Metzger, "Fourth Book of Ezra."

25. Stone, *Fourth Ezra*, 193.

26. Cf. 4 Ezra 8:52; 10:27, 42, 44, 54; 13:36; Collins, *Apocalyptic Imagination*, 203; Lee, *New Jerusalem*, 132; Stone, *Fourth Ezra*, 213.

27. Lee, *New Jerusalem*, 133; Stone, *Fourth Ezra*, 214.

28. Scholem, *Major Trends in Jewish Mysticism*, 46, 358; Stone, *Fourth Ezra*, 72. Cf. Hurowitz, "YHWH's Exalted House," 63–110; Kasher, "Anthropomorphism, Holiness and Cult," 192–208.

elaborated, "In 4 Ezra, we should observe, heavenly Jerusalem is usually related to the 'messianic kingdom' complex of ideas."[29]

That the messianic figure occupies the location typically reserved for the temple is particularly relevant for the current study. However, Lee argued that the reason for the omission of the temple is the implicit connection between Jerusalem and the temple. He wrote, "The author does not distinguish the city from the temple. For the author, the city is the temple and *vice versa*."[30] Indeed, Jewish authors often conflated Jerusalem and the temple. For example, in Psalm 79:1, the temple is set in parallel with Jerusalem: "They have defiled your temple;[31] they have turned Jerusalem to ruins." The author of 2 Baruch also seemed to use the concepts interchangeably at times: "Do you think that this is the *city* of which I said: 'On the palms of my hands have I graven thee?' This *building* now built in your midst is not that which is revealed with Me, that which was prepared beforehand here from the time when I took counsel to make Paradise" (2 Bar 4:2–3, italics added).[32] Therefore, although the temple never is mentioned in 4 Ezra 7, 8, or 13, the presence of the structure seems to be implied.

The city-temple of 4 Ezra is also part of the "world to come." Such a belief in two worlds is present in 4 Ezra, as in most apocalypses. The author explicitly stated, "The Most High has made not one world but two" (4 Ezra 7:50).[33] Thus, the author conveyed the idea of two ages as well as the notion that the "world to come" was created by God in advance.[34] In chapter 8, a listing of features that will be a part of the world to come is provided: the tree of life, goodness, rest, and wisdom (4 Ezra 8:52).[35] Phenomena that will be absent are listed as well: evil, illness, death, and sorrow (4 Ezra 8:53–54).

Considerable debate exists over whether the verses are literal or figurative. Joseph Keulers argued that the terms are spiritualized,

29. Stone, *Fourth Ezra*, 287.

30. Lee, *New Jerusalem*, 130–31; emphasis his. Cf. Hamerton-Kelly, "Temple and the Origins," 4; Nir, *Destruction of Jerusalem*, 37.

31. הֵיכָל.

32. Murphy, *Structure and Meaning*, 85. Cf. 11QT XLV, 13–14; XLVII, 3–6, 10–11, where the city is held to the same stringent purity regulations as the temple.

33. Collins, *Apocalyptic Imagination*, 204.

34. Stone, *Fourth Ezra*, 286.

35. Rest, paradise, and fruit are "a traditional combination of elements" expected in the eschatological age (Stone, *Fourth Ezra*, 286). Cf. T. Levi 18:9–10.

representing eschatological rewards in general.[36] Conversely, "It should be recalled that for authors of the age of 4 Ezra, heavenly objects were no less real than earthly ones, so that opposed categories 'material' and 'spiritual' seem irrelevant."[37] Lee concurred, noting the overlap between spiritual and material realities in the passage.[38] Therefore, much like the Qumran sectarians, the author of 4 Ezra blurred the distinction between material and spiritual. However, for the *yahad*, the spiritual and material were merging already, but for the author of 4 Ezra, such categories would blend in the eschaton.

Chapter 10 begins with a complex vision of a dead son and a grieving mother alongside the ravaged Jerusalem. The woman, symbolizing Zion, shortly transforms into a shining city. In verses 25–27 and 42–48, the author indicates that Zion will replace the city built by Solomon. The city, as before, likely represents both city and temple.

In 4 Ezra 10:38–54, the nature of the city is exceedingly difficult to discern. The ambiguity is reflected in the text itself. At first, the city seems to be the historical Jerusalem, as the complex is built by Solomon (4 Ezra 10:46). Alternately, the author stated that "no work of human construction could endure in a place where the city of the Most High was to be revealed" (4 Ezra 10:54), and that the "building" in the city is splendorous and vast. Stone wrote, "Questions as to whether the city is the heavenly Jerusalem or an eschatological one should probably be answered with an ambiguous 'Yes!'"[39] Thus, the author continued his propensity for blending material and spiritual realities.

Considering the various references to the temple-city in chapters 7, 8, and 10, the author of 4 Ezra seemed to expect the heavenly Jerusalem to appear on earth. Frederick Murphy explained, "The emphasis seems to be on the divine origin of a future Temple which will be built in order to replace the Second Temple."[40] Upon death, the righteous leave the physical creation and dwell with God in the realm of the spiritual, but only for an interim period (4 Ezra 7:78). Those who are with the messiah in the hidden city will return to earth with him in the eschaton (4 Ezra 7:27–28).

36. Keulers, *Die eschatologische Lehre*, 181–88.

37. Stone, *Fourth Ezra*, 286.

38. Lee, *New Jerusalem*, 133.

39. Stone, *Fourth Ezra*, 335.

40. Murphy, *Structure and Meaning*, 87.

2 Baruch

A general consensus exists that 2 Baruch was composed between the Jewish revolts of 70 and 132 CE. Collins explained, "As in 4 Ezra, the destruction at the hands of the Babylonians serves as an allegory for the fall of 70 CE."[41] The author probably made use of various sources, as evidence of different, sometimes conflicting, perspectives on the temple can be found.[42]

A number of parallels can be identified between 2 Baruch and 4 Ezra, although the latter is more optimistic in nature. Bruce Metzger argued that 2 Baruch was written in response to 4 Ezra from "a theological outlook somewhat more in accordance with later rabbinical Judaism."[43] Conversely, similarities may be the result of a common source.[44]

The author of 2 Baruch addressed a Jewish ideology in which the welfare of the temple was linked to the welfare of the people. The author directly confronted and denied such thinking.[45] According to Murphy, "The author's purpose is to take attention away from the earthly Temple *per se* and direct it toward the heavenly sphere."[46]

Contemporary authors often criticized the Second Temple by contrasting the institution with the first temple or the eschatological temples.[47] The author of 2 Baruch utilized a different strategy by contrasting the earthly temple with the heavenly one. For the author of 2 Baruch, the present world is inherently corruptible. Because Jerusalem and the temple are part of the world, they will pass away along with the current order.[48]

Rivka Nir provided an alternate interpretation of 2 Baruch. She argued that the author's perspective on Jerusalem and the temple is

---

41. Collins, *Apocalyptic Imagination*, 212. Cf. Kirschner, "Apocalyptic and Rabbinic Responses," 29–30; Knibb, *Essays on the Book*, 399; Murphy, *Structure and Meaning*, 71; Murphy, "Temple in the *Syriac Apocalypse*," 671–83; Nir, *Destruction of Jerusalem*, 3–4; Stone, "Apocalyptic Literature," 383–41.

42. Klijn, "2 (Syriac Apocalypse of) Baruch," 615–52.

43. Metzger, "Fourth Book of Ezra," 522.

44. Klijn, "2 (Syriac Apocalypse of) Baruch," 619–20.

45. Murphy, *Structure and Meaning*, 84–85.

46. Murphy, *Structure and Meaning*, 87. Cf. Hamerton-Kelly, "Temple and the Origins," 4.

47. 1 En. 89:73; T. Mos. 4:8; Tob 14.

48. Murphy, *Structure and Meaning*, 37.

distinctively Christian.[49] As such, the author of 2 Baruch was not re-
sponding to the crisis of CE 70, but was emphasizing the "inferiority
and transience of the earthly Jerusalem and temple."[50] The destiny of the
temple in 2 Baruch is similar to that which is described in the NT: the
earthly temple must be destroyed so that the heavenly one can be established.[51] Although Nir's hypothesis is innovative, not enough evidence
exists to conclude that 2 Baruch is a Christian document. Further, the
level of attention given to the fate of the temple and temple implements in
2 Baruch is unheard of in other Christian texts. Yet, regardless of whether
the work is Jewish or Christian, the most salient feature for the current
study is the rejection of the earthly temple.

From the outset of 2 Baruch, the author intimated that some of the
functions of the temple are actually in the purview of the people. In a
statement reminiscent of Qumran sectarian thought, the Lord says to the
fleeing exiles: "For your works are for this city like a firm pillar and your
prayers like a strong wall" (2 Bar. 2:2).[52]

Pillars are a ubiquitous temple feature. The precise symbolic content
of Baruch's pillars is unknown, but possibilities include "strength, solid-
ity, binding efficacy, endurance, continuity, [and] cosmic order."[53] In the
passage at hand, the righteous of Jerusalem serve such functions rather
than the temple.[54]

In chapter 4, attention is directed toward the heavenly temple. The
purpose of the chapter is to make a distinction between heavenly and
earthly realities. In 2 Baruch 4:2–4, Baruch laments that he would sooner
die than see Zion destroyed. God, however, assures Baruch that the
earthly Jerusalem is not the city of promise. The real temple-city is the
eternal one that exists in heaven. Collins explained, "The destruction of
the earthly temple, then, is not as great a catastrophe as it might seem."[55]

49. Nir, *Destruction of Jerusalem*, 4, 40.

50. Nir, *Destruction of Jerusalem*, 21.

51. Nir, *Destruction of Jerusalem*, 33–34. See Mark 13; Matt 24; Luke 21.

52. Translations of 2 Baruch are reproduced from Klijn, "2 (Syriac Apocalypse of)
Baruch."

53. Lundquist, "Temple, Covenant, and Law," 300. Cf. Barker, *Gate of Heaven*,
29–30; Briggs, *Jewish Temple Imagery*, 67–74; Hurowitz, "YHWH's Exalted House,"
83; Patai, *Man and Temple*, 108–10.

54. Cf. Rev 3:12, where faithful Christ followers become pillars in the temple. Cf.
Briggs, *Jewish Temple Imagery*, 69–70.

55. Collins, *Apocalyptic Imagination*, 216. Cf. Lee, *New Jerusalem*, 146–47; Murphy,

Verse 2 is a quotation of Isaiah 49:16, which was written for Jewish exiles after the destruction of Solomon's Temple. In the original context, the author of Isaiah promised a literal rebuilding of Jerusalem. The author of 2 Baruch, however, made the startling assertion that the original passage did not refer to the earthly Jerusalem but to the heavenly abode. Murphy elaborated, "One can only conclude that all similar promises concerning Zion also refer to the heavenly one and not the earthly one ... At the very least, the 'forever' of the promises found in the Psalms, in Chronicles, in Ezekiel, and elsewhere are shown to pertain only to the building preserved with God."[56] Thus, the author of 2 Baruch validated God's promises by redirecting expectations.

Similarly, in chapter 5, Baruch worries that the destruction of Zion will tarnish the divine name. The Lord assures Baruch that "my name and my glory shall last unto eternity ... And you shall see with your eyes that the enemy shall not destroy Zion and burn Jerusalem" (2 Bar. 5:2). Indeed, the true Jerusalem cannot be destroyed because the city is heavenly and eternal.

Also of interest is the removal of the temple vessels in 2 Baruch 6:4—8:2.[57] The verses seem to allow for a literal restoration of Jerusalem: "Earth ... receive the things which I commit to you, and guard them until the last times, so that you may restore them when you are ordered, so that strangers may not get possession of them" (2 Bar. 6:8). Klijn explained that the angels removed vessels from the earthly temple in order to preserve them until a new temple could be built.[58] Supporting Klijn's interpretation is Jewish tradition, which has precedent for the vessels being hidden to preserve them for future use.[59]

However, most of 2 Baruch places emphasis only upon a heavenly Jerusalem. In fact, the final chapters provide a completely different reason for the hidden vessels. In chapter 80, the author indicated that the implements were hidden so that they would not be defiled (2 Bar. 80:2). Klijn resolved the discrepancy by explaining that multiple traditions existed in Jewish thought in regard to the future of the temple.[60] Collins

---

Structure and Meaning, 35.

56. Murphy, *Structure and Meaning*, 86–87. See Ps 125:1–2; 2 Chr 6:2; Ezek 43:9.

57. Murphy, *Structure and Meaning*, 93–96.

58. Klijn, "2 (Syriac Apocalypse of) Baruch," 617.

59. 2 Macc 2:1–9; Josephus, *Ant.*, 18:85–87.

60. Klijn, "2 (Syriac Apocalypse of) Baruch," 617.

also sought to resolve the ostensible disagreement. He explained that the author anticipated both an eschatological temple and a heavenly temple. The vessels would be preserved for the eschatological temple, but "the heavenly Jerusalem and temple are ultimately more important for the author's own time."[61] Murphy disagreed: "Although the author did not care to deny *explicitly* the possibility of a third Temple, it was of no ultimate significance to him."[62]

In short, the point of 2 Baruch is not to formulate doctrine, but to offer hope.[63] Therefore, the legends pertaining to the temple vessels and Jerusalem could be utilized to suggest that an earthly temple might be preserved in some manner. Although the author placed emphasis on the heavenly temple, he also provided a glimmer of hope for a physical restoration.

A second tradition found in chapters 6–8, the departure of God's presence, is relevant as well. Murphy asserted that the author of 2 Baruch "graphically depicts the absence of God from the Temple, and therefore from the midst of his people. It makes the meaning of the destruction of Jerusalem absolutely clear. The people are no longer to look to Zion for the presence of God in their midst."[64] Just as in Ezekiel, God's presence is not linked to the earthly temple.

The next relevant subject matter can be found in chapters 31–32, which present interpreters with no small challenge. The significant verses are as follows:

> Do not forget Zion but remember the distress of Jerusalem. For, behold, the days are coming, that all that has been will be taken away to be destroyed, and it will become as though it has not been. You, however, if you prepare your minds to sow into them the fruits of the law, he shall protect you in the time in which the Mighty One shall shake the entire creation. For after a short time, the building of Zion will be shaken in order that it will be rebuilt. That building will not remain; but it will again be uprooted after some time and will remain desolate for a time. And after that it is necessary that it will be renewed in glory and that it will be perfected into eternity. (2 Bar. 31:4—32:5)

---

61. Collins, *Apocalyptic Imagination*, 215. Cf. Lee, *New Jerusalem*, 147.

62. Murphy, "Temple in the *Syriac Apocalypse*," 682.

63. Murphy, *Structure and Meaning*, 89.

64. Murphy, *Structure and Meaning*, 96.

In 2 Baruch 31:4, the admonition to "forget not Zion" is given. Murphy queried, "If indeed the intent of the author is to distract the attention of his readers away from the destruction, how does this command fit?"[65] Indeed, in 2 Baruch 32:4–5, the author affirmed that the focus remains on the heavenly temple. Murphy proposed that just as Paul used the slogans of his opponents, the author of 2 Baruch used the words of his rivals to address a mind-set he wished to counter.[66] Thus, in 2 Baruch 31:4–5, the author utilized Zion as an example of the current, transitory world. The entire creation is shaken, including Zion. Once the earthly Zion is destroyed, a time of desolation must elapse before the heavenly Zion is experienced.

The corresponding renewal of creation (2 Bar. 32:4–6) does not accord well with the stark contrast between the two worlds present in the previous chapters. Murphy explained, "It would appear that our author did not wish to replace the eschatology of the tradition of Isaiah wholesale. Rather, he is trying to bolster the hope of the people in the future. In doing so, he can still refer to a renewed Zion. Nonetheless he tempers this with his own novel solution to the problem of the distress of the present time."[67] As before, the author may have hinted at an eschatological restoration, but his primary focus remained on the eternal heavenly realm. The same tension is therefore reflected in 2 Baruch 31–32 as in 2 Baruch 6–8.

In chapters 35–52, the author continued to offer hope with a discussion of the two worlds, represented by the heavenly and earthly planes. Chapter 35 begins with a lament over the destroyed temple, or "holy place" (2 Bar. 35:1). In the following chapters, Baruch is comforted with visions of the ultimate defeat of evil. Accordingly, in chapters 44–46, exhortations to follow the law are offered. Individuals who inherit the future reward are those who do not "withdraw from the commandments of the Mighty One" (2 Bar. 44:3). The section concludes with a reassurance that the righteous will take their place with God after death: "There is nothing that will be destroyed unless it acted wickedly, if it had been able to do something without remembering my goodness and accepting my long-supporting. For this reason surely you will be taken up" (2 Bar. 48:29–30;

65. Murphy, *Structure and Meaning*, 96.
66. Murphy, *Structure and Meaning*, 104.
67. Murphy, *Structure and Meaning*, 105.

cf. 51:1–3). Thus, the righteous depart the earthly realm to dwell with
God.

Chapters 53–77 are a review of history from creation to the messianic age, which is an interim before the final heavenly state. The sequence
of events is unique in that the author rigorously depicted alternating periods of good and evil. He continued to stress personal responsibility by
indicating that the quality of each period is related directly to the behav-
ior of the people residing in that time period. The author thus co-opted
apocalyptic structures for paraenetic purposes.[68]

The temple plays a major role in chapters 53–77, as the condition of
Jerusalem is indicative of the nature of the age.[69] In summary, following
the destruction of Zion (2 Bar. 67:1–5), evil will increase (2 Bar. 67:5–8).
This eventuality reflects the common apocalyptic theme that evil multi-
plies prior to the end of time. Correspondingly, in chapter 68, the author
exhibited a negative disposition toward the Second Temple. However,
the reason for the negativity is not due to the inferiority of the Second
Temple to the First Temple. Rather, the author hinted that the golden age
of the temple will never be an earthly eventuality.[70]

The closing epistle of 2 Baruch, chapters 77–87, serves as a summary of chapters 1–77. The author reiterated his main points—that Zion
was destroyed because of Israel, that God was the agent of destruction,
and that Israel should not be distressed over the loss. Instead of an occasion for mourning, however, the destruction of the temple was a necessary step toward the heavenly goal. Robert Kirschner explained, "The
destruction of the Temple signifies not the defeat of God but the hidden
design of God."[71] Unlike Revelation (and 4 Ezra and 1 Enoch), however,
the author of 2 Baruch nowhere indicated that the heavenly Jerusalem
will descend to earth.

68. Murphy, *Structure and Meaning*, 109–11. Cf. Kolenkow, "Introduction to II
Bar. 53," 144.

69. God is absolved of responsibility for the catastrophe of Jerusalem, as the destruction of the city is described as the result of immorality. Resultantly, both 2 Baruch
and 4 Ezra defend "the omnipotence and benevolence of God" (Kirschner, "Apocalyptic and Rabbinic Responses," 35).

70. Murphy, *Structure and Meaning*, 112–13; Murphy, "Temple in the *Syriac
Apocalypse*," 683.

71. Kirschner, "Apocalyptic and Rabbinic Responses," 38.

Pseudo-Philo

Liber Antiquitatum Biblicarum (LAB), or Pseudo-Philo, bears similarities with 4 Ezra and 2 Baruch, although the lack of explicit mention of the fall of Jerusalem makes a pre-70 CE date possible.[72] Like Jubilees, Pseudo-Philo can be categorized within the rewritten Bible genre. The author of Pseudo-Philo surveyed Scripture from the garden of Eden to the institution of the monarchy.

On the surface, Pseudo-Philo is related only peripherally to the current study. However, the work outlines a pattern for dealings between God and humanity that is relevant.

> For example, the golden calf episode in ch. 12 establishes a paradigm for subsequent dealings between God and Israel. Accordingly, the author intends to show that the Second Temple was destroyed on account of the idolatrous sin through the golden calf story and then to provide the clue for the restoration from the Temple destruction at the same time: to remove the idolatrous sin.[73]

Similarly, Israel's identity as a nation depends upon their exclusive fidelity to Yahweh. Murphy opined, "The function of this story is to recall Israel to its true identity at a time when that identity is under attack in numerous and subtle ways."[74] If Jerusalem is destroyed, then the very existence of Israel is in peril.[75]

Even more striking, the existence of the universe is connected to the welfare of Israel (LAB 9:3; 12:8). Specifically, in Pseudo-Philo 12:4, the author linked the welfare of humanity with the existence of the temple. In the passage, Moses gives Israel instructions from Mt. Sinai. However, the language implies that the location should be identified as Zion, with phrases like "thy house" and "thy throne," as well as imagery of precious stones and perfumes.[76] Additionally, Moses reveals that Israel, "the vine,"

---

72. Much debate exists as to the exact dating of the work, with proposals ranging from 50 CE to 150 CE. Regardless of whether composition took place pre- or post-70, LAB likely was written in the first century (Jacobson, *Commentary on Pseudo-Philo's Liber*, 99). Cf. Harrington, "Pseudo-Philo," 297–377; Murphy, *Pseudo-Philo*, 3–6; Murphy, "Retelling the Bible," 275–87.

73. Lee, *New Jerusalem*, 181.

74. Murphy, "Retelling the Bible," 284.

75. Murphy, *Structure and Meaning*, 82–83.

76. Murphy, *Structure and Meaning*, 83.

derives life-giving water from the throne that sits atop the mountain (LAB 12:8–9). Murphy wrote, "Note the strange imagery of the throne refreshing the vineyard. This could be a combination of the images of Zion as God's throne and God as the bringer of rain."[77] Conversely, the author may have been alluding to the tradition that the waters of the deep flowed from beneath the temple and throne of God. Regardless, humanity and creation are in danger.

Moses informs the people that after a period of exile they will return to the land and build a temple, which will be destroyed because of their sin. When the "house" is destroyed, "the race of men will be to [God] like a drop from a pitcher and will be reckoned like spittle" (LAB 12:4).[78] Howard Jacobson commented, "The language strongly suggests that this is a reference to the destruction of the second temple . . . though the flow of the context makes it hard to see how a *second* temple could be referred to here."[79] Nonetheless, the author most likely drew upon the understanding of the temple as God's dwelling place, as well as the universe in microcosm.[80] Thus, the sin of Israel places the entire creation at risk.

In the following chapter, similar themes of blessing through obedience continue. In Pseudo-Philo 13:9, fidelity to God's commands is equated to walking in the ways of paradise, and in Pseudo-Philo 13:10, the blessings of paradise are actualized in the annual Feast of Tabernacles. Thus, events in the history of Israel provide a paradigm for eschatological restoration, which cannot take place until the sin that caused the temple's destruction is removed.[81]

Skipping forward a few chapters, in Pseudo-Philo 19:2, punishment is expressed through the departure of God from the land and foreign domination, just as in Ezekiel 9–11. Also like Ezekiel, the destruction of the Jerusalem Temple is referenced in chapter 19. In Pseudo-Philo 19:7, the author warned that the "place where they will serve me," will be destroyed by enemies. Thereafter, Moses is given a glimpse of a new temple: "And [God] showed him the place from which the manna rained upon the people, even until the paths of paradise. And he showed him

---

77. Murphy, *Structure and Meaning*, 83. Cf. Patai, *Man and Temple*, 86.

78. Translations of LAB are reproduced from Harrington, "Pseudo-Philo."

79. Jacobson, *Commentary on Pseudo-Philo's Liber*, 489 (emphasis his).

80. Jacobson, *Commentary on Pseudo-Philo's Liber*, 498–500.

81. Lee, *New Jerusalem*, 183–86; Murphy, *Pseudo-Philo*, 75.

the measurements of the sanctuary and the number of sacrifices and the signs by which they are to interpret the heaven" (LAB 19:10).

Verse 10 may be regarded as a brief ascent narrative.[82] That the vision is of the heavenly temple is reinforced in verse 13, in which the author referred to the site as "the immortal dwelling place." Further, the author reiterated the idea that the earthly temple is discredited, as sacrifices being performed in the heavenly temple "are prohibited for the human race because they have sinned against [God]" (LAB 19:11).

In the following verses, the author implied that the heavenly paradise will be established on earth one day (LAB 19:13). Israel's future restoration to "the place of sanctification" seems to represent a restored relationship between God and Israel, which simultaneously functions as a restoration to the promised land with a restored sanctuary.[83] Although the presence of the temple is only implied here, the importance attached to the temple earlier in the narrative indicates that the sanctuary would be necessary for the safety of humanity.

Overlap between the heavenly and earthly realms can also be found in the bizarre narrative of Kenaz and the twelve stones in chapter 26. Kenaz, a fictitious leader of Israel, finds twelve stones that are engraved with the names of the twelve tribes. He eventually brings them into the tabernacle and places them into the ark. The Lord explains that when Israel's sin reaches "full measure," he will remove the stones and "store them in the place from which they were taken in the beginning," presumably the heavenly temple. In the eschaton, God will return the stones to the earth so that they may provide light to the righteous.

> It is significant that the precious stones accompany the tablets of the covenant in their placement in the ark and their removal to paradise at the destruction of the Temple because this co-existence of the tablets with the precious stones emphasizes the covenantal feature of the precious stones. In this case, the replacement of the precious stones with the tablets in Paradise demonstrates that the covenant is not cancelled even in the situation of the Temple destruction.[84]

82. Jacobson, *Commentary on Pseudo-Philo's Liber*, 634–36.

83. Lee, *New Jerusalem*, 189.

84. Lee, *New Jerusalem*, 193.

Additionally, the author utilized the stones to allude to the edenic state that humanity lost as a result of sin, but which will be regained by the righteous at the end of time.[85]

The Apocalypse of Baruch

The Apocalypse of Baruch (3 Baruch) is an apocalyptic work likely written in response to the fall of Jerusalem.[86] The interweaving of Christian and Jewish tradition indicates that the text was composed in the first or second century.[87] The original language was likely Greek, although the text is well attested in Slavonic as well. The two versions vary somewhat in that the Greek typically provides more detail. Therefore, where distinctions need to be made, verse references will be accompanied by a "G" (Greek) or "S" (Slavonic).

As the book opens, Baruch is lamenting over the destruction of Jerusalem. He queries, "Lord, why have you set fire to your vineyard and laid it waste" (3 Bar. 1:2G)?[88] In other words, Baruch wants to know how the Jewish people can maintain a proper relationship with God without the temple and sacrifices. An angelic guide appears and responds "Know, O man, greatly beloved man, and do not concern yourself so much over the salvation of Jerusalem" (3 Bar. 1:3G). Thus, as in 2 Baruch, attention is shifted away from the earthly Jerusalem. The author of "3 Baruch makes a point of discouraging both excessive mourning over the loss of Jerusalem and unrealistic hope for the city's restoration."[89]

Michael, an angelic guide, takes Baruch on a tour of heaven. In the first three heavens, the fate of individuals who rebel against God is revealed, and in the fourth heaven an edenic landscape appears. Baruch is shown a "very wide mountain" (3 Bar. 10:2S; "unbroken plain," 10:2G)

85. Murphy, *Pseudo-Philo*, 152.

86. Collins, *Apocalyptic Imagination*, 248; Gaylord, "3 (Greek Apocalypse of) Baruch," 653–79; Harlow, *Greek Apocalypse of Baruch*, 11; Knibb, *Essays on the Book*, 399.

87. Debate exists as to whether the Apocalypse of Baruch is Jewish or Christian, although consensus seems to lean toward the work being a Christian composition. See Collins, *Apocalyptic Imagination*, 248; Gaylord, "3 (Greek Apocalypse of) Baruch," 657; Ginzberg, "Greek Apocalypse of Baruch," 551; Harlow, *Greek Apocalypse of Baruch*, 32; James, "Apocalypse of Baruch," li–lxxi.

88. Quotations of 3 Baruch are reproduced from Gaylord, "3 (Greek Apocalypse of) Baruch."

89. Harlow, *Greek Apocalypse of Baruch*, 16.

with a "large lake of water" (3 Bar. 10:2S). Birds surround the lake, praising God ceaselessly. In the Greek version, righteous souls also surround the lake "living together choir by choir," which could indicate that they join the birds in praise. Alternately, the birds may symbolize the righteous souls. That the lake is not simply a body of water is indicated by its provision of rain for the earth. The angelic guide explains that the water is "dew from heaven" that causes plants and fruit to grow (3 Bar. 10:6, 9).

Michael proceeds to the fifth heaven, where Baruch is shown the heavenly temple (chapters 11–16). Baruch sees that prayers and good deeds are offered in the heavenly temple, and thus, the absence of the Jerusalem Temple does not mean that God is absent from his people.[90] Himmelfarb explained that the prayers and good deeds are the primary answer to the crisis of the temple's destruction, "Like Revelation, 3 Baruch has no interest in the restoration of the earthly temple."[91]

Three types of people are represented by the prayers and virtues: those who offer sufficient virtues, those who offer part measure, and those who offer none (3 Bar. 12:1–8). So important are the offerings that the angels tremble with fear as they serve. The importance of prayer is highlighted also by the severe punishment upon those who do not pray:

> It may be because the author views prayer, which was previously one of the Temple acts, as the unique and only instrument to approach God, and even as that which takes the place of the function of the Temple (building). Therefore, without prayer, there is no way to communicate with the heavenly God . . . God's people do not necessarily have to long for the destroyed Temple building because they can meet God wherever and whenever they pray.[92]

Further evidence that service in the heavenly temple provides the solution to the crisis of 70 CE is found as the book concludes. Baruch's initial mourning is turned into praise as he exhorts his brethren to glorify God (3 Bar. 17:3–4G).

The heavens in 3 Baruch are unique among Jewish apocalypses. Typically, otherworldly journeys culminate in the seventh heaven with a vision of the divine presence.[93] The Apocalypse of Baruch has neither.

90. Gaylord, "3 (Greek Apocalypse of) Baruch," 659.

91. Himmelfarb, *Ascent to Heaven*, 34.

92. Lee, *New Jerusalem*, 163.

93. Harlow, *Greek Apocalypse of Baruch*, 3.

Some scholars argue that the ending is truncated—that the account of the sixth and seventh heavens has been lost.[94] Indeed, the author seemed to imply that the journey would culminate in a vision of God upon his throne in the heavenly temple. However, the journey abruptly ends at the fifth heaven. Harlow argued that the unexpected ending is an intentional literary device, as the sudden termination "coheres with the narrative logic of the work as a whole."[95] In aborting the ascent, the author polemicized against other apocalyptic works that place the temple at the center of eschatological hope.[96]

Unlike 2 Baruch, 4 Ezra, and Pseudo-Philo, the author of 3 Baruch gave no hint of restoration for Jerusalem or the temple.[97] Whereas the authors of the former works dealt with the loss of the Jerusalem Temple by shifting attention to the heavenly one, the author of 3 Baruch denied the importance of the temple altogether. Harlow contended, "Baruch's being denied a vision of God in the heavenly temple underscores the dispensability of the earthly Temple."[98]

That the author of 3 Baruch offered a way to commune with God without the temple is particularly relevant for the study of Revelation and Ezekiel.[99] Both Ezekiel and Revelation detach the presence of God from the Jerusalem Temple (Ezek 10:18; Rev 21:22). Other parallels are especially noticeable in the fourth heaven. The location on a high mountain with a body of water that provides nourishment for the earth's vegetation is found in both Ezekiel and Revelation (Ezek 47:1–12; Rev 21:10; 22:1–2). Further, the ceaseless worship of God and the bowls full of prayer, which are offered without a temple, evoke similar patterns of worship in Revelation (Rev 4:10–11; 5:8).

94. Bauckham, "Early Jewish Visions of Hell," 355–85; Himmelfarb, *Ascent to Heaven*, 90.

95. Harlow, *Greek Apocalypse of Baruch*, 72.

96. Harlow, *Greek Apocalypse of Baruch*, 72.

97. Collins, *Apocalyptic Imagination*, 250.

98. Harlow, *Greek Apocalypse of Baruch*, 73.

99. Lee, *New Jerusalem*, 159.

The Apocalypse of Abraham

Aside from 2 Baruch and 4 Ezra, the Apocalypse of Abraham is one of the most important post-70 works.[100] The author offered yet another perspective on the destruction of the Jerusalem Temple. Much as in 2 Baruch, the author intimated that the destruction of Jerusalem was the result of the sin of Israel and its leaders.[101] Accordingly, the chief problem addressed in the text is evil, specifically idolatry. The fate of the temple is used to bring such issues into focus, although the temple is not the central concern of the narrative.[102]

Like 4 Ezra and 2 Baruch, the Apocalypse of Abraham is concerned with theodicy. However, the book does not begin with mourning over the loss of the temple. In the first eight chapters of the text, the author provides a narrative account of Abraham's youth, in which Abraham rejects idolatry. In chapter 9, the Lord commands Abraham to provide a sacrifice "on a high mountain" (Apoc. Ab. 9:8).[103] At first glance the location seems to be a normal mountain, as Abraham's sacrifices in Genesis 15 and 22 are recalled. However, through subsequent events, the author indicated that Abraham has left the earthly plane.

The Lord sends Iaoel to guide Abraham on a heavenly tour (Apoc. Ab. 10:3, 8). The angel seems to be an incarnation of the divine presence, as he has power on heaven and earth (Apoc. Ab. 10:8–10), and power over the dead (Apoc. Ab. 10:11).[104] Iaoel is also "the one who ordered your father's house to be burned" (Apoc. Ab. 10:12). Further, "the appearance of his body was like sapphire, and the aspect of his face was like chrysolite, and the hair of his head like snow. And a kidaris[105] (was) on his head, its look that of a rainbow, and the clothing of his garments (was) purple; and a golden staff (was) in his right hand" (Apoc. Ab. 11:2–4).

---

100. "It is commonly held that [the Apocalypse of Abraham] was composed at the end of the first century A.D" (Rubinkiewicz, "Apocalypse of Abraham," 683). Cf. Box, *Apocalypse of Abraham*, xv; Collins, *Apocalyptic Imagination*, 225; Ginzberg, "Apocalypse of Abraham," 92.

101. Rubinkiewicz, "Apocalypse of Abraham," 682–85.

102. Collins, *Apocalyptic Imagination*, 225–27.

103. Translations of the Apocalypse of Abraham are reproduced from Rubinkiewicz, "Apocalypse of Abraham."

104. Barker, *Gate of Heaven*, 153.

105. A headdress or cap.

Elements of the description can be found elsewhere in descriptions of God, but also in relation to high priestly vestiture.[106]

Thus, Iaoel plays the role of God and high priest in a covenant ceremony with Abraham. The patriarch makes his sacrifices in a narrative that seems to draw from both Genesis 15 and 22. As such, Lee proposed that temple restoration is portrayed in terms of the Abrahamic covenant. The new people of God will come from Abraham's seed, and "through them the New Temple will be rebuilt and right sacrifice will be performed in the newly rebuilt Temple."[107]

In addition to sacrifices, worship takes place on the mountain: "And [the angel] said, 'only worship, Abraham, and recite the song which I taught you.' Since there was no ground to which I could fall prostrate, I only bowed down, and I recited the song which he had taught me. And he said, 'Recite without ceasing.' And I recited, and he himself recited the song" (Apoc. Ab. 17:4–7). The worship continues in chapter 18 with a passage that finds numerous parallels in the *merkabah* vision of Ezekiel 1.[108] Unlike Ezekiel, however, no mention is made of a human-like figure who occupies the throne.[109] The throne's occupant is only heard, not seen, as he speaks to Abraham (Apoc. Ab. 18:14—19:1).

Several features indicate that Abraham is not only in heaven but in the heavenly temple.[110] Although no architectural elements are present, the angelic guide, the sacrifices, the worship, and the throne are all common features of the temple in heaven.[111] Additionally, in the Apocalypse of Abraham 17:19, the author described the locale as God's "heavenly dwelling place." Lee explained, "The ascent of Abraham demonstrates the existence of the Heavenly Temple as the counterpart of the earthly Temple. Moreover, his ascent establishes the organic connection of the earthly sacrifice with the Heavenly Temple because he ascends to the

106. Exod 24:10; 28:39; Ezek 1:26–28; Rev 19:12; Himmelfarb, *Ascent to Heaven*, 61–62.

107. Lee, *New Jerusalem*, 174.

108. Chapters 18–25 are influenced by Ezekiel 1 and 10 as well as 1 Enoch 1–36. See also Rubinkiewicz, "Apocalypse of Abraham," 685.

109. Rowland, *Open Heaven*, 87.

110. Himmelfarb, *Ascent to Heaven*, 66; Lee, *New Jerusalem*, 176.

111. The worship bears a remarkable similarity to Revelation 4:6–11, 5:8–14, and 7:11–12, where all manner of heavenly beings and saints worship around the throne. However, the similarities are more likely the result of a common apocalyptic milieu than direct influence.

heaven just as the sacrifice performed on the earthly place goes up to the Heavenly Temple."[112]

The continuing narrative serves as a medium to convey theological principles. From the heavenly temple Abraham is shown snapshots of history, beginning with the garden of Eden and moving through the history of Israel. In the Apocalypse of Abraham 26:3, idolatry results in the burning of Terah's house. The event is used to explain the burning of the temple, which is a consequence of idolatry (ch. 27). Conversely, in chapter 9, Abraham is allowed to enter heaven because of sacrifices properly offered (ch. 9). Thus, idolatrous sacrifice leads to the destruction of the temple, while sacrifices rightly offered lead to the fulfillment of God's promises and restoration of the temple.[113]

Next, Abraham circumspectly asks whether the temple will be restored soon (Apoc. Ab. 28:2). The angel's response is based upon the appearance of a righteous man who will be beaten by some people and worshipped by others (Apoc. Ab. 29:5–13). The man is clearly a messianic figure, but his connection to the temple is ambiguous. Lee proposed that in the Apocalypse of Abraham 29:17–19, the restoration of the temple is inaugurated by the messianic figure.[114] The author hinted at the restoration of a temple in describing "righteous men . . . who strive in the glory of my name toward the place prepared beforehand." Further, the place is described as the one "which you saw deserted in the picture," i.e., the temple. The faithful then will be "affirmed by the sacrifices and the gifts of justice and truth" and "rejoice forever" (Apoc. Ab. 29:18–19).

While the temple described could be a material structure in the eschaton, as Lee proposed, the verses also could be interpreted as figurative. Indeed, the "sacrifices" are linked with justice and truth. Even Lee conceded that at no point does the author explicitly present a restored temple.[115] Regardless, the author may have left his earthly temple purposely ambiguous so that whatever the fate of the Jewish people, they could have confidence that God still reigns in his heavenly dwelling.

---

112. Lee, *New Jerusalem*, 176.

113. Lee, *New Jerusalem*, 170.

114. Lee, *New Jerusalem*, 178.

115. Lee, *New Jerusalem*, 170n10.

Sibylline Oracles 1 and 2

Sibylline Oracles (Sib. Or.) 1 and 2 comprise a unit by structuring history into ten generations. The two oracles consist of original Jewish material with Christian redactions.[116] Two major views exist for dating. Johann Geffken dated all of the text to the third century CE.[117] Alfons Kurfess, however, dated the Jewish material to the turn of the millennium and the Christian material to before 150 CE.[118] Collins pointed out, "The Jewish sub-stratum is the only extensive document we have from the Judaism of Asia Minor in this period."[119] Thus, Sibylline Oracles 1 and 2 are of particular significance for studies of Revelation.

Lines 324–86 of Sibylline Oracle 1 consist of a Christian passage on the incarnation of Christ. Here, the author alluded to various messianic Scriptures such as Isaiah 35:5 and Matthew 11:5 in which "the blind will see and the lame will walk" (Sib. Or. 1:353).[120] The author also described the messiah walking on water, driving out demons, and feeding the hungry (Sib. Or. 1:355–59). The messiah then is rejected by the Jewish people and executed. At his time of death the "temple of Solomon will effect a great sign for men," although the author did not specify the nature of the sign (Sib. Or. 1:376). After his resurrection, Christ journeys to heaven on the clouds (Sib. Or. 1:381).

In the following lines, the sibyllist referred to "Solomon's" Temple (i.e., the Second Temple). In Sibylline Oracle 1:393–400, the fall of Jerusalem and exile of the Jews are narrated. The destruction is attributed to an unnamed "evil deed" committed by the Jewish people, presumably their execution of the messiah.

In lines 214–37 of Sibylline Oracle 2, the author provided a description of a general resurrection that is reminiscent of Ezekiel 37. As in Ezekiel, the individuals do not ascend to heaven, but are transformed on the earth. Lines 2:221–24 read, "Then the heavenly one will give souls and breath and voice to the dead and bones fastened with all kinds of joinings . . . flesh and sinews and veins and skin about the flesh, and the former hairs." At the time of resurrection, the Lord of Hosts rests upon a

---

116. Collins, *Apocalyptic Imagination*, 238; Collins, "Sibylline Oracles," 317–472.

117. Geffken, *Komposition und Entstehungszeit*, 49.

118. Kurfess, "Oracula Sibyllina I/II," 151–65.

119. Collins, "Sibylline Oracles," 332.

120. All translations of Sib. Or. 1, 2, 4, and 5 are reproduced from Collins, "Sibylline Oracles."

heavenly throne "and establishes a great pillar, Christ, imperishable himself," who will sit in judgment over the world (Sib. Or. 2:240–41).

The symbolic content of pillars has been mentioned already. Here, as in 2 Baruch, Christ embodies what the temple represented—strength, order, and divine presence.[121] Most noteworthy for the current study is the building imagery that is applied to Christ.

Sibylline Oracle 4

The original body of Sibylline Oracle 4 (Sib. Or. 4) was composed shortly after the time of Alexander, by 300 BCE. However, the document attests numerous redactions, which seem to have been completed around 80 CE. Collins contended that nothing in the book suggests Christian influence or authorship. However, emphasis upon baptism indicates that "the book was presumably written in Jewish baptist circles."[122]

Sibylline Oracle 4 begins with a rejection of idolatry, sexual sin, and violence (Sib. Or. 4:1–48). God is lauded as creator, and people who love him are blessed. The distinctive doctrine of lines 1–48, however, is the rejection of the temple. In lines 8–11, God does not have a temple of stone, but "one which it is not possible to see from earth nor to measure with mortal eyes, since it was not fashioned by mortal hand" (Sib. Or. 4:10–11). Further, in lines 27–30, the sibyllist indicated that the pious "reject all temples" as well as the sacrifices that are performed in them. Collins wrote, "While these passages are not specifically an attack on the Jewish Temple (which no longer existed), they undermine temple worship and make no allowance for the possibility of an acceptable temple."[123]

The temple is mentioned again in Sibylline Oracle 4:115–29. Jerusalem is sacked and the temple is destroyed because of violent acts committed in front of the temple. No mention is made of restoration. Instead, in the concluding lines of the oracle, the author described a bodily resurrection upon a renewed earth without a temple (Sib. Or. 4:179–92). Thus, Sibylline Oracle 4 sharply contradicts books 3 and 5, in which the author anticipated a restored eschatological temple.

---

121. Barker, *Gate of Heaven*, 29–30; Lundquist, "Temple, Covenant, and Law," 300.

122. Collins, "Sibylline Oracles," 383.

123. Collins, "Sibylline Oracles," 383.

Sibylline Oracle 5

The fifth Sibylline Oracle (Sib. Or. 5) consists of two primary strata. The first stratum exhibits little historical detail. Thus, Stephen Felder suggested that the material could have been written at any point between 300 BCE and 70 CE.[124] The second stratum seems to have been written between the Jewish revolts of 70 and 135 CE. However, the prophecies cannot be dated with specificity, as the verses "could have come from numerous 'authors' at various times and in various places."[125]

The author of Sibylline Oracle 5 engaged in a vitriolic critique of Rome, which is blamed for the destruction of Jerusalem.[126] Retribution will be carried out against the Romans by a messianic figure. The messiah will rule the world and defeat Nero, who is portrayed as an eschatological enemy. Finally, Jerusalem and the temple will be restored (Sib. Or. 5:386–433).[127]

The temple is discussed in many passages throughout Sibylline Oracle 5. In lines 150–54, the author described the destruction of Jerusalem by Nero:[128] "He seized the divinely built Temple and burned the citizens and peoples who went into it, men whom I rightly praised. For on his appearance the whole creation was shaken and kings perished, and those in whom sovereignty remained destroyed a great city and righteous people." After the fall of the city, a "great star" appears. The star (i.e., messianic figure) will destroy not only Rome, but the entire earth (Sib. Or. 5:115–35, 155).

In the next oracle, a "man from the sky" who shines like the sun comes to deliver the Jewish people. Apparently, the man had come once before, but his fate is unclear. When he returns, however, the man will bring peace and prosperity for the Jewish people, who will reside in the "city of God" (Sib. Or. 5:250). The city appears to be a restored earthly Jerusalem with walls that extend all the way to Joppa (Sib. Or. 5:249–55).

---

124. Felder, "What Is *The Fifth Sibylline Oracle*?," 363–85.

125. Felder, "What Is *The Fifth Sibylline Oracle*?," 368. Cf. Collins, *Apocalyptic Imagination*, 234; Helyer, *Exploring Jewish Literature*, 443.

126. Collins, *Apocalyptic Imagination*, 234; Collins, "Sibylline Oracles," 391; Collins, "The Sibylline Oracles," 362.

127. See Revelation 18–22; Ezekiel 26–27, 40–48; Felder, "What Is *The Fifth Sibylline Oracle*?," 380; Helyer, *Exploring Jewish Literature*, 444–45.

128. Although Nero did not lead the siege of Jerusalem, the revolt began during his reign.

That crops grow upon the land further points to a literal expectation (Sib. Or. 5:281–84). Further, the great city seems to function as the entire earth, as any land that the Jewish people do not occupy is laid waste.[129]

In Sibylline Oracle 5:260, the focus of the oracle shifts abruptly from a messiah to the city. Lee suggested, "This sudden change of the object of the oracles functions to maximize the effect of the appearance of the Messiah which causes blessings of the new Jerusalem in the following lines."[130] Thus, the author of the oracle may have hinted that the messiah establishes the city.

No temple is mentioned, but the city may function as the temple. First, the city is pure, as no uncleanness, violence, or lawlessness are present (Sib. Or. 5:253–74). Second, sacrifices and prayers are offered in the city (Sib. Or. 5:268). Third, the land is referred to as "holy" (Sib. Or. 281).

The next oracle contains a clear passage about the destruction of Jerusalem (Sib. Or. 5:397–413).[131] The ideology of the oracle is consistent with the previous two. In Sibylline Oracle 5:414, "a blessed man" comes from heaven to destroy all evildoers and rebuild the city of God. Unlike the previous oracles, however, the messianic figure himself builds a temple: "And he provided ornament and made a holy temple, exceedingly beautiful in its fair shrine, and he fashioned a great and immense tower over many stadia touching even the clouds and visible to all" (Sib. Or. 5:423–25). That the messiah here constructs the temple strengthens the case that the city of the previous oracle functions as the temple. Thus, the author of Sibylline Oracle 5 did not provide an alternate temple or shift focus away from the temple, but promised a glorious future restoration in which the Jewish people, from their city and temple, will rule the earth.[132]

Several relevant points can be gleaned from Sibylline Oracle 5. First, as in Revelation, Nero and Rome are cast as eschatological enemies who will be defeated by the messiah. Second, the messiah inaugurates a

---

129. Cf. Isa 2:2–4; Mic 4:1–5.

130. Lee, *New Jerusalem*, 200.

131. The use of past tense in the midst of oracles about the future is unusual. Geffken proposed that the author of the oracle was a personal witness to the destruction of Jerusalem. Upon writing of the event, the sibyllist was so overcome with grief that he or she momentarily slipped into the past tense (Geffken, *Komposition und Entstehungszeit*, 24). Cf. Felder, "What Is *The Fifth Sibylline Oracle*," 381.

132. The author of Sib. Or. 5 mentioned another temple in lines 501–7. A "great holy temple" will be built in Egypt, but then destroyed because of the sin of the people.

completely new age on earth. Third, the messiah builds an eschatological city that encompasses the entire earth and serves the function of the temple.

The Mishnah

The Mishnah came to final form later than the book of Revelation, but the traditions described in the text are much older.[133] Of greatest relevance to the current study is tractate Middoth, which provides architectural details for a temple. Klawans noted that the portrait of the temple and priests in the Mishnah is "rather idyllic," as "the rabbis seem willing to blame the Second Temple's destruction on almost anything but the defilement of the temple."[134] In view of their positive attitude toward the Jerusalem Temple, the rabbis seem to have anticipated a literal rebuilding. Indeed, few rabbinic sources describe a future without a Jerusalem Temple.[135] Thus, tractate Middoth seems to have been written shortly after the destruction of the temple in order to preserve the details for a future rebuilding.[136]

Debate exists as to whether the temple of the Mishnah was a description of Herod's Temple or an earlier structure. Much of the dispute stems from inconsistencies between Josephus's description of Herod's Temple and that which is described in Middoth.[137] However, variations between Middoth and the account in Josephus may be due to Josephus's propensity for exaggeration: "wherewith Josephus sought to magnify the great work of Herod, and to impress upon the gentiles the magnificence of the Temple and its surroundings."[138] Additionally, discrepancies may

---

133. Jacob Neusner argued that the Mishnah reached final form around 200 CE. Neusner, *Mishnah: Religious Perspectives*, 193. Cf. Neusner, *Mishnah: Introduction and Reader*, 5–7; Neusner, *Transformations in Ancient Judaism*, 37–40; Schiffman, "Temple Scroll," 13.

134. Klawans, *Purity, Sacrifice, and the Temple*, 178, 186. In contrast, Josephus expressly connected the departure of God's presence and the destruction of the temple to defilement (*J.W.* 5:402–12; 6:300; *Ant.* 20:165–66).

135. Klawans, *Purity, Sacrifice, and the Temple*, 200.

136. Ehrman, "Middot," 180; Neusner, *History of the Mishnaic Law*, 6:210.

137. Josephus, *J.W.* 5:184–226; *Ant.* 15:380–425.

138. Hollis, *Archaeology of Herod's Temple*, 19.

be due to changes in the layout of the temple, as structural work on the complex continued until the time of the outbreak of the revolt in 66 CE.[139]

Another feature that makes identification of the Mishnah's temple difficult is that the author appears to have drawn upon Ezekiel's temple vision. References to Ezekiel's temple can be found in m. Mid. 2:1, 4, 6; 3:1; and 4:1, 2, most of which are pertinent to architectural details. However, Frederick Hollis did not believe that tractate Middoth was a rabbinic interpretation of Ezekiel 40–48. Few measurements agree, and the gates are highly dissimilar. He contended, "The use made of the Holy Scripture in the tractate is not such as to give the impression that somehow or other the words of Scripture are being followed, and violence done to the fact, but rather that there was a fairly clear recollection of the Temple as it had been, with Holy Scripture appealed to to illuminate the fact, not as authority to prove it."[140] Hollis further argued that the author of Middoth described the reality of the Jerusalem Temple that had been destroyed.[141] The citations of verses from Ezekiel likely are used to support instances where the dimensions agreed with Scripture. In other words, accord with Scripture prompted the allusion.[142] Therefore, whether or not Middoth preserves the dimensions of the First or Second Temple, most scholars agree that the passage does indeed reflect the architecture of a historical temple. Further, the "Jewish sages who compiled [tractate Middoth] expected that future generations would rebuild the Temple according to the specifications transmitted."[143]

Little warrant for eschatological interpretation can be found with the exception of m. Mid. 2:6, in which the author discussed the "water gate." The author indicated that the gate is named such because "through it do they bring in the glass of water for the water libation on the Festival [Sukkot]."[144] Alternately, the name of "the water gate" is linked with Ezekiel 47:1–2. Rabbi Eliezer ben Jacob articulated the expectation that in the future, water will flow from beneath the temple.[145] The idea of water

139. John 2:20; Josephus, *Ant.* 17:254–267; 20:219; Levine, *Jerusalem*; Levine, "Josephus' Description," 233–46.

140. Hollis, *Archaeology of Herod's Temple*, 354.

141. Ehrman, "Middot," 180; Hollis, *Archaeology of Herod's Temple*, 20.

142. Hollis, *Archaeology of Herod's Temple*, 352.

143. Avi-Yonah, "Facade of Herod's Temple," 329.

144. Cf. m. Sukkah 4:9. Translation reproduced from Neusner, *Mishnah: A New Translation*.

145. m. Mid 2:6.

flowing from the temple bears both primordial and eschatological associations. Therefore, the passage may hint at an eschatological expectation
in association with the Mishnaic temple.

The Ezekiel Targum

The *targumim* likely reached their final form in the tenth century CE.[146]
Yet, the documents are still relevant, as the *terminus a quo* can be dated to
around 150 BCE.[147] Additionally, Samson Levey explained, "The process
by which the official Targum originally came into being may not have
applied to Ezekiel."[148] The wariness of the rabbis toward Ezekiel resulted
in a tight control over the transmission of the text. Thus, little alteration
in the ideology of the Targum took place as the centuries passed. Moreover, Levey proposed that the Ezekiel Targum reflects the situation of the
period immediately following the destruction of 70 CE, as the message
of Ezekiel was uniquely suited to stimulate hope and perseverance in the
Jewish people.[149]

A nonliteral temple expectation might be implied in the Ezekiel
Targum. In the Targum, the land is described in the same language as
the temple—"the place of the abode of God's Shekinah."[150] Perhaps the
meturgeman was indicating a shift from God's presence being only in the
temple to being wherever his people are. Such a theory fits well with the
mobility of God in Ezekiel, as well as the situation of post-70 Jews, who
had lost their temple.

Summary and Evaluation

As is well recognized, Second Temple Judaism was a multifaceted, complex entity. Multiple strands of tradition are attested in regard to the

146. Pinkhos Churgin argued for a date no later than 641 CE (Churgin, *Targum
Jonathan to the Prophets*, 28–30), but Levey refuted Churgin's argument definitively
(Levey, "Date of Targum Jonathan," 186–96).

147. Levey, "Date of Targum Jonathan," 190; Pfeiffer, *Introduction to the Old Testament*, 77–79.

148. Levey, *Targum of Ezekiel*, 2.

149. Levey also proposed that evidence of "the redactive hand of R. Johanan b.
Zakkai" can be identified in the Targum" (Levey, *Targum of Ezekiel*, 2). Cf. Levey, "Targum to Ezekiel," 142–43.

150. Translation from Levey, *Targum of Ezekiel*. Cf. Ezek 36:5, 20; 38:6; 43:7; 48:35.

temple and the messiah. The authors of the various documents examined above attributed the destruction of Jerusalem to different factors. The author of 4 Ezra indicated that adversity is required to attain eschatological blessings. The authors of 2 Baruch, Pseudo-Philo, the Apocalypse of Abraham, and Sibylline Oracle 4 all indicated that the sinfulness of the Jewish people was the cause of the destruction. The author of Sibylline Oracle 5 cast the blame squarely on Rome.

Consolation is offered along various avenues. The authors of 2 Baruch, 3 Baruch, and Sibylline Oracle 4 diverted attention to the heavenly temple and in doing so denied that the destruction of the Jerusalem Temple was of great consequence. The authors of Pseudo-Philo, 4 Ezra, the Apocalypse of Abraham, and Sibylline Oracle 5 offered hope through a vision of a heavenly city that will replace the earthly Jerusalem in the eschaton.

Several of the works surveyed exhibit some form of messianic expectation. The author of the Similitudes anticipated a messianic figure who would usher in the eschaton and transform the earth. Although the messiah is enthroned, no indication is given that he reigns from a temple. In fact, the "son of man" is described in terms usually reserved for the temple. Likewise, in 4 Ezra, God sends his son to deliver creation, after which the son will stand upon Mt. Zion in victory. That the messianic figure occupies the location typically reserved for the temple is particularly relevant for the current study. However, the implicit connection between Jerusalem and the temple may indicate that the temple is present, if not mentioned.

Sibylline Oracles 1, 2, and 5 exhibit an overt messianism. In Sibylline Oracles 1–2, a Christian composition, the eschatological blessings that resulted from Christ's ministry on earth are described. After his ascension and second coming, Christ will be established as a "great pillar" on the earth and judge its inhabitants. The building imagery applied to Christ is particularly germane in seeking to demonstrate that Christ embodied what the temple represented. Similar phraseology is used in Revelation 3:12: "I will make the one who overcomes a pillar in the temple of my God." Just as Christ overcomes the sin of humanity and will return in strength, so will his people (according to Revelation) be established as pillars by resisting evil (Rev 3:7–13).

Sibylline Oracle 5 exhibits similarities with Revelation in casting Nero and Rome as eschatological enemies who will be defeated by the messiah. As in Sibylline Oracles 1–2, the messiah inaugurates a completely new age on earth. However, where the author of Sibylline Oracles 1–2 made no mention of an eschatological temple, the author of Sibylline Oracle 5 indicated that the messiah will build an eschatological city that encompasses the entire earth and serves the function of the temple.

Overall, both literal and figurative temple imagery can be identified. The expectations can be broken down as follows. First, the authors of Pseudo-Philo, 4 Ezra, and Sibylline Oracle 5 anticipated that the heavenly Jerusalem would be established on the earth in the eschaton. In Pseudo-Philo and Sibylline Oracle 5, a temple is said to be present. In 4 Ezra, however, no explicit mention of the temple is made. Although the sanctuary's presence could be implicit, the messiah may serve such a function. Second, like Revelation, the authors of 2 Baruch and 3 Baruch had no interest in a restored temple, whether literal or symbolic, but the author of 2 Baruch did apply building imagery to righteous Jews. Further, the author of 3 Baruch implied that righteous living, prayer, and worship are favorable ways to commune with God in the absence of the temple—as in the Qumran sectarian literature. Third, the Apocalypse of Abraham is somewhat ambiguous in regard to temple expectations. The author placed emphasis upon the overlap between the heavenly and earthly temples. However, the restoration or replacement of the earthly temple never is articulated clearly. Fourth, the author of Sibylline Oracles 1–2 was silent on the ultimate fate of the temple, possibly indicating that no restoration is expected. Further, Christ appears to embody that which the temple represents. As Sibylline Oracles 1–2 originated in Asia Minor, the information is especially relevant for studies of Revelation. That both documents offer similar messianic expectations may indicate that such thought was well-attested in the region. Fifth, the author of the Mishnah provided details for a material temple that would be built prior to the eschaton. References to Ezekiel do not indicate that the authors of tractate Middoth viewed their temple and Ezekiel's as the same entity. Rather, brief portions of Ezekiel were used to bolster the validity of the plan in Middoth. Sixth, the most promising example for the current study is the messiah of the Similitudes, who seems to be the embodiment of the temple. Seventh, distinctions between material and spiritual are somewhat artificial. Like the Qumran sectarians, most Second Temple period authors did not draw stark distinctions between earthly and heavenly realities.

A few other implications for the study of Ezekiel and Revelation can be identified. In Sibylline Oracle 4, the Apocalypse of Baruch, and 2 Baruch, the presence of God is detached from the Jerusalem Temple. Just as in Ezekiel, Revelation, and the Qumran sectarian literature, God's presence can be accessed through prayer, worship, and righteous living.

As in Revelation, the heavenly Jerusalem often appears on the earth in the eschatological age.[151] That John implied that his temple-city is the same as that of Ezekiel may imply that John, like other Second Temple period authors, understood Ezekiel's city as some form of the heavenly sanctuary. Further, considering the absence or demotion of the temple in much of the literature surveyed here, John's omission of a temple may not have been surprising to his readers. The portrayal of Christ at the center of the heavenly city and the embodiment of the temple is at home fully in the literary and theological milieu of the time. Like Ezekiel before him, John drew upon the language that was at his disposal. Yet, whereas Ezekiel may not have conceived of a nonmaterial fulfillment of his temple, John was not confined by strictly literal interpretations. John referenced and expanded upon the material from Ezekiel 40–48, while also molding the broader traditions about the new Jerusalem into his own vision.[152]

Just as the destruction of the Jerusalem Temple in 586 BCE and 70 CE required a theological reorientation for the Jewish people, the destruction of Christ's body, the metaphorical temple, required a reorientation for Christian proselytes. John's work helped provide a new orientation to the world by shifting focus to spiritual realities, much like the Jewish sages and rabbis sought to readjust their own ideology in the aftermath of the temple's destruction.

---

151. See Revelation 21:2.

152. Beale, *Book of Revelation*, 1108; Schüssler Fiorenza, *Book of Revelation*, 111.

6.

The Visions of Ezekiel and John

IN THE CURRENT CHAPTER, the relationship between Ezekiel 40–48 and Revelation 21–22 will be examined synchronically. The analysis will proceed in two phases. First, broad parallels between the entirety of Ezekiel and Revelation will be outlined. Second, intertextual parallels between Ezekiel 40–48 and Revelation 21:1—22:5 will be examined with the goal of determining precisely how John utilized the Ezekielian material. Before proceeding, however, criteria that will aid in identifying allusions will be discussed.

Intertextual Foundations

Despite the inherent subjectivity of intertextuality, as well as the mosaic of theories in regard to the term, some consensus does exist as to the process for identifying an intertextual reference. Scholars generally agree that "the likelihood for intertextuality grows on a scale of cumulative evidence."[1] In other words, the possibility of an intertextual reference increases as structural, stylistic, thematic, and linguistic patterns emerge.[2] Along such lines, "sustained lexical linkages" can increase the certainty of an allusion.[3] Further, the likelihood of lexical parallels increases if

1. Postell, *Adam as Israel*, 66.

2. Hays, *Echoes of Scripture in the Letters*, 30; Paulien, "Elusive Allusions," 45; Sommer, *Prophet Reads Scripture*, 35.

3. Fishbane, *Biblical Interpretation in Ancient Israel*, 285. Cf. Briggs, *Jewish Temple Imagery*, 41; Hultberg, "Messianic Exegesis in the Apocalypse," 42; Leonard, "Identifying Inner-Biblical Allusions," 246–56; Manning, *Echoes of a Prophet*, 10; Sommer,

structural parallels are present.[4] In sum, "the more parallels one finds to a particular source, the more likely it is that the author had that source in mind as he wrote."[5]

The most objective criteria for identifying parallels are lexical linkages.[6] Jeffery Leonard provided helpful guidelines for identifying lexical connections:

> (1) Shared language is the single most important factor in establishing a textual connection. (2) Shared language is more important than non-shared language. (3) Shared language that is rare or distinctive suggests a stronger connection than does language that is widely used. (4) Shared phrases suggest a stronger connection than do individual shared terms. (5) The accumulation of shared language suggests a stronger connection than does a single shared term or phrase. (6) Shared language in similar contexts suggests a stronger connection than does shared language alone. (7) Shared language need not be accompanied by shared ideology to establish a connection. (8) Shared language need not be accompanied by shared form to establish a connection.[7]

Leonard elaborated on his eight criteria. First, additional unshared language "*in no way* undermines the possibility of a connection."[8] Second, early Christian authors "allude *constantly* to earlier texts and traditions, yet they apparently felt perfect liberty to push those allusions in new and unexpected directions."[9] Third, the different *Sitz im Leben* of later authors "would have prompted them to use the elements of the earlier traditions in quite different ways."[10]

Leonard's criteria are useful, especially in an intertextual study of Revelation. John drew on traditions with which he was familiar, yet

---

Prophet Reads Scripture, 35.

4. Paulien, "Elusive Allusions," 42–45.

5. Paulien, "Elusive Allusions," 41. Cf. Beale, *John's Use*, 71; Hays, *Echoes of Scripture in the Letters*, 30; Hultberg, "Messianic Exegesis in the Apocalypse," 40.

6. Leonard, "Identifying Inner-Biblical Allusions," 241–65; Nurmela, "Growth of the Book, 245–59.

7. Leonard, "Identifying Inner-Biblical Allusions," 246. Cf. Manning, *Echoes of a Prophet*, 9–11.

8. Leonard, "Identifying Inner-Biblical Allusions," 249; emphasis his..

9. Leonard, "Identifying Inner-Biblical Allusions," 256; emphasis his.

10. Leonard, "Identifying Inner-Biblical Allusions," 256.

creatively reshaped them to present his own vision of the eschaton. That he relied on numerous sources does not diminish the relevance of each precursor in contributing to the finished whole.

One final area of correspondence should be mentioned. Manning noted that "resonance" between texts increases the likelihood of allusory material in that "two texts can be said to resonate when their *contexts* deal with similar themes and ideas."[11] Accordingly, both John and Ezekiel described an eschatological city in which the presence of God brings life. Further, Ezekiel and Revelation share a historical resonance. Both books were composed in the wake of the destruction of Jerusalem. The Jewish people were scattered and the source of their pride and hope—the temple—was gone. Although the loss of the temple was not as devastating for Christ's followers, both John and Ezekiel sought to offer hope to people who were facing persecution and hardship.

Structural Parallels

Numerous scholars have noted that Ezekiel and Revelation exhibit parallel structures.[12] While John was not slavish in his use of Ezekiel, he did link Revelation with broad sections of the prophetic book.

Table 1. Structural Parallels between Ezekiel and Revelation		
Ezekiel	Revelation	Content
1	1, 4	Introductory vision
2–3	5, 10	Prophetic commission
9–10	7–8	Judgment on non-sealed
16, 23	17	Judgment on harlot
26–28	18	Judgment on Tyre/Babylon
38–39	19–20	Final battle
40–48	21–22	New Jerusalem

Ian Boxall contended that Ezekiel served as a key text for John, such that the substance of the book became part of his psyche and served as a determining influence upon his own visions. He asserted that Ezekiel

---

11. Manning, *Echoes of a Prophet*, 13; emphasis his. Cf. Beale, *Use of Daniel*, 307–8.

12. Goulder, "Apocalypse as an Annual Cycle," 343–48; Mathewson, *New Heaven*, 29; Moyise, *Old Testament in the Book*, 74, 78; Presser, "La Escatología Apocalíptica de Ezequiel," 129–46; Vanhoye, "L'utilization du livre d'Ezéchiel," 440–41; Vogelgesang, "Interpretation of Ezekiel," 68.

"was at least one of John's major texts for meditation, such that he has thoroughly imbibed not only its spirit and its imagery, but even something of its order."[13]

The fourfold ending of both books correlates closely as well.[14] In Revelation 20–22, John drew upon material from the last twelve chapters of Ezekiel. A careful examination of the parallel structures reveals that John exhibited a tendency to collapse and condense OT texts and visions[15]:

> The broad structure of the city from 21:12 through 22:5 is based on the vision in Ezekiel 40–48 . . . Rev. 21:12–22:5 interprets the future fulfillment of Ezekiel by collapsing temple, city, and land into one end-time picture of the one reality of God's communion with his people. This identification is based on Ezekiel's own identification of temple, city, and land as representing the same truth . . . And the concluding statement of Ezekiel's vision likewise interprets the ultimate meaning of the restored city to be God's presence with his people . . . That John "saw no temple" in the new Jerusalem . . . is partial but clear evidence of his method of interpretive distillation.[16]

John Sweet, likewise, contended that John distilled and clarified Ezekiel's vision while remaining faithful to the prophet's original intent.[17]

Table 2. Structural Parallels between Ezekiel 37–48 and Revelation 20–22		
Ezekiel	Revelation	Content
37a	20:4	Resurrection

13. Boxall, "Exile, Prophet, Visionary," 155. Debate exists as to which source exerted the greatest influence on John. Goulder suggested Ezekiel ("Apocalypse as an Annual Cycle," 348). Beale suggested Daniel, going so far as to contend that Revelation is a midrash on Daniel (Beale, *Use of Daniel*, 154–305). Swete determined that Isaiah received the greatest number of references (*Apocalypse*, clii).

14. Beale, *Book of Revelation*, 977; Beale, "Millennium in Revelation 20:1–10," 29–62; Decock, "Scriptures in the Book," 379–80; Goulder, "Apocalypse as an Annual Cycle," 347–48; Mathewson, *New Heaven*, 30; Osborne, *Revelation*, 712; Presser, "La Escatología Apocalíptica de Ezequiel," 134; Tanner, "Rethinking Ezekiel's Invasion by Gog," 29–45.

15. Beale, *Book of Revelation*, 1090; Son, "Background of Exodus 15," 56–60; Sweet, *Revelation*, 39–40, 308; Vogelgesang, "Interpretation of Ezekiel," 85–115.

16. Beale, *Book of Revelation*, 1061–62. Cf. Sweet, *Revelation*, 308.

17. Sweet, *Revelation*, 39–40. Cf. Mathewson, "Re-examination of the Millennium," 237–51.

37b	20:4–6	Messianic reign
38–39	20:7–10	Final battle
40–48	21:1—22:5	New Jerusalem

John may have been so familiar with Ezekiel that he unwittingly took on something of the prophet's persona.[18] Boxall contended that John assumed three aspects of Ezekiel's self-presentation—visionary, prophet, and exile.[19] Richard Bauckham also saw John as a figure who took up the mantle of the OT prophets:

> Certainly, John sees himself as a prophet in the Old Testament tradition of prophecy and receives a revelation given to him as a prophet. But just as late Old Testament prophecy already takes up, interprets and develops the authoritative oracles of its predecessors, so John's prophecy gathers up and interprets all the prophecies of the Old Testament prophets which he regarded as relating to the eschatological coming of God's kingdom. Because the Old Testament prophecies are authoritative for him, his fresh revelation cannot be discontinuous with them, but must be closely related to interpretation of them, thereby providing the culmination of the whole prophetic tradition.[20]

Thus, John, in the light of his prophetic persona and authority, was "able to articulate more clearly in the light of the Christ event what the old texts were saying less clearly."[21]

Gog and Magog

A discussion of each structural parallel between Ezekiel and Revelation would require a monograph. However, the parallels between Ezekiel 38–39 and Revelation 19–20 will be given attention due to their proximity to the final vision. The battle described in these chapters prepares the way for the eschatological era that follows.[22]

---

18. Boxall, "Exile, Prophet, Visionary," 149; Moyise, *Old Testament in the Book*, 78–84.

19. Boxall, "Exile, Prophet, Visionary," 155. Cf. Beale, *John's Use*, 67; Boxall, *Revelation*, 32–34; Moyise, *Old Testament in the Book*, 78–84.

20. Bauckham, *Climax of Prophecy*, 262–63.

21. Decock, "Scriptures in the Book," 392.

22. Some scholars propose that Revelation 19:17–21 and 20:8–10 comprise two different battles that fulfill the singular event of Ezekiel 38–39 (Deere, "Premillennialism

Numerous parallels can be identified between Revelation 19–20 and Ezekiel 38–39. Most noteworthy, Revelation 20 and Ezekiel 38–39 contain the only references to Gog and Magog in Scripture.[23] A slight difference in wording should be noted, however. In Ezekiel 38:1, the prophet described Gog *of the land of* Magog. In Revelation 20:8, John referenced Gog *and* Magog.

The unit "Gog and Magog" is attested in extrabiblical sources as a referent for eschatological enemies of Israel.[24] Presser explained that Gog and Magog may be considered a hyperonym for the multitude of evil forces that gather for the final battle.[25] Thus, in Revelation, the appellations Gog and Magog do not function to indicate geography or ethnicity. Rather, the unit serves a literary function. In Revelation, the reference points "to the parallel eschatological scenario on Ezekiel 38."[26] John desires that his readers recognize the events of 19–20 as the events prophesied by Ezekiel.[27]

Several other distinctive parallels appear in Revelation 19–20. Innumerable enemies come against the people of God (Rev 20:8; Ezek 38:6, 9, 15, 22) and are consumed by fire (Rev 20:9; Ezek 38:22). Most striking are the birds eating flesh (Rev 19:17–21; Ezek 39:4, 17–20) until they are gorged (Rev 19:21; Ezek 39:18–20). [28] Thus, while John seemed to be aware of other traditions, the sustained lexical and thematic linkages imply that John drew upon Ezekiel heavily here.

Further support that John alluded to Ezekiel 38–39 is provided by an examination of the place name "Hamonah." In Ezekiel 39, the location where the dead will be buried is described:

---

in Revelation 20:4–6," 58–73; Mealy, *After the Thousand Years*, 187–88; Mounce, *Book of Revelation*, 352; Walvoord, "Millennial Kingdom," 291–300). However, John tended to condense, not expand, the oracles upon which he drew. For a detailed rebuttal see Beale, *Book of Revelation*, 974–76.

23. Goulder, "Apocalypse as an Annual Cycle," 347.

24. Sib. Or. 3:319–23; 1QM XI, 15.

25. Presser, "La Escatología Apocalíptica de Ezequiel," 146.

26. Mealy, *After the Thousand Years*, 130. Cf. Mathewson, "A Re-examination of the Millennium," 241; Milgrom and Block, *Ezekiel's Hope*, 5–11. To the contrary, Rieuwerd Buitenwerf argued that John incorporated common oral traditions about Gog and Magog rather than drawing upon Ezekiel ("Gog and Magog Tradition," 165–81).

27. Mealy, *After the Thousand Years*, 130–31.

28. Buitenwerf, "Gog and Magog Tradition," 167; Goulder, "Apocalypse as an Annual Cycle," 347.

> Thus, it will come about, on that day I will give to Gog a place
> of burial there in Israel . . . And they will bury Gog there with
> all his horde, and they will call it the valley of Hamon-Gog . . .
> When those who pass through the land pass through and see
> a man's bone, then they will erect a marker beside it, until the
> buriers have buried it in the valley of Hamon-Gog. And also
> (גַּם), the name of the city is Hamonah. Thus, they will cleanse
> the land. (Ezek 39:11, 15–16)

As a noun, הָמוֹן can be translated as "turmoil" or "agitation."[29] Yet, the
appellation Hamonah has long puzzled interpreters.[30]

Margaret Odell's proposal that Hamonah symbolizes Jerusalem has
met with widespread support.[31] Odell contended that the corruption
of the city "defies the order which has been intended by God's statutes
and ordinances."[32] Correspondingly, Ezekiel 39:16 should be translated
as "Even though the name of the city is Hamonah they will purify the
land."[33] Thus, Ezekiel used the metaphorical place name to highlight the
transformation of the city from ruins to "the eschatological city of divine
presence."[34]

> Although the city has acquired a pejorative name because of
> the abominations of its former inhabitants, the eschatological
> inhabitants will no longer contribute to this reputation. Instead
> they will get a new name for themselves as an obedient people
> who purify the land (cf. 39:13).[35] Not only do the people get a
> new name for themselves: Jerusalem also receives a new name.
> When Jerusalem is renamed at the end of chap. 48, the sentence
> structure echoes that of 39:16 . . . The new name of 48:35 im-
> plies, of course, that the city had gone by another name until
> that time.[36]

29. HALOT 250.

30. Blenkinsopp, Ezekiel, 188–89; Eichrodt, Ezekiel, 528–29; Zimmerli, Ezekiel 2, 317.

31. Odell, "City of Hamonah," 479–90. In most commentaries published after Odell's article, her argument is accepted. See Block, Book of Ezekiel: Chapters 25–48, 472; Joyce, Ezekiel, 217; Milgrom and Block, Ezekiel's Hope, 26; Tuell, Ezekiel, 269–70.

32. Odell, "City of Hamonah," 483.

33. Odell, "City of Hamonah," 488. Odell translates the גַּם concessively rather than conjunctively.

34. Odell, "City of Hamonah," 480.

35. The new "name" (וְהָיָה לָהֶם לְשֵׁם) is obscured in most English translations.

36. Odell, "City of Hamonah," 488.

Similarly, in Revelation 21:1–2, the battlefield is replaced by the new Jerusalem.[37] Further, in Revelation 2:17, John indicated that the saints who overcome will receive a new name, and in Revelation 22:4, the saints receive God's name upon their foreheads. Thus, the pervasive allusions to Ezekiel 38–39 in the chapters directly preceding John's vision of the new Jerusalem prepare readers to understand Revelation 21–22 in the light of Ezekiel 40–48.[38]

The Messiah in Ezekiel

Although no direct lexical link exists between Christ in Revelation 21–22 and the נָשִׂיא, or "prince," in Ezekiel 40–48, the potential parallel merits discussion. Ezekiel, in his final vision, described the functions and land allotments of a tribal ruler (Ezek 44–46; 48). However, Ezekiel's portrait of the ruler, and possible messiah, is intricate and difficult to decode.

In the chapters preceding his final eschatological vision, Ezekiel inscribed three messianic oracles: Ezekiel 17:22–24, 34:11–31, and 37:15–28, all of which anticipate a restored Davidic king.[39] However, the restrictions placed upon the prince in chapters 40–48 do not seem to coincide with the previous expectations. Manning opined, "Although Ezekiel uses messianic imagery in other parts of his book, such imagery is muted in Ezekiel 45–48. There is discussion of the prince and his role in the new Temple, but he is overshadowed by the description of the new Temple."[40] Levenson, to the contrary, contended that a messianic reign is the subject of chapters 40–48 and the culmination of the entire book.[41]

Further complicating matters is the difficulty in determining whether Ezekiel made a distinction between the terms נָשִׂיא and מֶלֶךְ, or "king." In Ezekiel, נָשִׂיא is portrayed often in a positive light,[42] whereas

37. Like Ezekiel, John made no initial identification of the city that is under attack.

38. For further scholarship on the relationship between Ezekiel 38–39 and Revelation 19–20, see Beale, *Book of Revelation*, 965–71; Bøe, *Gog and Magog*; Buitenwerf, "Gog and Magog Tradition," 165–81; Tanner, "Rethinking Ezekiel's Invasion by Gog."

39. Ezekiel 29:21 may contain a reference to the messiah as well. See Block, *Book of Ezekiel: Chapters 25–48*, 152; Fohrer and Galling, *Ezechiel*, 170; Joyce, *Ezekiel*, 182. Tuell and Zimmerli argued to the contrary; Tuell, *Ezekiel*, 208–9; Zimmerli, *Ezekiel 2*, 120.

40. Manning, *Echoes of a Prophet*, 94.

41. Levenson, *Theology of the Program*, 90.

42. Princes of other nations: Ezek 26:16; 27:21; 30:13; 32:29; 38:2, 3; 39:1, 18;

מֶלֶךְ is portrayed almost uniformly negatively.[43] The messianic oracle of Ezekiel 17 does not use either term, but Levenson suggested that verse 23 may contain a play on words that subtly connects the prince with the anticipated messiah.[44] Similarly, in Ezekiel 34:22, God affirms that a Davidide will be restored one day as a נָשִׂיא of Israel.

Conversely, מֶלֶךְ is portrayed positively in only two instances. In Ezekiel 20:33, God states that at the time of judgment and restoration, he himself will be king over Israel. In Ezekiel 37:22–24, God pronounces that he will gather the people of Israel and unite the tribes under a Davidic king. Some scholars attribute the atypical usage of מֶלֶךְ to different redactional strands.[45] Alternately, the usages in chapters 20 and 37 may serve to foreshadow the people's restoration to full nationhood in the future.[46]

Despite the positive portrayal of the king in Ezekiel 20:33 and 37:22–24, Ezekiel's preference for נָשִׂיא may reflect a polemic against the monarchy.[47] Block, however, argued that Ezekiel was not fundamentally opposed to the office of king, but only the manner in which the monarchy had operated historically.[48] He contended that Ezekiel largely avoided מֶלֶךְ because of the term's association with independence and arrogance, while נָשִׂיא more appropriately conveys "the king's status as a vassal of YHWH."[49] Block further contended that the function of the נָשִׂיא is facili-

---

officials of Judea who will be punished: Ezek 7:27; 12:10, 12; 19:1; 21:12, 25; 22:6; anticipation of a messianic or Davidic ruler: Ezek 34:24; 37:25; 44:3; 45:7–9, 16, 17; 45:22; 46:2, 4, 8, 10, 12, 16–18; 48:21, 22.

43. Kings of other nations: Ezek 17:12, 16; 19:9; 21:24, 26; 24:2; 26:7; 27:33, 35; 28:12, 17; 29:2, 3; 29:18, 19; 30:10, 21, 22, 24, 25; 31:2; 32:2, 10, 11, 29; Jehoiachin: Ezek 1:2; king of Judea who will be punished: Ezek 7:27; harlotrous kings of Israel: Ezek 43:7, 9; Davidic king: Ezek 37:22, 24.

44. Levenson, *Theology of the Program*, 81. "On the high mountain of Israel I will plant it, and it will raise its branches (וְנָשָׂא עָנָף) and bear fruit and become a great cedar" (Ezek 17:23). Similarly, Block argued that נָשִׂיא derives from נָשָׂא, i.e., the prince is the "promoted one" (Block, *Beyond the River Chebar*, 82).

45. Gese, *Der Verfassungsentwurf des Ezechiel*, 116–23; Tuell, *Ezekiel*, 103–20; Zimmerli, *Ezekiel 2*, 278.

46. Block, *Book of Ezekiel: Chapters 25–48*, 413–14.

47. Stevenson, *Vision of Transformation*, 109–23, 151–54. Iain Duguid argued that in Ezekiel 40–48, the prophet used נָשִׂיא as a subtle critique of Israelite kings, while in Ezekiel 1–39, the prophet used מֶלֶךְ and נָשִׂיא interchangeably (Duguid, *Ezekiel and the Leaders*, 18–27, 31–33).

48. Block, *Beyond the River Chebar*, 74–94. Cf. Blenkinsopp, *Ezekiel*, 176–77.

49. Block, *Beyond the River Chebar*, 83.

tative rather than political. The prince is a religious figure and cult patron who ensures harmonious relations between the nation and Yahweh. In short, Ezekiel did not seek to eliminate hierarchies but to redefine existing institutions.[50] Further, Block viewed the נָשִׂיא as a messianic figure who, as the representative of the Lord, "symbolizes the presence of YHWH in the midst of his people."[51]

Similarly, Levenson argued that Ezekiel's prince is a reinterpretation of Israel's messianic expectation.[52] The messianic figure was increasingly absorbed into the personality of God, as "the Exilic community saw the historical monarchy fulfilled in the eschatological theocracy."[53] The messiah rules in subjection to the will of Yahweh, and no other administrative structures are needed. Further, the title נָשִׂיא does not conflict with a Davidic expectation. "On the contrary, the lesser title makes sense within the framework of a theology of monarchy common to Ezekiel and other literature in the Hebrew Bible as the designation of a messianic individual shorn of the structural temptations to commit abuses."[54] Levenson went so far as to compare the persona of the messianic figure in Ezekiel 17 and 34 to the Christ child of the nativity. The figures evoke "a sense of that rarest intersection of all human affairs—the intersection of humility and power."[55]

Vogelgesang, following Levenson, also viewed Ezekiel's prince as messiah. He explicitly connected the נָשִׂיא to the Lamb of Revelation. Just as God and the prince govern Ezekiel's new Jerusalem, so also God and the Lamb govern John's.[56]

Various other proposals have been suggested for the identity of the prince. Tuell argued that the prince "belongs most immediately to historical and political reality, rather than eschatological hope of proto-apocalyptic fancy."[57] He contended that the prince was, in fact, "a Judean governor, under Persian hegemony."[58] Conversely, Stevenson argued that

50. Block, *Beyond the River Chebar*, 74–94.
51. Block, *Book of Ezekiel: Chapters 25–48*, 680.
52. Levenson, *Theology of the Program*, 57–101.
53. Levenson, *Theology of the Program*, 99.
54. Levenson, *Theology of the Program*, 67.
55. Levenson, *Theology of the Program*, 88.
56. Vogelgesang, "Interpretation of Ezekiel," 129.
57. Tuell, *Law of the Temple*, 108.
58. Tuell, *Law of the Temple*, 116. Tuell's conclusions are based on proposed redactional layers.

Ezekiel removed the traditional office of the monarchy altogether. The prince's limited role in the cult and government points to the sovereignty of Yahweh as the sole king of Israel.[59] Brian Boyle also understood the utopia of Ezekiel 40–48 as a theocracy in which the prince is "a central figure in Ezekiel's plan of the restored sphere of the sacred. He is the principal lay worshipper and cult patron in this theocratic vision of society," although he has no official political or cultic role.[60]

To conclude, space does not allow for a more thorough analysis of Ezekiel's prince and king. As in the previous section, a full investigation would require a monograph. Nonetheless, a few conclusions can be drawn. First, Ezekiel does appear to anticipate a messiah, even if the precise function of the figure is difficult to ascertain. Second, Ezekiel's messiah appears to hold a subservient role to Yahweh. Third, the prince plays some role in the cult and the government, although he does not operate with the full power of the historical Davidic monarchs, and neither does he fit the OT descriptions of a messiah who will reign in power.[61] Fourth, Ezekiel's prince bears only a slight resemblance to the Lamb of Revelation 21–22, in that both figures serve a mediatorial role between God and his people.

Though an intertext is desirable for the current study, no linguistic or structural parallels exist. Only vague topical parallels can be identified: (1) that of a messianic figure who rules in conjunction with or in submission to the Lord, and (2) that of a cult patron who facilitates the relation between Yahweh and the people. Further examination might unearth additional parallels, but for now, no direct allusion to the נָשִׂיא seems to be present in Revelation.

Nonsequential Parallels

In addition to broad structuring around the content of Ezekiel, John also felt the freedom to modify and rearrange Ezekielian themes to suit his own theological and compositional purposes. A few of the more obvious examples will be iterated here. First, in Revelation 1:15, God's voice is like

---

59. Stevenson, *Vision of Transformation*, 3, 119–23.

60. Boyle, "Figure of the *NĀŚΪ*," 1. Cf. Klawans, *Purity, Sacrifice, and the Temple*, 96.

61. See Gen 49:10; Ps 110:1–4; Isa 9:6–7; Dan 7:13–14.

the sound of many waters (cf. Ezek 43:2).[62] Second, in Revelation 1:17, John falls on his face before the presence of God (cf. Ezek 43:3).[63] Third, in Revelation 5, the inability of John to open his scroll (Rev 5:3–4) mirrors Ezekiel's inability to speak to the people of Israel (Ezek 2:1—3:27). Both instances represent a failure to fulfill the prophetic commission.[64] Fourth, in Revelation 10, John is recommissioned and given a second scroll, which is reminiscent of Ezekiel 2–3.[65] Both prophets are directed to eat the scroll, which is sweet to the taste (Ezek 2:8—3:3; Rev 10:9). Fifth, in Revelation 11:1–2, John is told to measure the temple (cf. Ezekiel 40–48).

Sixth, the Greek text of Revelation 11:11–13 closely follows that of Ezekiel 37:7–10. In Revelation 11:11–13, a great earthquake (σεισμός) comes upon Jerusalem just as the two martyred witnesses are resurrected.[66] Similarly, in Ezekiel 37:7, the earth shakes (σεισμός) as the corpses of slain Israelites rise from the dead.[67] In both passages, the spirit of life causes the dead to rise to their feet.[68] Thus, John appears to draw upon LXX Ezekiel to portray a resurrection that is instigated by the Spirit and accompanied by an earthquake.

Seventh, in Revelation 21, the portrayal of a marriage ceremony between God and the new Jerusalem (Rev 21:29) may serve as an antithetical parallel to Ezekiel 16–18 and 23, in which the Lord is married to Jerusalem the whore (Ezek 16:8–22; 23).[69] The personification of Jerusalem as a wife "provided Ezekiel with a powerful metaphor with which to describe the pollution of the Jerusalem temple."[70] Conversely, the city-temple-bride of Revelation 21 is pure and undefiled.

---

62. Beale, *Book of Revelation*, 931.

63. Goulder, "Apocalypse as an Annual Cycle," 347.

64. Tuell, "Should Ezekiel Go to Rehab?," 289–302.

65. Boxall, *Revelation*, 152.

66. Cf. Rev 6:12; 8:5; 11:13, 19; 16:18. Beale, *Book of Revelation*, 596–97.

67. The connection is obscured in the Hebrew, which reports that the resurrection is accompanied by a rattling *sound* (קוֹל).

68. A total of six parallel terms or cognates are present between Revelation 11:11–13 and Ezekiel 37:7–10: σεισμὸς, πνεῦμα, ζωῆς/ἔζησαν, εἰσῆλθεν, ἔστησαν, and πόδας. Further, the phrase καὶ ἔστησαν ἐπὶ τῶν ποδῶν αὐτῶν is nearly identical in both passages.

69. Fekkes, "Bride has Prepared Herself," 269–87.

70. Galambush, "Jerusalem in the Book," 223.

Eighth, in Revelation 22:4, the name written on the foreheads of believers is reminiscent of Ezekiel 9:4, in which those who mourn over the idolatry in Jerusalem receive a mark on the forehead.[71] Further, the mark of the beast in Revelation 13:16–17 is the inverse of the mark that indicates loyalty to God.[72]

To conclude, Revelation resonates with a wealth of themes and topics also found in Ezekiel. Numerous structural, stylistic, thematic, and linguistic patterns have been identified. Although the discussion here has not been exhaustive, the cumulative weight of parallels that have been noted increases the likelihood of further parallels.

Ezekiel 40–48 in Revelation 21:1—22:5

With structural and topical parallels established, the groundwork is set for an examination of Ezekiel 40–48 in Revelation 21:1—22:5. A detailed exegesis will not be provided for the entirety of Ezekiel 40–48 and Revelation 21:1—22:5. Only potential instances of intertextuality will be examined. Terminology relevant to the current study will be identified and discussed in context. Relevance is determined by the presence of a parallel lexeme, the presence of synonymous lexemes, or temple-related terminology. After discussion, the contextual function and relative certainty of each reference or group of references will be determined using categories proposed by Beale.

The analysis will follow a roughly chronological order through Revelation 21:1—22:5, although the overlap of topics throughout the section will necessitate some nonsequential discussion. In particular, Revelation 21:9—22:5 seems to be a recapitulation and expansion of Revelation 21:1–8.[73] Sweet explained, "It is a common trait of biblical narration to state a theme, and then restate it in more detail as if recounting a subsequent event; 21:1–8 can be seen as a text which is expounded in 21:9ff. almost verse by verse."[74] However, where Revelation 21:1–9 is dominated

71. Beale, *Book of Revelation*, 1114.

72. Aune, *Revelation 6–16*, 767.

73. Jan du Rand regarded Revelation 21:1–8 as a transitional hinge ("New Jerusalem as Pinnacle," 275–302). Cf. Aune, *Revelation 17–22*, 1120; Beale, *Book of Revelation*, 1062; Decock, "Scriptures in the Book," 380; Mathewson, *New Heaven*, 94; Vogelgesang, "Interpretation of Ezekiel," 119. Rissi argued to the contrary (*Future of the World*, 54).

74. Sweet, *Revelation*, 296–97.

by allusions to Isaiah, Ezekiel 40–48 comes to the forefront in Revelation 21:9–17.[75]

City and Mountain (Rev 21:2, 10; Ezek 40:1–2)

Revelation 21:2, 10, and Ezekiel 40:1–2 consist of a conglomeration of topics and lexemes. The first topic to be discussed will be the city, the new Jerusalem. In Revelation 21:2 and 21:10, the new Jerusalem descends from heaven, which John sees from a mountain, and in Ezekiel 40:1–2, Ezekiel sees a city upon a mountain:

Καὶ τὴν πόλιν τὴν ἁγίαν Ἰερουσαλὴμ καινὴν εἶδον καταβαίνουσαν ἐκ τοῦ οὐρανοῦ ἀπὸ τοῦ θεοῦ ἡτοιμασμένην ὡς νύμφην κεκοσμημένην τῷ ἀνδρὶ αὐτῆς. (Rev 21:2)[76]

Καὶ ἀπήνεγκέν με ἐν πνεύματι ἐπὶ ὄρος μέγα καὶ ὑψηλόν, καὶ ἔδειξέν μοι τὴν πόλιν τὴν ἁγίαν Ἰερουσαλὴμ καταβαίνουσαν ἐκ τοῦ οὐρανοῦ ἀπὸ τοῦ θεοῦ. (Rev 21:10)[77]

Ἐν τῇ ἡμέρᾳ ἐκείνῃ ἐγένετο ἐπ’ ἐμὲ χεὶρ κυρίου καὶ ἤγαγέν με ἐν ὁράσει θεοῦ εἰς τὴν γῆν τοῦ Ισραηλ καὶ ἔθηκέν με ἐπ’ ὄρους ὑψηλοῦ σφόδρα, καὶ ἐπ’ αὐτοῦ ὡσεὶ οἰκοδομὴ πόλεως ἀπέναντι. (Ezek 40:1b–2)[78]

Immediately obvious is that Revelation 21:2 bears little resemblance to Ezekiel 40:2. The only parallel lexeme is πόλιν (city), which is such a common term that the lexical parallel is virtually irrelevant. Further, in Revelation 21:2, John drew upon imagery similar to Isaiah 61:10 and 62:1–5, in which Isaiah indicated that Jerusalem will be adorned as a bride and called by a new name in the eschaton.[79] The affinities with

75. Mathewson, *New Heaven*, 94; Vanhoye, "L'utilisation du livre d'Ezéchiel," 440–42.

76. "And I saw the holy city, the New Jerusalem, coming down out of heaven from God, having been prepared as a bride adorned for her husband" (Rev 21:2).

77. "And he bore me in spirit to a great and high mountain, and he showed me the holy city, Jerusalem coming down from heaven, from God" (Rev 21:10).

78. "On that same day, the hand of the Lord was upon me, and he brought me in a vision of God into the land of Israel. Thus, he set me on a very high mountain, and upon it there was a structure like a city before me" (Ezek 40:1b–2).

79. Aune, *Revelation 17–22*, 1121; Beale, *Book of Revelation*, 1044; Fekkes, "Bride has Prepared Herself," 270; Mathewson, *New Heaven*, 44–49.

Isaiah do not preclude a reference to Ezekiel, but the Isaianic themes are dominant here.

Nonetheless, a minor parallel can be identified in the city imagery of Revelation 21:2 and Ezekiel 40:1–2. Both passages describe the restoration of a city that was destroyed previously. In Revelation 11:2, the holy city was trampled by the gentile nations, and in Ezekiel 33:21, Jerusalem had fallen to Babylon. Then in Revelation 21–22 and Ezekiel 40–48, the prophets are shown a restored Jerusalem, eschatologically transformed and full of God's presence.

Additionally, Revelation 21:2 is helpful in determining the nature of the new Jerusalem. In Revelation 21:2, 9–10, John described the city as a bride, but in Revelation 19:7–8, the bride had been identified already as the saints.[80] Fekkes contended that the imagery of a bride is "best taken as a relational metaphor, whose primary referent is the salvation community."[81] Similarly, Beale argued, "The image of the city is probably figurative, representing the fellowship of God with his people in an actual new creation."[82]

As noted above, both John and Ezekiel exhibited a tendency to identify people with cities. Ezekiel 16–18 and 23 may be in the background of Revelation 21 with the bride of Christ providing an antithesis to the harlotrous wife of God.[83] Just as Jerusalem the whore represents a nation who rebelled against God, so also the new Jerusalem of Ezekiel 40–48 embodies a reality in which God's people are restored to fellowship with him. Accordingly, in Revelation, "just as Babylon symbolizes the socio-economic and religious culture arrayed in antagonism to God, so the bride, portrayed as the new Jerusalem, represents the redeemed community, which stands on God's side."[84]

---

80. Cf. Rev 20:9; Gundry, "New Jerusalem," 254–64; Kistemaker, "Temple in the Apocalypse," 433–41; Spatafora, From the "Temple of God," 229.

81. Fekkes, "Bride has Prepared Herself," 272. Cf. Isa 49:18; 54:5–6; 62:4–5; Jer 2:2; Ezek 16:32; Hos 2:19–20; Eph 5:22–23; 2 Cor 11:2.

82. Beale, Book of Revelation, 1045. Cf. McKelvey, New Temple, 167–76; du Rand, "New Jerusalem as Pinnacle," 294; Rissi, Future of the World, 57, 60; Stevens, Revelation, 527.

83. Fekkes argued that John did not draw on Ezekiel 16 and 23 here, as John had already used Ezekiel 23:25 to describe Babylon. The scholar did argue however for the influence of Ezekiel 17–18 on Revelation 21 (Fekkes, "Bride has Prepared Herself," 272–83).

84. Beale, Book of Revelation, 1064. Cf. Gundry, "New Jerusalem," 256; McKelvey, New Temple, 171–73; Vogelgesang, "Interpretation of Ezekiel," 5.

Similarly, in Revelation 3:12, the saints are identified with the new Jerusalem.[85] Christ promises that those who overcome will become a pillar in the temple of God and receive a new name: "I will make the one who overcomes a pillar in the temple of my God and he will not go out anymore, and I will write upon him the name of my God and the name of the city of my God, the new Jerusalem, which comes down from heaven from my God, and I will write upon him my new name" (Rev 3:12).[86] Just as the gates boast the names of the tribes, and the foundation stones shine with the names of the apostles, so also the pillars are inscribed with the names of faithful believers.[87] Beale explained, "That was the first substantial hint in the Apocalypse that later in ch. 21 the concepts of city and temple would be collapsed into the one concept of the presence of Christ and God with his people."[88] Along similar lines, in Ezekiel 48:35, the prophet indicated that the name of the city is "the Lord is there." Just as the city-saints in Revelation are inscribed with a new name—the name of the Lord—so also the city in Ezekiel 40–48 receives a similar new name.

Thus, the cities in both Ezekiel and Revelation are relational rather than spatial entities. The new Jerusalem represents the locus of God's rule, but in Revelation 21–22, John revealed that such a locale is "God's dwelling place in the saints rather than their dwelling place on earth."[89] Just as God had made Israel his abode in the past, so also he will make the saints his abode in the new heavens and earth.[90]

Having established the nature of the city of Revelation 21:2 and 21:10, a comparison of Revelation 21:10 and Ezekiel 40:2 can now be undertaken. Both prophets experienced their vision of the city (πόλιν) while on a high mountain: ἐπὶ ὄρος μέγα καὶ ὑψηλόν (Rev 21:10) and ἐπ' ὄρους ὑψηλοῦ σφόδρα (Ezek 40:2).[91] Although none of the terms are particularly distinctive, the similar phraseology, sustained lexical linkages, and comparable literary contexts add weight to the allusion.

85. Gundry, "New Jerusalem," 256.

86. Cf. Rev 22:4.

87. The application of temple language to the community is reminiscent of Qumran texts: 1QS III, 2; VIII, 5–10; 1QS IX, 3–6; 4QS VI, 5–7; 4Q164 I, 2–3; 1QSa I, 26–28; 4QFlor I, 3–6; 4QD III, 19–IV, 5; 1QH XIV, 24–27; cf. Deutsch, "Transformation of Symbols," 114.

88. Beale, *Book of Revelation*, 1070.

89. Gundry, "New Jerusalem," 256. Cf. Beale, *Book of Revelation*, 1079.

90. Cf. Gal 4:21–27; Heb 12:22–24.

91. Cf. T. Levi 2:5.

In Revelation 21:10, John seemed to draw on Ezekiel 40:2, but the structure that Ezekiel sees is *like* a city in that it has walls and gates, but is actually the temple.[92] Thus, at first glance, John sees a city, while Ezekiel sees a temple. However, John's new Jerusalem is, in fact, a temple, as will be borne out in the following discussion. Gundry explained, "Ordinarily, God dwells in the temple and the temple is located in the city. Here, he and the Lamb are the temple, so that the city, since it is the cubically shaped Holy of Holies, is located in the temple—a striking reversal which means that the saints will dwell in God and the Lamb just as God and the Lamb will dwell in them."[93]

Further, the symbol system of the city and the temple has shifted from a nation-centered reality to a more universal expectation based on a Christian worldview—a worldview in which the Messiah embodies what the temple had represented.[94] As a temple and holy of holies, the entire city radiates the glory of God, as the division between holy and profane dissipates, at least within the confines of the city.

The separation between heaven and earth is gone as well. Heretofore in Revelation, heaven and earth have been distinct entities. However, as cultic liminal space, the new Jerusalem collapses boundaries between realms.[95] Such a collapse of thresholds also helps explain how "a space that while meant to be inhabited is not meant to be built."[96]

The location of the temple of Revelation also reflects the dissipation of boundaries. Ezekiel's temple rests upon a mountain, whereas John's is descending from heaven. Some commentators argue that John's city comes to rest upon the mountain, even though the location never is stated.[97] However, a more straightforward interpretation takes the descent as it stands. Gerald Stevens explained, "New Jerusalem descends (21:2). Humans do not have to scale the impossibly scalable mountain of God.

---

92. Aune, *Revelation 17–22*, 1151; Block, *Book of Ezekiel: Chapters 25–48*, 514; Tuell, *Ezekiel*, 284.

93. Gundry, "New Jerusalem," 262.

94. Deutsch, "Transformation of Symbols," 122.

95. Spatafora, *From the "Temple of God*," 29.

96. Palmer, "Imagining Space in Revelation," 42. Cf. Cook, "Ezekiel's God Incarnate!," 147; Liss, "Describe the Temple," 135; Rissi, *Future of the World*, 56.

97. Bauckham, *Theology of the Book*, 132–33; Beale, *Book of Revelation*, 1065; Ford, *Revelation*, 339; Mathewson, *New Heaven*, 95–100; Thomas and Macchia, *Revelation*, 374.

Such mountains were too high to climb; thus, gods lived there. Instead, heaven comes down."[98]

The presence of the divine upon the mountain is closely related to the importance of the temple.[99] As the place where heaven meets earth, the temple is "the locus of divine-human encounter" and the place where new life and meaning can be found[100]:

> It is not at all surprising that the holy mountain should be the place where the new age becomes visible. It is the site of creation where forces hostile to order were quelled. Though chaotic forces could gain the upper hand for a time, people believed that the high gods of order and fertility would impose order once again. Implicit in the concept of creation was the return to the original state of creation.[101]

The holy mountain is the site where the presence of the divine ushers in a new age of order and peace. However, in John's vision, the abode of God has descended to the earth.

As observed in the previous chapter, the idea of a heavenly Jerusalem that would appear in the eschaton is fairly common in apocalyptic Jewish literature.[102] That John clearly references Ezekiel's temple throughout the vision may indicate that he envisions Ezekiel's as the heavenly temple that finally is descending to the earth.

To conclude, the passages under consideration bear both lexical and thematic connections. Further, the shared language in Ezekiel 40:1–2 and Revelation 21:10 comes within a shared context, with both serving as an introduction to the eschatological vision of the new Jerusalem. Thus, the reference to Ezekiel in Revelation 21:10 can be regarded as a clear allusion. However, Revelation 21:2 shared only one parallel lexeme with

98. Stevens, *Revelation*, 527–28. Cf. Bar 5:7–9, in which the author indicated that every mountain will be made low so Israel can dwell securely with God. Cf. Sim, *Das himmlische Jerusalem*, 96; Vogelgesang, "Interpretation of Ezekiel," 86.

99. Levenson, *Theology of the Program*, 10.

100. Levenson, *Theology of the Program*, 17. Cf. Bittell, "Hittite Temples and High Places," 63–72; Clifford, *Cosmic Mountain in Canaan*, 131–60; Eliade, *Myth of the Eternal Return*, 12; Tuell, "Temple Vision of Ezekiel 40–48," 102.

101. Clifford, "Temple and the Holy Mountain," 107–24.

102. See Exod 25:9, 40; 27:8; 4 Ezra 7:26; 10:25–28, 54; 13:36; 2 Bar. 4:2–6; LAB 19:13; 4QFlor I, 3–6; 4QD III, 19–IV, 5, and possibly 1 En. 18, 24–26; 90:20–29; Jub. 1:17–29; 4QNJ; although John's city *descending* seems to be unique. Cf. Aune, *Revelation 17–22*, 1121; Beasley-Murray, *Book of Revelation*, 309–10; Sweet, *Revelation*, 303.

Ezekiel 40:1–2, and the contexts were dissimilar. Thus, Revelation 21:2 bears only a possible allusion to Ezekiel.

As for contextual function, the idea of a holy mountain is a recurring theme throughout the OT and Second Temple Jewish literature. In the OT, the mountain is typically the place where God resides, and where his presence can be sought.[103] Authors of apocalyptic literature further developed the theme to portray the mountain as the place where heaven and earth meet, and the location from whence eschatological blessings spread to the rest of creation.[104] John's usage of the concept builds upon such imagery, which is reflected in Ezekiel as well, to describe the union of the heavenly and earthly realms. The allusion can be classified therefore as a thematic use.

Closely related is the concept of the holy city. The restoration of Jerusalem was an expectation frequently articulated by the OT prophets. Viewed against the broader context of the OT, John's imagery of the restored city could be a thematic use. However, John drew upon prophetic expectations—those of Ezekiel in particular—to present his new Jerusalem as the culmination and fulfillment of such hopes.

In the Spirit (Rev 21:10; 40:1–2; 43:5)

In addition to the mountain and city imagery, a rapture in the Spirit takes place in Ezekiel 40:1–2 and Revelation 21:10. In Revelation 21:10, John appears to have drawn on a cluster of similar terms from Ezekiel 40:1, 43:5, and 11:1, 5, 24, with Ezekiel 11:24 being one of only two usages of the exact phrase ἐν πνεύματι in Ezekiel.[105]

Bauckham offered several possible options for interpreting ἐν πνεύματι. "In early Christian literature the phrase ἐν πνεύματι commonly means 'in the Spirit's control,' with various connotations. Frequently, it denotes temporary experience of the Spirit's power in prophetic speech or revelation."[106] Additionally, ἐν πνεύματι may describe the author's narrative of a visionary experience in which the Spirit is the agent of the vision,

---

103. Exod 19:3–24; 24:1–15; 34:2–4; Deut 10:1; Ps 24:3; Isa 2:3; Jer 31:6; Mic 4:2.

104. T. Levi 2:5–6; 1 En. 18:6–10; 24–26; 4 Ezra 13:36; LAB 12:8–9; 3 Bar. 10:2S; Apoc. Ab. 9:8.

105. Cf. Ezek 37:1.

106. Bauckham, *Climax of Prophecy*, 150–51.

taking over the faculties of the human author.[107] However, such was not John's experience. He remained a free agent throughout his visions.[108]

In Revelation 21:10, the phrase ἐν πνεύματι refers to transportation by the Spirit.[109] Similarly, Ezekiel is transported by the Spirit in Ezekiel 11:1, 11:2, 37:1, and 43:5. In Ezekiel 40:1–2, however, Ezekiel is transported by the χεὶρ κυρίου, "hand of God." Found at key points throughout Ezekiel, the hand of the Lord links the introductory visions (Ezek 1:3; 3:22), the vision of abomination in the temple and God's departure (Ezek 8:1), the vision of national resurrection (Ezek 37:1), and the final vision of God's return (Ezek 40:2).[110] In each case, the hand of the Lord implies "concrete manifestations of a physical or psycho-physical nature."[111] Additionally, the hand of the Lord is connected closely with transportation in the Spirit in Ezekiel 37:1: Καὶ ἐγένετο ἐπ᾽ ἐμὲ χεὶρ κυρίου, καὶ ἐξήγαγέν με ἐν πνεύματι κύριος.[112] Thus, the hand of the Lord, much like the Spirit, seems to designate a physiopneumatic visionary experience.

Bauckham observed that pneumatic transportation is not attested widely.[113] Yet most of the passages that describe a physical movement by the Spirit "copy the language of Ezekiel."[114] Thus, John's experience seems to mirror that of Ezekiel.[115] Boxall went further to suggest that "John is in effect re-enacting Ezekiel's vision."[116]

---

107. See 1 En. 91:1; Jub. 25:14; 31:12; LAB 32:14; 4 Ezra 14:22.

108. Bauckham, *Climax of Prophecy*, 151–52; Spatafora, *From the "Temple of God*," 226.

109. Cf. Rev 4:2 and 17:3 for similar usage. Ἐν πνεύματι is used also in Revelation 1:10, but not in the sense of being transported (Barr, "Apocalypse as a Symbolic Transformation," 39–50; Bauckham, *Climax of Prophecy*, 154–55).

110. Χεὶρ κυρίου is used similarly in Ezekiel 33:22 to denote a prophetic vision, although the actual vision never is recounted (Kasher, "Anthropomorphism, Holiness and Cult," 202–3).

111. Roberts, "Hand of Yahweh," 251.

112. "And the hand of the Lord was upon me, and he brought me in the Spirit of the Lord" (Ezek 37:1a).

113. See 2 Bar 6:3; 1 En. 70:2; Acts 8:39–40; 1 Kgs 18:12; 2 Kgs 2:16.

114. Bauckham, *Climax of Prophecy*, 157.

115. Aune, *Revelation 17–22*, 934; Bauckham, *Climax of Prophecy*, 156–57; Beale, *Book of Revelation*, 1065; Mathewson, *New Heaven*, 96–97; Moyise, *Old Testament in the Book*, 79; Osborne, *Revelation*, 748; Rissi, *Future of the World*, 60; Stevens, *Revelation*, 531; Sweet, *Revelation*, 303; Thomas and Macchia, *Revelation*, 374.

116. Boxall, "Exile, Prophet, Visionary," 157. A further indication that John's use of ἐν πνεύματι mirrors that of Ezekiel can be found in Revlation 4:2, where John, "in the spirit," receives a vision of the heavenly *merkabah*, much as in Ezekiel 1.

Indeed, the repeated raptures by the Spirit underscore the prophetic authority of both Ezekiel and John.[117] "John's claim to prophetic inspiration could also be seen as one of the reasons why he was able to use the Scriptures with such great freedom and creativity"[118] John experienced raptures in the Spirit like Ezekiel and Isaiah, and drew on their language to describe his own visions.[119] Thus, John presented himself as an heir to prophetic traditions.

Along similar lines, both Ezekiel and John saw what was to happen in the future. The prophets saw a similar final reality, in which God's presence would come to dwell permanently with his people.[120] Yet John's vision serves to interpret Ezekiel's.[121]

Each of the verses dealing with Ezekiel's rapture is also proximate to the movement of God's presence. In Ezekiel 11, the prophet depicted the departure of God's presence from the Jerusalem temple, whereas in Ezekiel 37, 40, and 43, he described God's return. Therefore, the parallel language of rapture in the Spirit may be an intentional literary device to foreshadow the return of God to his people. Although God's presence never departs in Revelation, neither does the Lord fully dwell with his people until the new Jerusalem descends in Revelation 21:10.

To conclude, the Greek parallels are inexact, but the verses bear strong conceptual and lexical affinities. Although Revelation 21:10 exhibits John's condensing tendencies, the verse almost could be considered a paraphrase of Ezekiel 40:1–2, as many of the same terms are used in the same manner. However, the conflation of terms from Ezekiel 43 seems to indicate that John drew on more than one passage. Thus, the reference can be regarded as a clear allusion to both Ezekiel 40:1–2 and Ezekiel 43:5. John seemed to be implying that he intended his vision to be interpreted in the light of Ezekiel 40–48 in its entirety.[122]

The three possible reference types here are literary prototype, thematic use, and analogical use. Viewed in isolation, the reference to rapture in the Spirit might be classified as an analogical use. However, in the broader context of the movement of the Spirit, the Ezekiel passages

---

117. Beale, *Book of Revelation*, 1065; Boxall, "Exile, Prophet, Visionary," 156–57; Mathewson, *New Heaven*, 98, 221.

118. Decock, "Scriptures in the Book," 392.

119. Decock, "Scriptures in the Book," 377. Mathewson, *New Heaven*, 122.

120. Briggs, *Jewish Temple Imagery*, 105.

121. Beale, *Book of Revelation*, 1065.

122. Mathewson, *New Heaven*, 98; Stevens, *Revelation*, 531n8.

appear to serve as a pattern through which the future eschatological fulfillment is conveyed. Both prophets convey a similar reality, and John drew upon Ezekiel's language to do so.[123] Therefore, the usage here would be classified as a literary prototype.

God's Tabernacling Presence
(Rev 21:3, 11, 23; Ezek 43:4–9; 44:4)

The next allusion can be found in Revelation 21:3, 21:11, and Ezekiel 43:7 and 43:9. The eschatological temple will be the site from which God will dwell among his people.[124] As discussed above, the dwelling is not a physical location but a restored relationship:

> Ἰδοὺ ἡ σκηνὴ τοῦ θεοῦ μετὰ τῶν ἀνθρώπων, καὶ σκηνώσει μετ᾽ αὐτῶν, καὶ αὐτοὶ λαοὶ αὐτοῦ ἔσονται, καὶ αὐτὸς ὁ θεὸς μετ᾽ αὐτῶν ἔσται [αὐτῶν θεός]. (Rev 21:3b)[125]

> καὶ κατασκηνώσω ἐν μέσῳ αὐτῶν τὸν αἰῶνα. (Ezek 43:9b)[126]

Unfortunately, determining the original Greek text of Revelation 21:3 is difficult. The final two words of the verse may have been omitted by some copyists due to redundancy.[127] Sweet suggested that if the phrase is original, "John may have meant 'and God-with-them (=Immanuel) himself will be their God.'"[128] If Sweet is correct, then John may be foreshadowing his christological focus, which will not be expressed fully until Revelation 21:22.

Either way, both verbal parallels and conceptual affinities can be identified in Revelation 21:3 and Ezekiel 43:9. The root σκηνόω is utilized in both passages, along with the idea of God dwelling μετ᾽ αὐτῶν, "with them" (Rev 21:3), or ἐν μέσῳ αὐτῶν, "in their midst" (Ezek 43:9).[129] The

---

123. Beale, *Book of Revelation*, 1065.

124. Cf. Ezek 37:26–28; Exod 29:45; Lev 26:11–12; Jub. 1:17. Beale, *Book of Revelation*, 1046.

125. "And I heard a great voice from the throne saying, "Behold, the dwelling of God with men, and he will dwell with them, and they will be his people, and God himself will be [their God] with them" (Rev 21:3b).

126. "And I will dwell in the midst of them forever" (Ezek 43:9b).

127. Metzger, *Textual Commentary*, 688–89.

128. Sweet, *Revelation*, 298. Cf. Thomas and Macchia, *Revelation*, 366; Isa 7:14; 8:8, 10.

129. John used versions of σκηνόω (Rev 7:15; 12:12; 13:6; 15:5; 21:3), while Ezekiel

two verses diverge in that John expressed the promise in the third person, while God himself speaks in Ezekiel.

In Ezekiel 37:26b–27, the prophet offered a verbal parallel with a slightly expanded lexical linkage:

> Καὶ θήσω τὰ ἅγιά μου ἐν μέσῳ αὐτῶν εἰς τὸν αἰῶνα. καὶ ἔσται ἡ κατασκήνωσίς μου ἐν αὐτοῖς, καὶ ἔσομαι αὐτοῖς θεός, καὶ αὐτοί μου ἔσονται λαός.[130]

In addition to the σκηνόω/κατασκηνόω parallel, in Ezekiel 37:27, God promises that αὐτοί μου ἔσονται λαός, "they will be my people," and in Revelation 21:3, John similarly expresses that αὐτοὶ λαοὶ αὐτοῦ ἔσονται, "they will be his people." The similar phraseology and eschatology could, in isolation, seem to indicate that John had Ezekiel 37 and 43 in mind.[131] However, the hope of God dwelling with his people is ubiquitous throughout the OT, especially in the prophetic corpus.[132] Ezekiel 37 and 43 are certainly not the only texts from which John could have drawn.

One such verse upon which John may have drawn is Zechariah 2:11. The verse reads, "Many nations will join themselves to the Lord on that day; and they will become my people. Then I will dwell in your midst, and you will know that the Lord of hosts has sent me to you" (Zech 2:11). Here, Zechariah provided an explicit portrayal of all nations dwelling with God, as did John in Revelation 21–22. Ezekiel's stance on the nations is less clear. Debate exists as to whether the prophet restricted his vision to Israel or extended eschatological restoration to the nations.[133] Yet a mediating position is possible. Ezekiel's perspective seems to be somewhere between a strictly universalistic or a completely inclusive outlook. For Ezekiel, the pathway to sharing in eschatological blessings was through God's covenant with Israel.[134] However, NT believers under-

---

preferred κατασκηνόω (Ezek 25:4; 37:27; 43:7, 9).

130. "And I will place my sanctuary in their midst forever. And my tabernacle will be among them, and I will be their God, and they will be my people" (Ezek 37:26b–27).

131. According to Mathewson, Revelation 21:3 is inspired primarily by Ezekiel 37:26b–27, but John has been influenced by other sources as well (*New Heaven*, 51). Cf. Decock, "Scriptures in the Book," 380–81.

132. See, for example, Lev 26:11–12; Jer 30:22; 31:1, 33; 32:38; Zech 2:10–11; 8:3, 8.

133. For a nationalistic perspective see Allen, *Ezekiel 20–48*, 194–95; Decock, "Scriptures in the Book," 385; Joyce, *Ezekiel*, 212; Pfisterer Darr, "Wall around Paradise," 271–79; Vogelgesang, "Interpretation of Ezekiel," 385. For a universalistic perspective see Eichrodt, *Ezekiel*, 415; Gundry, "New Jerusalem," 257.

134. Sweet, *Revelation*, 308.

stand that everyone who is sanctified through the Messiah is included in God's salvific promises.[135]

A comparison of the Greek text may support the conjecture that John expanded upon Ezekiel's more particularistic vision. In Revelation 21:3, the term λαοὶ, "people," is plural, whereas the λαός of Ezekiel 37:27 is singular.[136] Mathewson concluded that, in Revelation, "Inclusion in the covenant people of God is no longer nationalistically centered, but is extended to include all peoples of the world."[137] Correspondingly, in Revelation, worship of God is no longer restricted to a physical temple in the land of Israel.[138]

Closely related to God's tabernacling presence is his δόξα, or "glory." In Revelation 21:11, John indicated that the glory of God resides in the new Jerusalem. In verse 23, John elaborated:

καὶ ἡ πόλις οὐ χρείαν ἔχει τοῦ ἡλίου οὐδὲ τῆς σελήνης ἵνα φαίνωσιν αὐτῇ, ἡ γὰρ δόξα τοῦ θεοῦ ἐφώτισεν αὐτήν, καὶ ὁ λύχνος αὐτῆς τὸ ἀρνίον.[139]

Glory in the OT is associated commonly with God's presence in the sanctuary, as well as eschatological expectations.[140] As the new Jerusalem can be considered a type of temple, John's description of God's glory filling the city is roughly equivalent to Ezekiel's proclamation that the glory of the Lord filled the temple:[141]

---

135. Beale, *Book of Revelation*, 1047.

136. Some manuscripts read λαός instead of λαοὶ. Metzger gave λαοὶ a B rating, noting that the plural has "slightly superior manuscript evidence" (Metzger, *Textual Commentary*, 688).

137. Mathewson, *New Heaven*, 52. Cf. Aune, *Revelation 17–22*, 1123; Moyise, *Old Testament in the Book*, 81–82; Sweet, *Revelation*, 298; Swete, *Apocalypse of St. John*, 278; Thomas and Macchia, *Revelation*, 366; Vogelgesang, "Interpretation of Ezekiel," 4; Witherington, *Revelation*, 252.

138. Beale, *Book of Revelation*, 1047; Deutsch, "Transformation of Symbols," 120.

139. "And the city had no need of the sun or the moon to shine in it. For the glory of God illuminates it, and its lamp is the lamb" (Rev 21:23).

140. God's presence in sanctuary: Exod 40:34–35; Lev 9:23–24; 1 Kgs 8:10–11; Pss 26:8; 63:2; eschatological expectations: Pss 96:3–9; 102:16; Isa 6:3; 24:23; 35:2; 40:5; 43:7; 58:8; 66:18–19; Ezek 39:21; 43:1–5; 44:4; Hab 2:14; Hag 2:7; Zech 2:5. Cf. Mathewson, *New Heaven*, 162.

141. Vogelgesang, "Interpretation of Ezekiel," 86–87.

καὶ δόξα κυρίου εἰσῆλθεν εἰς τὸν οἶκον κατὰ τὴν ὁδὸν τῆς πύλης τῆς βλεπούσης κατὰ ἀνατολάς . . . Καὶ ἰδοὺ πλήρης δόξης κυρίου ὁ οἶκος. (Ezek 43:4–5)[142]

Additionally, both Ezekiel and John link the glory to God's personal presence.[143] Glory is a theophanic term that implies the physical substance of God himself, although glory "is never described in terms of human imagery."[144] Rimmon Kasher contended, "There is perhaps no other biblical prophet whose God is so corporeal as Ezekiel," which accords well with the idea of God incarnate (i.e., Jesus Christ) in Revelation 21–22.[145]

Thus, in Revelation 21:11, John seemed to be expanding upon Revelation 21:3 to describe the fulfillment of the prophetic promise that God would dwell among his people. "The presence of light and glory in the final visionary drama of Revelation (21.11, 23) functions as a climax to all these previous references, as God's luminous glory now comes down to fill the new creation and new Jerusalem."[146] No longer is a tabernacle or temple needed because God's glory can be encountered in the flesh.[147]

Just as the dwelling of God with his people in Revelation 21–22 is the climax of John's vision, so also is Ezekiel 43:2–5 the climax of Ezekiel's. In Ezekiel 43:2–5, the glory of the Lord returns to the temple. Ezekiel revealed that God's luminous presence is not restricted to Jerusalem, as the whole earth shines with the radiance of God's glory (Ezek 43:2). Correspondingly, in Ezekiel 48:35, the prophet indicated that God's presence inhabits the entire city: "And the name of the city from that day will be 'the Lord is there'" (Ezek 48:35).[148] Thus, in Ezekiel, just as in Revelation, God's presence returns to dwell with his people.

142. "And the glory of the Lord entered into the house by the way of the gate looking eastward . . . And behold, the glory of the Lord filled the house" (Ezek 43:4, 5). The phrase καὶ ἰδοὺ πλήρης δόξης ὁ οἶκος κυρίου is found also in Ezekiel 44:4.

143. Rev 15:8; 21:11, 23; Ezek 1:28; 3:23; 8:4; 9:3; 10:4, 18–19; 11:22–23; 39:21; 43:2, 4–5; 44:4. Most uses of δόξα in Revelation are in reference to glory being given to God: Rev 1:6; 4:9, 11; 5:12–13; 7:12; 11:13; 14:7; 16:9; 19:7. Beale, *Book of Revelation*, 1066; Mounce, *Book of Revelation*, 390.

144. Kasher, "Anthropomorphism, Holiness and Cult," 203.

145. Kasher, "Anthropomorphism, Holiness and Cult," 192.

146. Mathewson, *New Heaven*, 163.

147. Spatafora, *From the "Temple of God,"* 115.

148. Eichrodt, *Ezekiel*, 593; Mathewson, *New Heaven*, 114.

Although parallels with Ezekiel are present in Revelation 21:23, John drew more overtly on Isaiah 60:19. Both texts indicate that God's people will have no need for the sun or moon because the Lord himself will provide light in the eschaton.[149] John added to his Isaian source material with the illumination from a λύχνος, or "lamp":

> The introduction of a 'lamp' at this point is perhaps significant due to the important role the lamp played in the Old Testament sanctuary and temple to light the holy of holies. Its presence here to depict the light given by the Lamb coheres with the depiction of the city as a holy of holies (21.16) and with the fact that the Lamb replaces the temple (21.22), accentuating the nature of the city as God's dwelling place.[150]

In addition to Isaiah, Zechariah may have been a source upon which John drew for his depiction of God's glory. In Zechariah 2:1–5, an angelic figure measures the walls of Jerusalem, which house the glory of God. Then in Zechariah 14:6–8, the luminaries disappear and living water flows from Jerusalem. A number of parallels to Revelation 21:23 are present, along with parallels to Revelation 21:15–16 and Revelation 22:1–2. The similarity in imagery indicates that Zechariah 2 and Zechariah 14 might have been in John's mind.[151] Alternately, the prophecies in Zechariah may be based upon Ezekiel and Isaiah, in which case both Revelation and Zechariah were influenced by the same sources.[152] Either way, the confluence of Ezekielian themes in the surrounding verses implies that John had Ezekiel in mind, even if he also drew upon imagery from Isaiah and Zechariah.[153]

To conclude, the references to God's dwelling and God's glory represent a possible allusion. Parallel language was identified; yet the lexemes were not an exact match, and neither were they particularly distinctive. The attestation of other possible source material further prohibits the identification of a clear allusion to Ezekiel. Nonetheless, the idea of the spreading of God's glory in Ezekiel is close enough to John's portrayal of

149. Beale, *Book of Revelation*, 1094; Mathewson, *New Heaven*, 159; Smalley, *Revelation to John*, 557; Sweet, *Revelation*, 309; Thomas and Macchia, *Revelation*, 383.

150. Mathewson, *New Heaven*, 159. For the lamp in the tabernacle, see Exod 25:37; 27:20; 30:7–8; in the temple, 1 Chr 28:15; 2 Chr 4:20–21; 13:11; 29:7. In each case, the LXX uses λύχνος.

151. Mathewson, *New Heaven*, 161.

152. Tuell, *Ezekiel*, 284; Wevers, *Ezekiel*, 37–38.

153. Beale, *Book of Revelation*, 1094; Sweet, *Revelation*, 309.

the glory of God filling the city, that Ezekiel cannot be eliminated as one of John's sources.

The contextual function of John's use of Ezekiel and other OT passages in regard to the tabernacling presence and glory of God in Revelation 21:3 could be classified as a literary prototype, a thematic use, or a fulfillment use. As a literary prototype, both John and Ezekiel described a similar eventuality, in which God's presence comes to dwell among his people and his luminous glory fills all of creation. Yet, God's presence with his people is a common OT expectation, which renders the intertext a thematic use. At the same time, John depicted the ultimate fulfillment of such hopes. As such, the reference is most likely a fulfillment usage.

The Walls (Rev 21:12–21; Ezek 40:5–6)

The presence of walls and gates in the new Jerusalem evokes Ezekiel 28:13, 40:5, and 42:20. However, most architectural details from Ezekiel are omitted, as "the presentation of the structures of the New Jerusalem is radically abridged, streamlined, and simplified."[154]

In Revelation 21:12, John presented a large wall with twelve gates, whereas Ezekiel provided copious dimensions in Ezekiel 40:5 and beyond:

Ἔχουσα τεῖχος μέγα καὶ ὑψηλόν, ἔχουσα πυλῶνας δώδεκα καὶ ἐπὶ τοῖς πυλῶσιν ἀγγέλους δώδεκα καὶ ὀνόματα ἐπιγεγραμμένα, ἅ ἐστιν τὰ ὀνόματα τῶν δώδεκα φυλῶν υἱῶν Ἰσραήλ. (Rev 21:12)[155]

Καὶ ἰδοὺ περίβολος ἔξωθεν τοῦ οἴκου κύκλῳ, καὶ ἐν τῇ χειρὶ τοῦ ἀνδρὸς κάλαμος, τὸ μέτρον πηχῶν ἓξ ἐν πήχει καὶ παλαιστῆς, καὶ διεμέτρησεν τὸ προτείχισμα, πλάτος ἴσον τῷ καλάμῳ καὶ τὸ ὕψος αὐτοῦ ἴσον τῷ καλάμῳ. (Ezek 40:5)[156]

154. Vogelgesang, "Interpretation of Ezekiel," 89.

155. "It had a great and high wall, having twelve gates, and upon the gates twelve angels, and names were written on them, which are the names of the twelve tribes of the sons of Israel" (Rev 21:12).

156. "And behold, a wall around the house on the outside, and in the hand of the man a reed, the measurement of it six cubits by a cubit and a handbreadth, and he measured the outer wall, and the width was equal to the reed, and the height of it was equal to the reed" (Ezek 40:5).

John described a great and high wall—τεῖχος μέγα καὶ ὑψηλόν.[157] The τεῖχος is a strong outer wall that typically surrounded a city.[158] Eze-kiel, however, used two different terms for his wall: περίβολος and προτείχισμα, from the Hebrew חוֹמָה and בִּנְיָן, respectively. Like the τεῖχος, the περίβολος /חוֹמָה also refers to a strong outer wall.[159]

Προτείχισμα, from the root τεῖχος, is a bit more difficult to decipher. The term is not attested in the NT and is used only six times in the LXX outside of Ezekiel. The most common meaning seems to be "rampart," as found in 2 Samuel 20:15, 2 Kings 21:23, and Lamentations 2:8. In 2 Chronicles 32:5, the προτείχισμα is an outer city wall, and in Song of Songs 2:14, a steep pathway or cliff. Jeremiah 52:7 is particularly helpful in that the author used τεῖχος and προτειχίσματος in the same verse, seeming to refer to the same structure.[160] Similarly, in Ezekiel 40:5, προτείχισμα is used synonymously with περίβολος.[161] Thus, the determination can be made that τεῖχος, περίβολος, and προτείχισμα are roughly equivalent terms. In Revelation 21:12–13, Ezekiel 40:5–6 and 48:31–34, the authors described a strong outer wall of the city-temple.

In proximity to the wall is an angel with a measuring reed (Ezek 40:3, 5–16; Rev 21:15). Similar language can be found in Zechariah 2:1–5. However, the scene in Zechariah is different from those of Ezekiel and Revelation. Although an angelic figure with a measuring rod is pres-ent, Zechariah is informed that Jerusalem is without walls (Zech 2:4).[162]

157. Cf. Rev 21:15, 17–19.

158. L&N § 7.61.

159. HALOT 298; LSJ 1370.

160. The relevant portion in the Greek reads ἀνὰ μέσον τοῦ τείχους καὶ τοῦ προτειχίσματος, "between the wall and the rampart." However, ramparts typically would abut the city wall, so the sense is difficult to determine. The Hebrew text lends clarity, as the verse reads בֵּין־הַחֹמֹתַיִם (between the two walls), giving no indication that two different structures are in mind.

161. Ezekiel 42:20 is troublesome in that the author seemed to use προτείχισμα in a different manner than other attestations. In the Masoretic Text (MT), Ezekiel measures the wall (חוֹמָה) around the temple, which surrounds the complex לְהַבְדִּיל בֵּין הַקֹּדֶשׁ לְחֹל, "to divide between the holy and profane." The LXX rendering is somewhat different in that the outer wall (περίβολον) creates a separation between the holy space and profane space, rendered προτειχίσματος. The same designation is made between holy and profane in Ezekiel 48:15. Thus, προτειχίσματος seems to be translated as "profane space" in both Ezekiel 42:20 and 48:15. However, Block noted that the LXX rendering may be a mistranslation, in which the translator mistook חֹל, "profane," for חֵיל, "outer wall" (Block, Book of Ezekiel: Chapters 25–48, 730).

162. In the MT, the area is פְּרָזוֹת, "open country" (Zech 2:8). The LXX author did

Then in Zechariah 2:5, the Lord announces that he will be a wall (τεῖχος) of fire around the city (Zech 2:5). No such imagery is present in Revelation or Ezekiel. Therefore, the wall imagery of Revelation does not seem to hearken from Zechariah.

The walls (τεῖχος) of Jeruaslem are mentioned frequently in Isaiah also, but the context is different.[163] Isaiah 26:1–2 comes closest in the expectation for an eschatological city with walls, into which righteous nations enter. That other Isaianic references can be identified throughout Revelation 21 indicates that Isaiah 26 may be in the background here. Further, John used the same term for "wall" as does Isaiah.

Nonetheless, in both Revelation and Ezekiel, the walls serve a similar function. The walls in Ezekiel "delimit the boundary between the clean and unclean, between the holy and the common."[164] Similarly, in Revelation 21:8 and 21:27, John proclaimed that nothing unclean may enter the city, and that everything outside is part of the lake of fire.[165] Both authors exhibited a concern for the holiness of God's people. Although Ezekiel utilized various architectural structures and cultic regulations to safeguard the city, John's city is protected by a single wall. Nonetheless, the walls of both cities protect the sanctity of the space inside.[166]

Along such lines, the walls delimit the holy from that which is unholy. Erin Palmer explained that for space to be sacred, something profane also must be present to define the nature of the sacred. "The boundary between the sacred and the profane is imperative in the discussion of the relationship between the two. It can be articulated through interaction with the divine, through architectural delineation, or both."[167] Thus, the dividing wall is a literary device John used to articulate the difference between the true church and people who reject God.

---

not mention a wall or even the lack of a wall.

163. See Isa 2:15; 22:10–11; 26:1; 36:11–12; 49:16; 60:10, 18; 62:6.

164. Vogelgesang, "Interpretation of Ezekiel," 78. Cf. Ezek 42:20; 43:8; 44:1–22. According to Vogelgesang, the function of the walls of John's new Jerusalem is in stark contrast to the walls around Ezekiel's temple. Ezekiel's walls keep people out, while John's walls draw people in.

165. Rissi, *Future of the World*, 67–68. Vogelgesang, "Interpretation of Ezekiel," 103.

166. Boyle, "Holiness has a Shape," 5–6, 16; Mathewson, *New Heaven*, 111; Sweet, *Revelation*, 310.

167. Palmer, "Imagining Space in Revelation," 38.

Correspondingly, literary spaces can be a powerful tool to convey ideas.

> While imagined spaces draw upon known experiences of space and are understood through the language of spatial theory, they are separate from physical spaces. Imagined space is mentally conceived space, *but space that is not meant to be physically created* ... Still, authors who employ imagined space, including John and other visionaries such as the prophet Ezekiel, draw upon commonly understood and experienced spaces as they communicate very specific political and theological goals to their audiences.[168]

The idea of sacred space was utilized by John, Ezekiel, Isaiah, and Zechariah to communicate their theology. Whereas Zechariah seemed to use the imagery of a wall to convey God's protection, the other three prophets described God's glory, which renders evil obsolete. Yet further discussion is necessary to articulate precisely how John utilized his OT sources in regard to the wall.

Materials of the Wall

In Revelation 21:17–19, John described the construction materials of the wall. After the angelic guide takes John to see the bride, which turns out to be the holy city, the first structure described is the wall. Beale explained, "The city itself continues to be described in association with the wall because its figurative meaning is ultimately similar to the wall and its parts."[169] The figurative meaning is that God's presence dwells fully with his people inside the city.

The wall is made of jasper (Rev 21:11, 18), which John has identified already with the glory of God in Revelation 4:3. Further, the valuable construction materials of the city in Revelation 21:18–21 point to a dwelling fit for divinity and at the same time reflect God's luminescence.[170] David Aune asserted, "Since jasper is normally an opaque stone, the description of it being like crystal underlies its purity and value."[171] Thus, in addition

---

168. Palmer, "Imagining Space in Revelation," 38–39; emphasis hers.

169. Beale, *Book of Revelation*, 1079. Cf. Fekkes, "Bride has Prepared Herself," 269.

170. Beale, *Book of Revelation*, 1078–80, 1089–90.

171. Aune, *Revelation 17–22*, 1154. Cf. Boring, *Revelation*, 216; du Rand, "New Jerusalem as Pinnacle," 295; Stevens, *Revelation*, 532; Thomas and Macchia, *Revelation*,

to delimiting a sacred space where God dwells with his people, the wall also proclaims God's glory.

However, that God's glory shines from the city does not imply an open invitation to all who are outside. Both Vogelgesang and Rissi argued for a universalist interpretation of John's new Jerusalem. Vogelgesang contended, "The wall does not function by protecting the city from the unclean by shutting them out . . . but by announcing the glory of God to all who are yet outside."[172] Vogelgesang went on to postulate that those who have been consigned to the lake of fire continually stream into the new Jerusalem.[173] The current research does not adhere to such a view, as will be discussed in the section on the nations below.

Returning to the topic of the wall, John noted that the foundations are composed of a variety of precious stones (Rev 21:18–21). Most scholars agree that the stones are an allusion to Isaiah 54:11–12.[174] Isaiah 54:11–12 is part of a larger pericope that is heavy with nuptual imagery, "suggesting that the previous stones in vv. 11–12 function as part of this imagery by portraying the bride's adornment (Rev. 21.2)."[175] Additionally, the repetition of κοσμέω in 21:19 from 21:2 further ties the stones to nuptial imagery and thus Isaiah 54:11–12.[176]

Ezekiel 28:13 is also one of John's sources in Revelation 21:19.[177] In Ezekiel 28:13, the prophet provided a list of precious stones similar to that which is found in Revelation. In particular, the introduction to John's

375; Witherington, *Revelation*, 271.

172. Vogelgesang, "Interpretation of Ezekiel," 98.

173. Vogelgesang, "Interpretation of Ezekiel," 104–8. Cf. Rissi, *Future of the World*, 71–78. For a rebuttal, see Mathewson, *New Heaven*, 142.

174. Beale, *Book of Revelation*, 1069; Boxall, *Revelation*, 305; Mathewson, *New Heaven*, 127; Mathewson, "Note on the Foundation Stones," 487–98; Morris, *Book of Revelation*, 245; Stevens, *Revelation*, 536; Thomas and Macchia, *Revelation*, 381. Alternately, Caird suggested that the jewels were arranged in the reverse order of the zodiac as a polemic against pagan religion. Caird, *Revelation of Saint John*, 276–77. Glasson argued against the theory definitively. Glasson, "Order of Jewels in Revelation 21:19–20," 95–100.

175. Mathewson, *New Heaven*, 127. Cf. Fekkes, "Bride has Prepared Herself," 269.

176. Mathewson, *New Heaven*, 140.

177. Aune, *Revelation 17–22*, 1164; Fekkes, "Bride has Prepared Herself," 277; Mathewson, *New Heaven*, 130; du Rand, "New Jerusalem as Pinnacle," 285; Swete, *Apocalypse of St. John*, 291; Thomas and Macchia, *Revelation*, 381; Witherington, *Revelation*, 271.

list closely follows Ezekiel's.[178] With the allusion to Ezekiel 28:13, John contrasted the exploitative use of wealth in Babylon with the use of the stones to reflect God's glory. At the same time he contrasted the beauty of the spotless bride with the garish excess of the whore of Babylon.[179]

The precious stones in Ezekiel 28 and Revelation 21 also recall the breastplate of the high priest in Exodus 28:15–21 and 39:10–14[180]:

> To the extent that Ezek. 28.13 associates the precious stones with priesthood and paradise, its inclusion here in Rev 21.19 lends consistency to the vision, anticipating the use of stones from the high priest's breastplate from Exod 28.17–20, and providing coherence with the identification of the new Jerusalem as paradise where its inhabitants function as priests and kings (cf. 22.1–5).[181]

Thus, the jewels are an indication of the priestly nature of the Messiah and his church. As such they provide another indication of the city's sanctity and the status of the city as a temple.[182]

Dimensions of the Wall

The function of the walls in both Ezekiel and Revelation is related to their dimensions. Although Henry Swete suggested that the wall is present as a ubiquitous feature of ancient cities, John gave far too much attention to the wall for the structure to be included only as a standard city feature.[183] Most details in John's vision convey spiritual truths.

178. Παντὶ λίθῳ τιμίῳ κεκοσμημένοι, "being adorned with every kind of precious stone" (Rev 21:19); πᾶν λίθον χρηστὸν ἐνδέδεσαι, "you have covered yourself with every precious stone" (Ezek 28:13).

179. Mathewson, *New Heaven*, 131. Cf. Stevens, *Revelation*, 532; Thomas and Macchia, *Revelation*, 375; Witherington, *Revelation*, 271. To the contrary, Vogelgesang argued that the stones represent the redeemed wealth of Babylon (Vogelgesang, "Interpretation of Ezekiel," 97–100, 127).

180. Aune, *Revelation 17–22*, 1165; Fekkes, "Bride has Prepared Herself," 277; Mathewson, *New Heaven*, 132; Rissi, *Future of the World*, 72; Vogelgesang, "Interpretation of Ezekiel," 98–99.

181. Mathewson, *New Heaven*, 131.

182. Sweet, *Revelation*, 306. For further discussion of the precious stones see Beale, *Book of Revelation*, 1080–88; Mathewson, *New Heaven*, 127–49; Mathewson, "Note on the Foundation Stones," 487–98; Reader, "Twelve Jewels of Revelation 21:19–20," 433–57.

183. Swete, *Apocalypse of St. John*, 285. Mathewson and Rissi argued to the

However, disagreement over the dimensions of the wall have led to varying suggestions as to what John intended to convey. The crux of the problem is Revelation 21:17, in which the dimension of the wall is recorded as 144 cubits. The dimension cannot refer to length, as the length of the wall is determined by the size of the city.[184] However, whether 144 cubits describes the height or breadth of the wall is unclear.[185] If John described the height, then the size of the wall is shockingly small in comparison to the size of the city. Vogelgesang contended, "There is an outlandish disparity in a city 12,000 stadia long, broad and high, having a wall of only 144 cubits."[186] Such an incongruence serves to illustrate graphically that the city does not need protection.[187]

In Revelation 21:12, John indicated that the city has a "great and high wall." Thus, the 144 cubits most likely describes the thickness of the city's wall. As such, Stevens noted that the wall is "disproportionately thick" in comparison with other ancient city walls.[188] As such, the wall is an expression of God's power and a representation of the city's inviolability. At the same time, the purpose of the wall is clearly not protection since the gates never close (Rev 21:25; Isa 60:11).[189] Thus, just as jasper reflects the glory of God, the substantial breadth of the wall reflects the power of God.[190]

Accordingly, the dimensions of the wall are not meant to be taken literally.[191] The 144 cubits echoes the 144,000 of God's people in Revelation 7:4–9 and 14:1–3. The walls are the perfect size for the perfect

---

contrary; Mathewson, *New Heaven*, 110; Rissi, *Future of the World*, 67.

184. Swete, *Apocalypse of St. John*, 289.

185. Height: Mathewson, *New Heaven*, 110. Breadth: Aune, *Revelation 17–22*, 1162; Stevens, *Revelation*, 536. Beale contended the dimension given is likely the width, height, and length, as all three equal dimensions are provided in Ezekiel 40:5 and 42:20 (Beale, *Book of Revelation*, 1075–77).

186. Vogelgesang also noted that even if the dimension refers to breadth, the wall still would be exceptionally thin, as the height of the wall would be 1,500 miles (based on Rev 21:16) (Vogelgesang, "Interpretation of Ezekiel," 95–96). Cf. Morris, *Book of Revelation*, 244; Mounce, *Revelation*, 381.

187. Swete, *Apocalypse of St. John*, 289; Witherington, *Revelation*, 269–70.

188. Stevens, *Revelation*, 536.

189. Rissi, *Future of the World*, 67.

190. Palmer, "Imagining Space in Revelation," 44; Stevens, *Revelation*, 532; Vogelgesang, "Interpretation of Ezekiel," 90.

191. Mathewson, *New Heaven*, 110.

number of saints who will dwell in the city.[192] The wall also represents the inviolability of fellowship between God and his people.[193]

In sum, the walls and stones are pregnant with symbolism. The structures convey (1) the separation of the saints from the nonredeemed, (2) the holiness of the saints, (3) the hierocratic nature of the city's inhabitants, (4) the glory and power of God, and (5) the inviolability of the fellowship between God and his saints.

John conveyed such ideas through a complex mosaic of allusions. "The convergence of intertexts would convey the sense that, in the very foundations of the holy city of Jerusalem, a number of OT prophecies and ideas are fulfilled."[194] Allusions to Isaiah, Exodus, and Ezekiel are all likely. In Revelation 21:12–13, 27, John seems to have drawn upon Ezekiel 40:5 and 42:20. However, the verses bear little linguistic similarity. Even the terms used for *wall* are different. Nonetheless, both authors utilize the wall imagery in a similar manner. The walls delimit holy space from non-holy space. The glory of God dwells with his people inside the walls, and those who do not belong to the community of the saints remain outside. Thus, the allusion may be classified as probable.

John's use of allusions in Revelation 21:17–19 is more complex. References to Isaiah 54:11–12, Ezekiel 28:13, and Exodus 28:15–21 and 39:10–14 may be present. The jewels and nuptial imagery render the allusion to Isaiah highly likely. However, a nonsequential background reference to Ezekiel is probable as well. Ezekiel 28:13 and Revelation 21:19 bear similar phraseology in the introduction to the list of stones. Further, the allusion to the breastplate stones in Exodus may be filtered through Ezekiel 28. Either way, through the precious stones of Ezekiel 28 and Exodus 28, John emphasized the idea of the city as a holy place with priestly inhabitants. The contextual function therefore can be classified as a thematic use, as John allude more to a theme than any particular verse.[195]

192. Bauckham, *Climax of Prophecy*, 399; Beale, *Book of Revelation*, 1076; Smalley, *Revelation to John*, 552; Thomas and Macchia, *Revelation*, 379.

193. Beasley-Murray, *Book of Revelation*, 320.

194. Thomas and Macchia, *Revelation*, 381.

195. Beale, *John's Use*, 93.

The Gates (Rev 21:12–13, 25; Ezek 42:15–19; 48:30–34)

Both Ezekiel and John use the same root for gate: πυλών, but the lack of any other options for *gate* in Greek renders the lexical connection irrelevant. The gates of Jerusalem are mentioned throughout Ezekiel, especially in the final nine chapters. In fact, gates are mentioned in forty-three verses throughout Ezekiel 40–48.[196] In Revelation 21–22, the gates are mentioned in six verses.[197] Thus, John's allusion to Ezekiel's gates is another example of his tendency to condense OT source material. Further, consistent with John's condensing tendency, he merges the numerous gates of Ezekiel's vision into one group of twelve gates around the city-temple.[198]

The arrangement of the gates of the new Jerusalem, with three on each side of the city and each bearing the name of one of the tribes, corresponds to Ezekiel's layout.[199] As in Ezekiel 48:31–34, three gates face each cardinal direction. However, John lists the order of directions based on Ezekiel 42:15–19: east, north south, west.[200] Significantly, the order that John follows for his city is the order Ezekiel provided for the gates of temple complex.[201] The priority given the east gate in being listed first coheres with the idea of the city as a temple, "owing to the brilliant radiance of the glory of God present in it and its eastern orientation."[202]

An element of John's vision that does not cohere with Ezekiel's is the angelic presence at the gates (Rev 21:12). The allusion to angels may hearken from Isaiah 62:6–9, in which the angelic figures defend Jerusalem

---

196. Ezek 40:6, 9, 10, 13–15, 19–23, 27, 28, 32, 35, 38, 40, 41, 44; 42:1, 15, 16; 43:1, 4; 44:1–4, 17; 45:19; 46:1–3, 8, 9, 12, 19; 47:2; 48:31–34.

197. Rev 21:12, 13, 15, 21, 25; 22:14.

198. Beale, *Book of Revelation*, 1068.

199. Aune, *Revelation 17–22*, 1154; Beasley-Murray, *Book of Revelation*, 320.

200. In Ezekiel 48:30–34, the gates are listed in the order of north, east, south, west. For other possible sources for John's directional ordering, see Num 2:3–31; 1 En. 34–36; 72; 76:2–3; 77:1–4; 11QT XXXIX, 11–13; XL, 9–12.

201. Beale, *Book of Revelation*, 1068; Mathewson, *New Heaven*, 101–3; Mounce, *Revelation*, 391; Vogelgesang, "Interpretation of Ezekiel," 77.

202. Thomas and Macchia, *Revelation*, 376. The east gate is significant also in respect to the Messiah himself. Jesus' triumphal entry into Jerusalem proceeded through the east gate (Matt 21:1–11; Mark 11:1–11; Luke 19:29–38; Hays, *Temple and the Tabernacle*, 161). In Matthew 24:27, the author indicated that Jesus would return from the east upon his second coming. Correspondingly, segments of both Judaism and Christianity believe that the Messiah will return through the eastern gate of Jerusalem (Barker, *Gate of Heaven*, 149).

against enemies.[203] Aune suggested that in Revelation, the angels likewise serve to protect the city from the evil nations outside. "Because the gates are always open (21:25), guards are presumably necessary to keep those opposed to God on the outside."[204]

The angels may comprise a reference to Genesis 3:24 and Ezekiel 28:14 and 28:16, where angels guard the garden of Eden; "and since the New Jerusalem is the eschatological counterpart of Eden (see 2:7; 22:1–5), angelic guards at its gates seem appropriate."[205] Further, the proximate allusion to Ezekiel 28 in regard to the foundation stones indicates that John had the edenic setting in mind. Thus, in placing angels at the gates, John was depicting his city as a restored garden of Eden more so than indicating that the city needs protection.

That the gates are constructed of pearls is an image which also is not derived from Ezekiel. The "pearly gates" likely hearken from Isaiah 54:12.[206] In Isaiah 54, the gates and walls are closely connected to the security of God's people. The peaceful state enables the people within to learn of, or from, the Lord (לְמוּדֵי יְהוָה; Isa 53:13). Thus, the gates facilitate the relationship between God and his people.

The pearls also serve as a continuing polemic against Babylon. Similar to the precious stones, the pearls "function not only to point to the restored eschatological community, but also to provide a deliberate counterpoint to the jewels which adorn the harlot-Babylon in chapters 17–18."[207] Indeed, the only other mention of pearls in Revelation is in association with Babylon (Rev 17:4; 18:12, 16).

> In each case, the mention of pearls underscores the opulent wealth of the great whore, as she is bedecked in pearls, appearing to have no rivals. But here it is revealed that the woman with whom she is compared, the bride of the Lamb, is adorned to such an unbelievable extent that the great whore's claims to wealth are revealed to be almost laughable.[208]

---

203. Mathewson, *New Heaven*, 103; Mounce, *Revelation*, 379; Sweet, *Revelation*, 304; Swete, *Apocalypse of St. John*, 285.

204. Aune, *Revelation 17–22*, 1154.

205. Aune, *Revelation 17–22*, 1154–55.

206. Fekkes, *Isaiah and Prophetic Traditions*, 244; Mathewson, *New Heaven*, 149–50.

207. Mathewson, *New Heaven*, 150.

208. Thomas and Macchia, *Revelation*, 382.

Thus, whereas the walls proclaim the glory of God, the gates proclaim the glory of his bride.

The orientation of the gates of the new Jerusalem as *open* is significant as well (Rev 21:25). While some scholars interpret the open gates as an invitation for those in the lake of fire to repent and join the saints,[209] the open gates more likely point to the security of the city's inhabitants.[210] "John is not describing an eternally secure place. He is describing eternally secure peoples."[211] Further, that the gates open in all directions suggests "universal access" for the saints from every corner of existence.[212]

In contrast, one of Ezekiel's gates is to remain shut. The closing of the eastern gate is closely connected to the previous return of Yahweh through the same gate (43:1–5). Indeed, the entrance of Yahweh through the eastern gate is connected directly to the closing of the gate in Ezekiel 44:2. Most likely the closing of the gate signifies the completion of God's promise to be with his people. Never again will his presence depart the holy precincts.[213] By extension, the closing of the gate with Yahweh's eternal presence inside also communicates the permanent sanctity of the space.[214]

Surprising, then, is the pronouncement in Ezekiel 46:1–10 that the gate will be opened for the Sabbath and the new moon festival. However, no one, not even the prince who sits in the gateway, is allowed to enter or exit through the gate. "On these Sabbaths and new moon festivals the citizens of the restored community of faith shall gather and pay homage to Yahweh by prostrating themselves at the entrance of the inner gate."[215] Thus, the periodically opened gate may represent access to the divine presence. Tuell asserted, "The disproportionate size of the gates, and the disproportionate attention the text gives to their description, underscore

---

209. Vogelgesang, "Interpretation of Ezekiel," 104–8; Rissi, *Future of the World*, 71–78.

210. Mathewson, *New Heaven*, 176.

211. Gundry, "New Jerusalem," 260. Cf. du Rand, "New Jerusalem as Pinnacle," 294; Smalley, *Revelation to John*, 548; Stevens, *Revelation*, 540–41.

212. Thomas and Macchia, *Revelation*, 376.

213. Boyle, "Holiness has a Shape," 17; Cooper, *Ezekiel*, 388; Kasher, "Anthropomorphism, Holiness and Cult," 195; Tuell, *Ezekiel*, 57; Wevers, *Ezekiel*, 219; Zimmerli, *I Am Yahweh*, 122.

214. Block, *Book of Ezekiel: Chapters 25–48*, 614–15; Zimmerli, *Ezekiel 2*, 440.

215. Block, *Book of Ezekiel: Chapters 25–48*, 671.

the central concern of this entire vision complex: access to the divine presence."[216]

Open gates are found also in Isaiah 60:11.[217] As in Revelation 21:26, the nations enter the city through the gates.[218] Other similarities are also present, such as the kings bringing their wealth into the city. Thus, Isaiah 60:11 seems to present a clearer parallel than the sometimes-open, sometimes-closed gates of Ezekiel.

Nonetheless, John almost certainly drew upon Ezekiel 42:15–19 and 48:31–34 in the arrangement and orientation of the gates of the new Jerusalem in Revelation 21:13.[219] Therefore, the allusion in Revelation 21:12–13 can be classified as clear, with the function of a literary prototype. The Ezekielian imagery is used as a pattern for John's own composition.[220] As for Revelation 21:25, no allusion to Ezekiel appears to be present.

Foundation Stones (Rev 21:14; Ezek 40:30–34)

As in Ezekiel, the gates in Revelation bear the names of the tribes of Israel.[221] However, John adds his own innovation in that the foundations of the walls bear the names of the twelve apostles (Rev 21:14).[222] John's addition of the apostles' names is conspicuous. "Here, an element is added in a passage which otherwise is radically simplified and abridged."[223]

Yet the names on the foundation stones do not represent a different purpose than names on the gates in Ezekiel 48:30–34, but rather the consummation of Ezekiel's hope. "Israel's divine purpose from the beginning

216. Tuell, *Ezekiel*, 287. Cf. Odell, "Wall Is No More," 339–56.

217. du Rand, "New Jerusalem as Pinnacle," 297.

218. Incidentally, in Isaiah 60:12, the nations who do not serve God are destroyed. Only those who honor God enter Jerusalem. That John tended to be faithful to his OT precursors is an argument against a universalist interpretation of Revelation 21:24–26.

219. Ford, *Revelation*, 341.

220. Beale, *John's Use*, 75.

221. Ezek 48:30–35; Rev 21:12–13.

222. Most scholars see the apostolic foundation as a reference to Ephesians 2:20 (cf. Matt 16:18; Gal 2:9; 1 Pet 2:4–8); Aune, *Revelation 17–22*, 1157; Beasley-Murray, *Book of Revelation*, 321; Boxall, *Revelation*, 303; Mounce, *Revelation*, 379; Sweet, *Revelation*, 304; Witherington, *Revelation*, 270. Vogelgesang, however, saw a reference to Ezekiel even here. In Ezekiel 41:8, the author described a raised base around the temple, which Vogelgesang viewed as inspiration for Revelation 21:14. Mathewson argued to the contrary (Mathewson, *New Heaven*, 104–5).

223. Vogelgesang, "Interpretation of Ezekiel," 90.

was fulfilled. For John, Jerusalem is one way to tell the two-stage story of the people of God, from nation to incarnation. The movement from historical Jerusalem to eternal Jerusalem is the story of the twelve tribes, Messiah, and the twelve apostles."[224]

Nonetheless, Ezekiel made no mention of foundation stones. As noted above, Isaiah 54:11 is the most likely precursor for John's foundation stones.[225] In Revelation 21:14, the stones are identified with the apostles, much like the author of the Isaiah Pesher identified the stones of Isaiah 54:11 with the founding members of the sectarian community.[226] Thus, both Revelation 21:14 and the Isaiah Pesher reflect a similar understanding of Isaiah 54. "Furthermore, both texts associate the city gates of Isa. 54.12 with the gates belonging to the twelve tribes from Ezek. 48.30–35."[227]

John seemed to be working within a circle of tradition that utilized building imagery to describe a community of people. He combined passages such as Ezekiel 40–48, which has no precious building materials, with other OT prophecies such as Isaiah 54:11–12 to describe the glory of the future Jerusalem. "Indeed, John's city is a *temple-city*, and the redeemed eschatological community is the spiritual temple in which God and the Lamb dwell and are worshipped. Thus, when viewed through the prism of building imagery, the costly ingredients of the city may represent the eternal glory, purity, and durability of the perfected community."[228] Additionally, the significance of the twofold twelve is that John, rather

224. Stevens, *Revelation*, 535. Cf. Bauckham, *Theology of the Book*, 137; Beale, *Book of Revelation*, 1070; Beasley-Murray, *Book of Revelation*, 321; Mathewson, *New Heaven*, 111; Palmer, "Imagining Space in Revelation," 42; Spatafora, *From the "Temple of God,"* 230.

225. Fekkes contended that John's description of the stones comes primarily from Tobit (Fekkes, "Bride has Prepared Herself," 281–82). However, similarities just as likely could have come from a common tradition, such as Isaiah 54:11–12. Further, Tobit's description of the new Jerusalem seems to envision a literal city, whereas the authors of Isaiah 54 and Revelation 21 dealt with ideological and theological concepts. For a more detailed rebuttal, see Mathewson, *New Heaven*, 151–52.

226. 4QpIsa I, 5–6. Beale, *Book of Revelation*, 1069; Mathewson, *New Heaven*, 144; Mathewson, "Note on the Foundation Stones," 487.

227. Mathewson, *New Heaven*, 145.

228. Fekkes, "Bride has Prepared Herself," 286; emphasis his. Cf. Beale, *Book of Revelation*, 1070; Lee, *New Jerusalem*, 280–81; Mathewson, *New Heaven*, 148; Mathewson, "Note on the Foundation Stones," 497; Palmer, "Imagining Space in Revelation," 43.

than privileging one people group over another, unites all peoples and makes the blessings promised to Israel available to all of the saints.[229]

In sum, the imagery of foundation stones clearly alludes to Isaiah 54:11. Yet, John almost certainly drew upon the gates of Ezekiel as well. He utilized imagery from both passages "to redefine the people of Israel as those faithful to God and the Lamb."[230]

Thus, the allusion to Ezekiel 48:30–35 can be classified as possible, based on similar concepts. Greater certainty is not possible due to the absence of parallel lexemes. The contextual function is literary prototype, due to the continued references to architectural elements found in Ezekiel.

Measuring the Wall (Rev 21:15–17; Ezek 40:3–4; 45:1–5)

Most commentators agree that the act of measuring in Revelation 21:15–17 is a clear allusion to Ezekiel.[231] In Ezekiel 40:3–4, the prophet encounters an angelic figure who begins to measure the temple and city.[232] The figure seems to be the model for the angel who measures the city in Revelation 21:15–17.[233] Accordingly, the angels in both visions measure with a κάλαμος. The act of measuring is described with the same root, μετρέω, although Ezekiel prefers the compound verb διαμετρέω. Neither term is particularly distinctive, as μετρέω is the most common verb used of measuring.[234]

Variations between the two passages can be detected as well. First, the reed in Revelation is golden (Rev 21:15), which is "very appropriate for a golden city."[235] The reed in Ezekiel is flax, which is likewise fitting for his more realistic architecture. Second, in Revelation the angel mea-

---

229. Beale, *Book of Revelation*, 1070; Vogelgesang, "Interpretation of Ezekiel," 92.

230. Palmer, "Imagining Space in Revelation," 43.

231. Aune, *Revelation 17–22*, 1163; Beale, *Book of Revelation*, 1072; Boxall, *Revelation*, 303; Mounce, *Revelation*, 391; Sweet, *Revelation*, 304; Vogelgesang, "Interpretation of Ezekiel," 78.

232. Cf. Ezek 40:5, 6, 11, 13, 19, 20, 23, 24, 27, 28, 32, 35, 47, 48; 41:1–5, 13, 15, 26; 42:15–19; 45:3; 47:3–5.

233. Vogelgesang, "Interpretation of Ezekiel," 78.

234. See, for example, Num 35:5; Deut 21:21; Ruth 3:15; 2 Sam 8:2; Pss 60:6; 108:7; Isa 40:12. Conversely, σταθμόω, the primary alternative term for measuring, is used only in 1 Kings 6:23.

235. Witherington, *Revelation*, 270.

sures the walls of the city, whereas in Ezekiel, the angel measures the temple precincts. Third, Ezekiel's measurements are based on multiples of twenty-five, while John's are based on multiples of twelve.

Some of the discrepancies can be explained by recognizing that John is alluding to Zechariah in addition to Ezekiel.[236] As in Revelation, the angel in Zechariah measures the city, not the temple (Zech 2:1–2). Although the term for measuring is again the same as in Ezekiel, διαμετρέω, the "measuring line" is different: σχοινίον γεωμετρικόν. Nonetheless, John's propensity to combine referents indicates that he may have had both passages in mind. Further, as noted above, John often applied Ezekiel's temple imagery to the new Jerusalem.

Despite the differences, distinctive terminology links Revelation and Ezekiel. In Revelation 21:16–17, John informed readers that the length, width, and height of the city are equal, drawing upon Ezekiel 45:1–5. Though the measurements are different, a square shape predominates both visions. Both authors used the term τετράγωνος, or "foursquare," which is unique to Revelation in the NT.[237] The cubic dimensions in John's vision could derive from 1 Kings 6:20, the holy of holies in Solomon's temple, "which would fit in well with the changing of temple motifs into city motifs in this vision."[238] However, the author of 1 Kings 6:20 did not utilize the term τετράγωνος. Thus, John seems to have drawn more directly upon Ezekiel.

John's vision also represents an escalation from his precursors. In contrast to the two-dimensional measurements of Ezekiel and Zechariah, John's measurements are three-dimensional. Moreover, in Solomon's Temple, Herod's Temple, and Ezekiel's temple, a wall separated the inner and outer courts. "In contrast, there will be only one wall in the new Jerusalem, and it will surround the entire city, thus stressing the unity of the city's inhabitants with one another and with God."[239]

---

236. Mathewson argued that Zechariah 2:1–2 is John's primary source for the measuring (Mathewson, *New Heaven*, 105–6).

237. Rev 21:16; Ezek 41:21; 43:16; 45:2; 48:20; cf. Ezek 41:4; 48:16. Aune, *Revelation 17–22*, 1160; Beasley-Murray, *Book of Revelation*, 322; Smalley, *Revelation to John*, 551. Vogelgesang argued that John's tetragonal imagery only was minutely influenced by Ezekiel. Instead, he contended that the layout was derived from the ideal Hellenistic city model and the shape of Babylonian temples (Vogelgesang, "Interpretation of Ezekiel," 93–94, 124–28).

238. Vogelgesang, "Interpretation of Ezekiel," 93. Cf. Spatafora, *From the "Temple of God,"* 231; Stevens, *Revelation*, 536.

239. Beale, *Book of Revelation*, 1078.

The size of John's city is greater than those of his predecessors as well. The new Jerusalem is a staggering 12,000 stadia squared, which is roughly the size of the known Hellenistic world.[240] "The holy city would stretch across the known world and into the heavens itself, perhaps indicating that the new heaven and new earth unite in the New Jerusalem!"[241] Additionally, the area of the new Jerusalem may have been an intentional increase on the nine thousand stadia of Rome, continuing John's polemic against Babylon.[242]

Thus, the measuring, like most elements of John's vision, is ripe with symbolism. Measuring reveals the magnitude of the new Jerusalem and the insignificance of Babylon, as well as the "astronomically high number" of saints that the city represents.[243] Measuring also symbolizes protection and security.[244] "The destroyer cannot enter the place that God has marked off as holy and within whose boundaries his people are secure."[245] Further, the measuring in Revelation 21 functions in the same manner as the measuring in Ezekiel. The action communicates the security of the people of God, who dwell in his presence for eternity.[246]

Yet consistent with his tendency, John radically condensed Ezekiel's narrative. John succinctly communicated in three verses what Ezekiel described in roughly four chapters.[247] In sum, although John may have had Zechariah in mind as well, the image of measuring is a clear allusion

240. The dimension is approximately 1,500 miles in diameter. Cf. Sib Or. 5:251–52, 420–26, in which the city reaches the clouds and extends as far as Joppa, but is still nowhere close to the size of John's city. See also, Mathewson, *New Heaven*, 109; Smalley, *Revelation to John*, 552; Stevens, *Revelation*, 536; Vogelsang, "Interpretation of Ezekiel," 94–95; Witherington, *Revelation*, 269.

241. Thomas and Macchia, *Revelation*, 379. Cf. Beasley-Murray, *Book of Revelation*, 322; du Rand, "New Jerusalem as Pinnacle," 291.

242. Aune, *Revelation 17–22*, 1162; Stevens, *Revelation*, 536.

243. Gundry, "New Jerusalem," 260. Cf. Kistemaker, "Temple in the Apocalypse," 435–36; Smalley, *Revelation to John*, 548.

244. Bauckham, *Climax of Prophecy*, 269; Beale, *Book of Revelation*, 559, 1072; Kistemaker, "Temple in the Apocalypse," 435; Stevens, *Revelation*, 417; Thomas and Macchia, *Revelation*, 378.

245. Kistemaker, "Temple in the Apocalypse," 435.

246. Beale, *Book of Revelation*, 1072; Palmer, "Imagining Space in Revelation," 43. To the contrary, Witherington argued that in Ezekiel, the measuring reveals how much needs protection. In Revelation, the measuring reveals the magnitude of the new Jerusalem, where the saints are safe (Witherington, *Revelation*, 270).

247. Vogelgesang, "Interpretation of Ezekiel," 93.

to Ezekiel. John continued to use Ezekiel 40–48 as a literary prototype for his own vision.

Measuring in Revelation 11:1–2

The act of measuring in Revelation 11:1–2 should be mentioned briefly. In Revelation 11:1–2, John himself is given a measuring reed with which he is commanded to measure the temple and the people who worship inside. The outer court is not measured, as the nations will trample the area for forty-two months. The forty-two months is a reference to Daniel and a symbolic time of persecution for God's people.[248] As in Revelation 21, the temple represents the Messiah and the saints, but in Revelation 11:1–2, the outer court of the temple represents the people of God who will be persecuted prior to the consummation of history.[249]

In both Revelation 11 and 21, John drew upon the measuring imagery of Ezekiel. Yet while the events of the outer court being trampled in Revelation 11:2 do not cohere with Ezekiel 40–48, the measuring imagery does. "Measuring the temple symbolizes that the people of God will be protected by God even though under severe duress by their enemies."[250]

Also similar to Revelation 21:15–17, in Revelation 11, John appeared to draw upon both Ezekiel and Zechariah. That Zechariah may be in mind is borne out in Revelation 11:3. The olive trees and lampstands reference Zechariah 4:2–3, in which the prophet sees a golden lampstand and two olive trees, representing the anointed king and priest who would rebuild the temple.[251]

In Revelation 11, John also foreshadowed the idea of the Messiah as the temple. Through the allusions to Ezekiel, Zechariah, and Daniel in Revelation 11, John hinted that OT expectations are being fulfilled through the Messiah and the church. "Christ's work is now the dominant interpretive lens through which one understands OT expectations. In

---

248. See Dan 7:25; 12:7–13. See also, Beale, *Book of Revelation*, 565–68; Stevens, *Revelation*, 416–17.

249. Beale, *Book of Revelation*, 562–68, 1072; Bauckham, *Climax of Prophecy*, 272.

250. Stevens, *Revelation*, 416. For the trampling of God's people, cf. Dan 8:13; 1 Macc 3:34, 51; 4:60; 2 Macc 8:2; Isa 63:18.

251. Stevens, *Revelation*, 417–19.

Rev 11:1–2, the temple of the church is patterned after the cross of Christ, who is the true temple."[252]

Kings and Nations (Rev 21:24–27; Ezek 44:9; 47:21–23)

As is apparent from the nations trampling the holy city in Revelation 11:1–2, the portrayal of the nations throughout Revelation is generally negative.[253] Thus, the presence of nations and kings in the new Jerusalem is unexpected. Such a turn of events may comprise a parallel with Ezekiel 40–48, but first the presence of the nations in Revelation 21 must be explicated.

In Revelation 21:24, John indicated that the nations will walk by the light of the new Jerusalem and that the kings of the earth will bring their glory into the city.[254] The interpretive question is how one accounts for the presence of the nations in the new Jerusalem when the portrayal of the nations throughout Revelation has been consistently negative. Adding to the difficulty, in Revelation 19:17–21 and 20:7–10, John indicated that the nations and kings had been decisively destroyed.[255]

Both Rissi and Vogelgesang argued that the nations who persecuted the saints are granted a pardon. Those who were punished in the lake of fire are converted and redeemed, which enables them to inhabit the new Jerusalem.[256] However, the idea that those who reject God come to dwell in the new Jerusalem "renders the entire judgment cycle no more than overwrought divine angst over incurable evil."[257] Further, the apocalyptic Jewish backdrop for Revelation offers no basis for such an interpretation. In the works examined for the current study, faithful followers of the Lord always are redeemed and those who reject him always are punished, with there being no hope for reconciliation after final judgment has taken place.

252. Beale, *Book of Revelation*, 561.

253. Rev 2:26; 10:11; 11:2, 9, 18; 13:7; 17:15; 18:3, 23; 19:15; 20:3, 8.

254. The parallelism of the verse implies that *nations* is synonymous with *kings* (Aune, *Revelation 17–22*, 1170).

255. Aune, *Revelation 17–22*, 1154, 1171.

256. Rissi, *Future of the World*, 74–78, 110; Vogelgesang, "Interpretation of Ezekiel," 104–7. Cf. Caird, *Revelation of Saint John*, 279; Sweet, *Revelation*, 308–9.

257. Stevens, *Revelation*, 544.

It is more likely that the nations who enter the new Jerusalem are those who are redeemed *out of* the nations.[258] John offered only two possibilities for the nations: genuine repentance and worship of God, or refusal to repent and final judgment.[259] Further, in Revelation 21:27, John made explicit what he implied in verse 24: only those who have been purified of sin and experienced the salvation of God may enter the city.[260]

The terminology in Revelation 21:27 underscores the moral nature of the entry requirements. Those who lie and commit abominations are barred from the city. Further, nothing κοινὸν, or "unclean," may enter. Κοινὸν often denotes ritual impurity, but Aune explained that the term carried over into Christianity with exclusively moral overtones.[261] "Thus, John's prohibition for entrance . . . reflects the Old Testament concern for purity and holiness in the community . . . By stipulating the moral requirements for inclusion/exclusion, John is able to maintain the holiness of the city even while including the *nations* within its boundaries."[262]

As with the nations, the "kings of the earth" are portrayed negatively throughout Revelation.[263] Similar to the reversal with the nations, the presence of the "kings of the earth" in the new Jerusalem contrasts their former allegiance to the beast. That they "bring their glory" into the city indicates that they now worship God.[264]

That the nations "walk" by the light of the Lamb is significant also (Rev 21:24). The term *walk* reflects obedience to God's word, as in the Jewish sense of *halakha*:

> There could be little doubt that the hearers would understand this language to mean that the nations who walk in its light are those who have experienced his salvation . . . And this very word has been encountered earlier in Revelation to describe

258. In Revelation 5:9 and 7:9, John indicated that individuals from every nation would worship around the throne in the eschaton. He did not, however, indicate that *every person* from every nation will worship God (Beale, *Book of Revelation*, 1097, 1101; Stevens, *Revelation*, 544).

259. Repentance: Rev 11:13; 14:6; 15:4; refusal to repent: Rev 14:9–11; 16:9, 11, 21; 17:14; 19:17–21. Bauckham, *Climax of Prophecy*, 307–8.

260. Thomas and Macchia, *Revelation*, 386.

261. Aune, *Revelation 17–22*, 1174.

262. Mathewson, *New Heaven*, 179; emphasis his.

263. Rev 1:5; 6:15; 17:2, 18; 18:3, 9; 19:19.

264. Bauckham, *Climax of Prophecy*, 314; Decock, "Scriptures in the Book," 385; Fekkes, *Isaiah and Prophetic Traditions*, 269; Lee, *New Jerusalem*, 287; Mathewson, "Destiny of the Nations," 121–42; Thomas and Macchia, *Revelation*, 384–85.

fellowship with the resurrected Jesus (Rev 2:1), eschatological reward (3:4), and ethical conduct (16:15).[265]

In Revelation 22:2, John provided a hint that redemption has taken place. The "healing of the nations" in Revelation 22:2 involves a reversal of the carnage described in Revelation 11:5–12 and 19:17–21.[266] Those who formerly persecuted the Lamb and his followers are restored to fellowship with God.[267]

The juxtaposition of both judgment and salvation is a reflection of OT tensions.[268] Bauckham explained that the portrayal of the nations in Revelation 21–22 mirrors the fulfillment of the prophetic expectation that "all nations will become God's people. The history of the covenant people—both of the one nation Israel and of the church which is redeemed from all the nations—will find its eschatological fulfillment in the full inclusion of all the nations in its own covenant privileges and promises."[269] Similarly, the authors of 1 Enoch 90 and Sibylline Oracle 3 juxtaposed images of judgment and salvation of the nations. Thus, the dichotomous notions are a common feature of both OT and apocalyptic literature.[270]

With the imagery of nations entering the city, John once again utilized spatial imagery to convey theological ideas. "Consequently, it would be incorrect to infer that the picture of people making a pilgrimage into the new Jerusalem refers to a literal pilgrimage from outer spaces into the city's inner space."[271] Instead, in Revelation 21:24–27, entering the city represents the fulfillment of soteriological expectations and is equivalent to professing loyalty to God.[272] Bauckham explained, "Revelation 22:3a

265. Thomas and Macchia, *Revelation*, 384. Cf. Aune, *Revelation 17–22*, 1171; Decock, "Scriptures in the Book," 384.

266. Sweet, *Revelation*, 311.

267. Smalley, *Revelation to John*, 563.

268. See Ps 2:2; 86:9; Isa 24:1, 6, 21–23; 25:6–9; 66:14–16, 24. Mathewson, *New Heaven*, 174.

269. Bauckham, *Climax of Prophecy*, 131. Cf. Aune, *Revelation 17–22*, 1171–73.

270. Deutsch, "Transformation of Symbols," 120; Mathewson, "Destiny of the Nations," 137.

271. Beale, *Book of Revelation*, 1099. Cf. Fekkes, "Bride has Prepared Herself," 286; Gundry, "New Jerusalem," 264; Palmer, "Imagining Space in Revelation," 44.

272. Similar to entering into the kingdom of God/heaven: Matt 5:20; 7:21; 18:3; 19:23–24; 23:13; Mark 9:47; John 3:5; Acts 14:22. Aune, *Revelation 17–22*, 1174; Mathewson, "Destiny of the Nations," 134.

recalls the judgment of the nations that worshipped the beast and opposed God's kingdom, but declares that, with the coming of God's kingdom, the nations which have been converted to the worship of God and the acknowledgment of his rule need never again fear his judgment."[273] Correspondingly, being outside of the new Jerusalem does not entail spatial distance. To be outside of the city is to be outside of the whole dimension in which the saints rule. "It means to be on earth not at all; rather, in the lake of fire."[274]

As usual, in his portrayal of the nations, John drew on a variety of OT passages. First, John alluded to Isaiah 60:3 and Isaiah 2:2–5. The reference to Isaiah 60:3 highlights "*the reversal* that will ensue in the future: while the nations destroyed Jerusalem in the past, they will restore its wealth in the future; while the nations subjugated Israel in the past, they will serve them in the future."[275] Further, "The semantic effect of reading [Rev] 21:24 in light of Isaiah 2:2–5 is that the nations are not only drawn to the light of God and come to restore Zion's fortunes (Is. 60:3, 5, 6, 11), they also worship the true God and live according to his will (2:2–4)."[276]

Second, John drew upon Zechariah 14:7–21, in which the prophet described endless daytime, living water, nations entering Jerusalem, and the city as a place of holiness.[277] Zechariah depicted individuals who formerly had attacked Jerusalem coming to worship God. Those who refuse to worship the Lord receive a plague and remain outside the city with no rain. Such imagery supports the contention that John did not espouse universal salvation in Revelation 21:24–27.

Third, although no direct linguistic connection exists, Ezekiel offered a similar portrayal of the fate of foreigners. Throughout the book, the nations are portrayed as evil, just as in Revelation. Additionally, both Ezekiel and John depicted a total annihilation of the enemies of God, but also foresaw former enemies inside the future eschatological city.[278]

273. Bauckham, *Climax of Prophecy*, 318. Cf. Decock, "Scriptures in the Book," 384.

274. Gundry, "New Jerusalem," 263.

275. Mathewson, "Destiny of the Nations," 130; emphasis his. Cf. Beale, *Book of Revelation*, 1094.

276. Mathewson, "Destiny of the Nations," 131. Cf. Bauckham, *Climax of Prophecy*, 315; Beale, *Book of Revelation*, 1095.

277. Mathewson, *New Heaven*, 165.

278. Annihilation of enemies: Ezek 26:14, 21; 27:36; 28:19, 24–26; 35:9; Rev 19:17–21; 20:7–10.

Much attention has been given to Ezekiel's exclusion of foreigners from the temple precinct (Ezek 44:9), but lesser consideration is typically given to Ezekiel 47:21–23, in which the prophet specifically dictated that foreigners are to be regarded as native Israelites:

> And you shall divide this land among yourselves, according to the tribes of Israel. And it will be that you will allot it as an inheritance for yourselves and for the aliens who dwell among you, who have borne children in your midst. And they will be to you as full citizens among the children of Israel; with you they will be allotted an inheritance in the midst of the tribes of Israel. And it will be in the tribe in which the alien dwells, there you shall give his inheritance, declares the Lord Yahweh. (Ezek 47:21–23)

Rather than barring people from the temple, Ezekiel indicated that foreigners were to be welcomed into Israel as family. Ganzel proposed that the prohibition against foreigners in Ezekiel 44:9 was more specifically a proscription against idol worship. [279] The foreign peoples in view were associated inextricably with practices that were abominable to Yahweh.

Indeed, the verses surrounding the prohibition all mention various idolatrous practices. The prohibition should be viewed, then, as the exclusion of individuals who are not followers of Yahweh, as Ezekiel 44:9 reads "No son of a foreign land *uncircumcised of heart and uncircumcised of flesh* shall come into my sanctuary" (italics added). Although in Ezekiel 44:9, the prophet barred foreigners from entering the sanctuary, the delimitation on those with uncircumcised hearts indicates that the reason for barring is not nationality.

The Jewish people anticipated a time when God would restore their homeland and temple. Ezekiel added a dimension to their hope by including aliens (Ezek 47:22):

> The constant formula: 'They shall know that I am Yahweh', which keeps recurring in Ezekiel, and applies to the nations as well as to Israel, therefore implies a great deal more than a mere theoretical recognition of the truth of the prophet's message. Rather, it expresses how the light of the new fellowship which God bestowed upon Israel also shines out over the Gentile world.[280]

---

279. Ganzel, "Defilement and Desecration," 369–79. Cf. Joyce, "Temple and Worship," 145–63.

280. Eichrodt, *Ezekiel*, 585–86. Cf. Sweet, *Revelation*, 308. For an opposing position, see Pfisterer Darr, "Wall around Paradise."

Similarly, in Revelation 21:27, John indicated that nothing unclean would enter the new Jerusalem. Just as idolaters were excluded from Ezekiel's temple, only individuals who espouse allegiance to God and the Lamb have a place in the new Jerusalem. Thus, once again what formerly applied only to Ezekiel's temple now applies to the entirety of the new Jerusalem.

To conclude, the salvation of the nations bears little linguistic connection between Ezekiel and Revelation. Yet because the usages bear a heavy thematic similarity, the allusion will be categorized as possible. As for contextual function, both John and Ezekiel described a time when those who formerly persecuted God's people will repent and enter into fellowship with the Lord. Thus, John's usage of Ezekiel can be described as a literary prototype.

And I Saw No Temple (Rev 21:22; Ezek 40–48)

Given that John made extensive use of Ezekiel 40–48 throughout Revelation, the omission of a temple in Revelation 21:22 is unexpected, if not shocking. Some scholars argue that the omission is a deliberate reinterpretation on John's part. Ruiz suggested that the absence of a temple in Revelation is a polemic against the emperor worship that took place in most temples in Asia Minor.[281] Vogelgesang argued that the absence reflects a democratization of Israel's traditional forms of worship.[282] Yet while John's portrayal of the temple at first glance appears to be a reinterpretation of traditional Jewish expectations, the examination of Second Temple period literature in the previous chapter revealed that Jewish temple expectations were far from homogeneous.[283] Temple imagery was often applied to individuals and groups.[284] Further, the absence or demotion of the temple in much Second Temple Jewish literature indicates that John's omission of a temple may not have been surprising to his readers.

Along similar lines, first-century Christians had little reason to hope that a literal temple would be rebuilt.[285] Christ had rendered the

---

281. Ruiz, *Ezekiel in the Apocalypse*, 168.

282. Vogelgesang, "Interpretation of Ezekiel," 77, 128–31.

283. Beale, *Book of Revelation*, 1091–92.

284. 2 Bar. 2:2; 1QS III, 2; VIII, 5–10; 1QS IX, 3–6; 4Q164 I, 2–3; 1QSa I, 26–28; 4QFlor I, 3–6; 4QD III, 19–IV, 5; 1QH XIV, 24–27.

285. Cross, *Ancient Library of Qumran*, 240.

sacrificial system obsolete and made the presence of God available via the Holy Spirit. Yet while Jesus had eliminated the need for an earthly sanctuary, the common belief in a heavenly temple led some Christ followers to anticipate a temple in which God would dwell with his people in the eschaton. "But on further reflection it soon becomes apparent that any and all sorts of temples are but tokens of the old order in which special geographical points of contact between the Holy God and fallen humanity had to be established."[286]

Nonetheless, the temple was a robust source of symbolism for John. From the beginnings of Christianity, "there was a consistent use of this temple imagery to describe and interpret the life, death, and ascension of Jesus."[287] More than simply a source of imagery, however, John drew upon his OT predecessors to describe the Messiah as the fulfillment of all that the temple represented.[288]

John also made use of traditions that the heavenly Jerusalem and temple would come to the earth in the eschatological age. As John portrayed the descent of his city to the earth, he implied that the new Jerusalem was the heavenly temple. He combined such traditions with other strands of thought that understood Ezekiel's temple as the heavenly temple. Thus, John depicted his city as the fulfillment of Ezekiel's vision.

Correspondingly, the reason that John offered little in the way of architectural detail, as in Ezekiel, is that he did not expect the temple to be restored in an architectural structure.[289] Beale explained, "It is not that John saw no temple, but only that he saw no physical temple . . . The temple pictured in four detailed chapters of Ezekiel's prophecy (chs. 40–43) is now summarized and interpreted by this brief phrase affirming that God and the Lamb are the temple."[290] Even Ezekiel hinted that God fulfilled the function of the temple in Ezekiel 11:16, wherein the Lord promises to be a sanctuary for the exiles.[291]

Most of the differences between the visions of John and Ezekiel can be explained by John's application of city imagery to Ezekiel's temple

286. Briggs, *Jewish Temple Imagery*, 103–4.

287. Barker, *Gate of Heaven*, 177.

288. Barr, "Apocalypse as a Symbolic Transformation," 41; Clowney, "Final Temple," 156–89; Levenson, "Jerusalem Temple," 32–61; du Rand, "New Jerusalem as Pinnacle," 296; Smith, "Like Deities, Like Temples," 3–27.

289. Beale, *Book of Revelation*, 1091.

290. Beale, *Book of Revelation*, 1090.

291. Spatafora, *From the "Temple of God,"* 108.

complex.[292] Additionally, instances in which John omitted Ezekielian details often can be accounted for by John's condensing tendency. However,
such an explanation does not fare well with John's omission of the entire
three chapters of Ezekiel 44–46, and most of 48, which deal with land ap-
portionment and ritual ordinances. By way of explanation, Vogelgesang
accurately observed that throughout Revelation 21–22, John focused on
the primary features of Ezekiel.[293] Yet, his contention that John omitted
Ezekielian features in order to democratize and universalize Ezekiel's
message is overstated. John did, indeed, universalize imagery applied
to Israel at points, but he did not depart from Ezekiel's original intent.
Alternately, Mathewson suggested that John omitted portions of Ezekiel
"that cease to function in his vision of the unmediated presence of God
and the Lamb."[294] The shift in *Heilgeschichte* resulted in the fulfillment of
some visionary details and the obsolescence of others.

The temple is certainly one area of fulfillment, and not one of obsolescence. John understood the OT prophecies about the temple to be
fulfilled by the Messiah. In Revelation 1:12–20, John foreshadowed the
culmination of his vision with the Son of Man as the central feature in
the heavenly temple.[295] Further, Robert Gundry suggested translating
Revelation 3:12 as "a pillar in the temple *that is* my God," with the ap-
positional genitive, instead of "the temple *of* my God."[296]

Indeed, for the Jewish people, the temple and tabernacle symbolized
the presence of God himself. Yet the difference in *Sitz im Leben* between
Ezekiel and John required a different articulation of the fulfillment of
God's promise to dwell with his people:

> Not only were Ezekiel and his audience down and out in exile,
> but they were also not far enough along the revelatory time line
> to cope with the idea that the temple institution, the very heart
> of their religious life, was to be altogether abandoned. Even
> though such was always a part of God's plan, it could be no more
> than hinted at in the days prior to Christ.[297]

292. Decock, "Scriptures in the Book," 386; Mathewson, *New Heaven*, 117.

293. Vogelgesang, "Interpretation of Ezekiel," 116.

294. Mathewson, *New Heaven*, 118.

295. Beale, *Book of Revelation*, 1091.

296. Gundry, "New Jerusalem," 262; emphasis his.

297. Briggs, *Jewish Temple Imagery*, 105.

Briggs further suggested, "It might even be said that Revelation 21–22 fulfills Ezekiel 40–48 in a manner akin to the multi-faceted way that Jesus Christ fulfills the whole of the Law and the prophets."[298] In Revelation 21–22, the symbol of the divine presence—the temple—has been fulfilled by the Lamb. Thus, the Lamb embodies the true substance of the temple.[299]

The lack of a temple inside the city lends credence to the idea that the entire city is holy.[300] Indeed, the city is portrayed as a holy of holies.[301] For the new Jerusalem, the saints are the most holy dwelling place of God.[302] The pervasive presence of God renders the entire city a vast ναός that "supersedes material structures."[303]

Ezekiel's city-temple likewise reflects several characteristics of the holy of holies as God's presence diffuses through the city. First, Ezekiel refer to the entire temple complex as a holy place. In Ezekiel 43:12, the prophet indicated that the mountain is holy, as well as the area "all around." According to Joyce, "The words 'whole' and 'all around' emphasize the breadth of the area of holiness, as though to diffuse the holiness that pertains not so much to place as to the God who dwells."[304] Second, in Ezekiel 45:3, the portion of the holy district that contains the temple is designated as a holy of holies: ἅγια τῶν ἁγίων.[305] Third, in Ezekiel 48:12 and 48:14, the entire tract of Zadokite land bears the same designation. "This conception of the supreme sanctity of the Temple and its environs is unique to Ezekiel; nowhere else in biblical literature do we find the term 'holy of holies' as a designation for an area outside the Temple proper."[306] Fourth, the appellation for the entire city is יְהוָה שָׁמָּה, or "God is There."[307]

298. Briggs, *Jewish Temple Imagery*, 107.

299. Aune, *Revelation 17–22*, 1189; Deutsch, "Transformation of Symbols," 115; Rissi, *Future of the World*, 60–61.

300. Palmer, "Imagining Space in Revelation," 44.

301. Boring, *Revelation*, 215; du Rand, "New Jerusalem as Pinnacle," 296; Rissi, *Future of the World*, 62–63.

302. Gundry, *Use of the Old Testament*, 261. Cf. Decock, "Scriptures in the Book," 386; Swete, *Apocalypse of St. John*, 288.

303. Swete, *Apocalypse of St. John*, 295. Cf. Thomas and Macchia, *Revelation*, 379.

304. Joyce, "Temple and Worship," 156.

305. קֹדֶשׁ קָדָשִׁים (Ezek 45:3).

306. Kasher, "Anthropomorphism, Holiness and Cult," 201–2.

307. Joyce, "Temple and Worship," 156.

Indeed, the presence of God throughout the city elevates the holiness of the entire region (Ezek 47:1–12).[308]

The term that typically denotes the holy of holies is ναός. Ναός can be used in reference to the entire temple as well, but ἱερός occurs most often in the NT to designate the temple complex.[309] Ezekiel utilized both ναός[310] and ἱερός,[311] as well as οἶκος.[312]

The only use of ναός outside Ezekiel 40–48 is Ezekiel 8:16. Here, τοῦ ναοῦ κυρίου designates "the area in which the sacrificial cult took place, an area therefore of special sanctity corresponding to the court of the priests in Herod's temple."[313] Thus, the ναοῦ in Ezekiel 8:16 is not the holy of holies, but a space just outside the adytum and still a place of special sanctity. The author of the Mishnah's tractate Kelim ranked the area eighth of the ten levels of sanctity.[314]

In the MT, ναός is translated from הֵיכָל, or "palace."[315] A nonsacral term, הֵיכָל can be used to describe any large, luxurious house.[316] "When used of the Israelite sanctuary, *hêkāl* highlights the building's role as the palace of Yahweh. In this context the term denotes not the temple as a whole but the great hall, the nave between the vestibule and the holy of holies."[317]

The only use of ἱερός in Ezekiel is Ezekiel 45:19. The priest is commanded to smear blood upon the lintels of τοῦ οἴκου[318] and upon the four corners of τοῦ ἱεροῦ.[319] Thus, ἱεροῦ seems to be used in parallel with οἴκου, as a designation for the temple as a whole, at least in the LXX.

308. Kasher, "Anthropomorphism, Holiness and Cult," 201.

309. *LSJ* 1160.

310. Ezek 8:16 (2x); 41:1, 4, 15, 21, 23, 25.

311. Ezek 45:19.

312. Ezek 8:14, 16; 9:3, 6 (2x), 7; 10:3, 4, 18, 19; 11:1; 23:39; 40:5, 45, 47, 48; 41:5, 6–10,13–16, 19, 26; 42:15 (2x), 20; 43:4–6, 10–12, 21; 44:4 (2x), 5 (2x), 11 (2x), 14; 45:5, 19, 20, 22; 46:24; 47:1 (2x); 48:11, 21. Other uses of οἶκος are attested in Ezekiel, but not in reference to the temple.

313. Blenkinsopp, *Ezekiel*, 56. Cf. Eichrodt, *Ezekiel*, 127. In Ezekiel 8:16, the τοῦ ναοῦ κυρίου seems to describe the same area as the τὴν αὐλὴν οἴκου κυρίου.

314. M. Kelim 1.9; Greenberg, *Ezekiel 1–20*, 171.

315. Ezek 41:1, 4, 15, 21, 23, 25.

316. *HALOT* 244–45.

317. Block, *Book of Ezekiel: Chapters 25–48*, 543.

318. MT: הַבַּיִת.

319. In the MT, the phrase is rendered differently, as the blood is to be smeared on the four corners of the altar's ledge: וְאֶל־אַרְבַּע פִּנּוֹת הָעֲזָרָה לַמִּזְבֵּחַ.

Although οἶκος is used often to designate the temple in Ezekiel and elsewhere, οἶκος is a nonspecific term whose meaning depends on usage.[320] For example, in Ezekiel 42:15, Ezekiel uses οἶκος to designate both the inner sanctuary and the entire temple. Additionally, "house" is used in other contexts, such as "house of Israel" (Ezek 3:4–5), and "rebellious house" (Ezek 12:2; 17:12; 24:3).

While Ezekiel frequently utilized both οἶκος and ναός, John used ναός exclusively.[321] Kistemaker argued that John's preference for ναός was intentional. "The place where the people are safe is God's temple, which throughout the Apocalypse means not the temple complex but the holy of holies and the holy place."[322]

Other usages of ναός throughout Revelation support such an interpretation. In Revelation 11:19, the heavenly ναός opens and John sees the ark of the covenant, indicating that he is seeing directly into the adytum. In Revelation 15:5, 16:1, and 16:17, John continued to receive visions of the inner sanctuary. Thus, when readers encounter the final use of ναός in Revelation 21:22, they should be prepared to understand that the city represents the very inner sanctum of God.[323]

To conclude, John did not reinterpret Ezekiel's temple vision, although he did reappropriate and reapply Ezekiel's imagery along several avenues. First, John applied Ezekiel's temple imagery to his entire city. Second, John radically distilled Ezekiel's overall description of the temple and the city to convey one central truth—God's presence with his people. Third, John drew upon traditions that portrayed Ezekiel's temple as the heavenly one to link his temple-city with Ezekiel's. However, instead of an architectural structure, John's temple is the Messiah and his people.

The holiness of both cities is a further conceptual link between the visions. Although Ezekiel's holy of holies is spatially distinct from the rest of the city, God's presence never is confined to the adytum. Similarly, the glory of God fills the new Jerusalem in Revelation. Thus, both cities function as an enlarged holy of holies, one which is not restricted to the high priest once a year, but accessible to all saints for all time.[324]

---

320. Οἶκος as temple: Isa 56:7; 60:7; Mark 2:26; Luke 2:49, 11:51; John 2:16. Cf. Michel, "οἶκος," 120–22; McCaffrey, *House with Many Rooms*, 30.

321. Rev 3:12; 7:15; 11:1, 2, 19 (2x); 14:15, 17; 15:5, 6, 8; 16:1, 17; 21:22 (2x).

322. Kistemaker, "Temple in the Apocalypse," 435.

323. Kistemaker, "Temple in the Apocalypse," 440.

324. Rissi, *Future of the World*, 63.

The linguistic links are not as strong as the conceptual ones, although both authors preferred ναός over ἱερός. Further, overt allusions to Ezekiel both before and after Revelation 21:22 indicate that John intended for his readers to understand the verse in connection with Ezekiel's vision.[325]

John maintained the timeless theological foundation of Ezekiel's vision—the presence of God with his people. Yet, in his presentation of a new Jerusalem without priests, land allotments, dividing walls, altars, or even a material temple, he presented God and the Lamb as the true substance of Ezekiel 40–48. Thus, the allusion will be categorized as clear, with a contextual function of fulfillment.

The Renewal of Creation (Rev 22:1–5; Ezek 47:1–12)

Due to the shift in imagery some scholars have contended that Revelation 22:1–5 constitutes a new vision.[326] However, the continuing allusions to Isaiah 60 and Ezekiel 40–48 indicate that no section break occurs.[327] Nonetheless, ἔδειξέν μοι (Rev 22:1) does indicate a topical shift, as in 21:9–10. As Mathewson explained, "Therefore, with 22.1–5 John introduces a new section which is contiguous with what has gone before, but which introduces fresh imagery to depict a new aspect of the reality of eschatological life in the new Jerusalem."[328] Similarly, Ezekiel 40–48 exhibits the same shift from building imagery to paradise imagery in chapter 47.[329]

Indeed, most scholars recognize the imagery in Revelation 22:1–5 as a continuing allusion to Ezekiel.[330] Further, John continued to simplify

---

325. Bauckham, *Climax of Prophecy*, x–xi; Briggs, *Jewish Temple Imagery*, 104–7; Mathewson, *New Heaven*, 32.

326. Aune, *Revelation 17–22*, 1148; Rissi, *Future of the World*, 54, 80.

327. Fekkes pointed out that Isaiah 60:19 is referenced in Revelation 21:23 and 22:5 (Fekkes, *Isaiah and Prophetic Traditions*, 98–99). Cf. Sweet, *Revelation*, 307–9.

328. Mathewson, *New Heaven*, 187.

329. Mathewson, *New Heaven*, 186. Spatafora, *From the "Temple of God,"* 242.

330. Aune, *Revelation 17–22*, 1175–79; Beale, *Book of Revelation*, 1103; Charles, *Critical and Exegetical Commentary*, 176–77; Goulder, "Apocalypse as an Annual Cycle," 347; Mathewson, *New Heaven*, 187; Mounce, *Revelation*, 398–99; Stevens, *Revelation*, 542; Swete, *Apocalypse of St. John*, 98; Vogelgesang, "Interpretation of Ezekiel," 108.

and condense Ezekiel's vision. Here, he has reduced Ezekiel's twelve-verse description into two verses.[331]

Water of Life (Rev 22:1–2; Ezek 47:1–12)

In Revelation 22:1–2, just as in Ezekiel, water flows from the temple, but now the temple is God and the Lamb.[332] Such a conception may not be completely foreign to the Ezekielian context either. In Ezekiel 47:1, the water flows from the threshold of the temple, which throughout Ezekiel is a space occupied only by God himself and the prince, God's representative.[333] Manning postulated, "We might speculate that [John] saw the מפתן, the source of the river, as the place for the glory of God."[334] Moreover, the course of the river retraces the path taken by the Lord upon his return to the temple in Ezekiel 43, likely indicating that the water flows from his very presence.[335] Thus, John's indication that the water flows from God's throne may reproduce Ezekiel's imagery even more closely than first imagined.

The Greek also exhibits parallels. In Revelation 22:1, John described a river of water of life (ποταμός, ὕδωρ, ζωή) that comes out (ἐκπορεύομαι) from the throne.[336] Similarly, Ezekiel described water that comes out (ὕδωρ, ἐκπορεύομαι) from the threshold of the temple (Ezek 47:1). Ezekiel's water, also called a river (ποταμός; Ezek 47:6–7, 9, 12), brings life (ζάω; Ezek 47:9) to the surrounding terrain. Although the grammatical forms are different, the roots ὕδωρ, ποταμός, ἐκπορεύομαι, and ζάω are used in both passages.[337]

---

331. Vogelgesang, "Interpretation of Ezekiel," 109.

332. Beale, *Book of Revelation*, 1104; Goulder, "Apocalypse as an Annual Cycle," 347; Mathewson, *New Heaven*, 189; Vogelgesang, "Interpretation of Ezekiel," 78.

333. God: Ezek 9:3; 10:4, 18; prince: Ezek 46:2.

334. Manning, *Echoes of a Prophet*, 183. Cf. Eichrodt, *Ezekiel*, 582; Zimmerli, *Ezekiel 2*, 514–15.

335. Allen, *Ezekiel 20–48*, 279.

336. Cf. 1 En. 26:1–3.

337. In addition to Ezekiel 47:1–12, John likely alluded to a variety of other biblical passages in his portrayal of the eschatological paradise. Such passages include Genesis 2:9–10; Isaiah 35:6–9; 51:3; Zechariah 14:8. Cf. Ps 36:8–9; Isa 35:6–9; 43:18–20; 41:18–20; 49:10; Joel 3:18; Zech 14:8, 11; John 7:38. Mounce, *Revelation*, 398–99; Stevens, *Revelation*, 542; Swete, *Apocalypse of St. John*, 98; Vogelgesang, "Interpretation of Ezekiel," 108.

Other Second Temple Jewish authors also associated such paradisal imagery with the new Jerusalem.[338] As in Ezekiel 47:1–12, paradise imagery is associated often with the cult.[339] In Jubilees 8:19, the garden of Eden is described as "the holy of holies and the dwelling of the Lord." The historical Jerusalem temple also was suffused with edenic imagery.[340]

Such themes derive largely from the primeval garden of Genesis 2:9–10.[341] Thus, both Ezekiel and John anticipated a restoration of the primeval paradise in which God dwelt in perfect communion with people. "Even the decorative palm trees and cherubim portrayed as part of Ezekiel's temple (41:18–26) allude to the garden setting of Eden."[342] The entire temple complex represents paradise, and the river that flows from the threshold represents the life that God's presence brings to creation.[343] "No amount of exegetical finesse or insistence on 'what the Bible plainly says' can transform the poetry of this passage into a topographically and ecologically realistic account of an event in time."[344] Similarly, in Revelation 22, the river, trees, and leaves do not simply provide nourishment, but rather eternal life, as in Genesis. Regardless of how one understands the significance of Ezekiel's vision, "it is abundantly clear that Rev. 22:2 interprets the Ezekiel picture in this manner."[345]

John drew upon texts such as Ezekiel 47:1–12 and Genesis 2:9 to depict his temple-city as a return to paradise and unmediated access to God's presence.[346] Additionally, John's use of paradise imagery in the eschatological city-temple creates a pan-biblical *inclusio*, which is a fitting conclusion for his own vision and Scripture as a whole.[347] Yet John's

---

338. 2 Bar. 4:1–6; T. Dan 5:12; 1 En. 24–32; 2 En. 8:1–8; T. Levi 18:10–11; 4 Ezra 2:12, 18–19; 7:123; 8:52.

339. Exod 25:33; 28:33–34; 1 Kgs 6:23–29; 7:18–29, 42; Ps. 36:7–9; Ezek 28:13; 41:18–26; Joel 3:18–20.

340. Barker, *Gate of Heaven*, 2, 57; Mathewson, *New Heaven*, 197.

341. Levenson, *Theology of the Program*, 28–29; Niditch, "Ezekiel 40–48," 217.

342. Beale, *Book of Revelation*, 1106. Cf. Barker, *Gate of Heaven*, 69; Blenkinsopp, *Ezekiel*, 231; Lee, *New Jerusalem*, 15; Levenson, *Theology of the Program*, 26–36.

343. Barker, *Gate of Heaven*, 30, 75; Goulder, "Apocalypse as an Annual Cycle," 347; Tuell, *Law of the Temple*, 69.

344. Blenkinsopp, *Ezekiel*, 231.

345. Beale, *Book of Revelation*, 1107.

346. Mathewson, *New Heaven*, 195; du Rand, "New Jerusalem as Pinnacle," 297.

347. Clifford, "Temple and the Holy Mountain," 122; Mathewson, *New Heaven*, 198; Smalley, *Revelation to John*, 563.

transformation of spatial imagery into relational imagery emphasizes that the point of restoration is not a place, but a person—Jesus Christ.

The Sea (Rev 21:1)

While representing the life-giving character of God, the waters flowing from the temple also signify the absence of evil in the new creation. The ancients believed that the temple was situated above the primeval deep and that the proper functioning of the temple "was necessary to ensure that sufficient [water] was released to ensure fertility, but not so much as to overwhelm the earth with a flood."[348] Thus, the temple was a bastion of order that prevented the eruption of chaotic waters.[349] The idea of the tamed waters of chaos recalls Revelation 21:1, in which John described a new heaven and earth where "the sea was no more."[350]

Ezekiel, in his enumeration of architectural details and temple appurtenances, likewise omitted the sea. The sea was a large, round bronze basin that stood upon twelve bronze cattle. In Solomon's Temple, the vessel measured ten cubits in diameter and five in height.[351] At half the width of the temple, the enormous basin dominated the temple courtyard. The absence of the vessel would have been conspicuous to those familiar with the layout of the Jerusalem temple.[352]

The function of the bronze sea is somewhat unclear. According to 2 Chronicles 4:6, the priests washed in the basin. However, "It is difficult to imagine that such a vessel would serve only for simple ablutions."[353] Instead, the priests may have "immersed in it before performing certain ceremonies . . . because it was deep enough to cover a man's entire body.

348. Barker, *Gate of Heaven*, 18.

349. Barker, *Gate of Heaven*, 19. Lundquist, "Temple, Covenant, and Law," 299. Cf. Ps 29:10; Let. Aris. 89–91; b. Yoma 77b, 78a; b. Sukkah 53a.

350. For the absence or destruction of the sea, cf. Sib. Or. 5:158–59, 447–48; T. Levi 4:1; Pss. 18:15; 106:9; Isa 44:27; 50:2; 51:10; Jer 51:36; Nah 1:4; Zech 10:11.

351. Roughly four and a half meters in diameter and two in height (1 Kgs 7:23–26, 39).

352. Patton, "Ezekiel's Blueprint for the Temple," 164; Tuell, *Ezekiel*, 289–90. Milgrom proposed that the sea is absent from Ezekiel's vision because the priests could wash their hands in the spring near the entrance to the temple. His supposition is based on the presence of a spring at the entrance to the Delphi temple (Milgrom and Block, *Ezekiel's Hope*, 46–47).

353. Hurowitz, "YHWH's Exalted House," 79.

If so, it must be assumed that a priest wishing to bathe would use a ladder or some other device at the side of the basin to reach its upper edge."[354]

Regardless of function, the sea likely symbolized the waters that the temple kept ordered.[355] Further, the river may replace the sea in Ezekiel's vision.[356] That Ezekiel's waters flow from the exact place that the bronze sea was located in Solomon's temple is support for such a proposal.[357] Resultantly, Ezekiel's river in Ezekiel 47:1–12 may represent the permanently tamed waters of chaos that had threatened the security of God's people previously.

Similarly, the absence of a sea in Revelation 21:1 represents the end of persecution and suffering for God's people.[358] In Revelation 21:4, such an understanding is confirmed in that "death will be no more, nor mourning nor crying nor pain will exist any longer, for the first things have passed away." Although the sea is gone in both Revelation and Ezekiel, the waters of paradise may represent the permanently transformed waters of chaos, which now bring life instead of evil.

To conclude, the absence of the sea cannot be categorized as an allusion, since Ezekiel did not actually state that the sea is absent in his temple. The absence is simply presumed from silence. Nonetheless, one can conjecture that John, noticing the omission, might have decided to make the lack of a sea more overt in his own vision of the eschatological temple.

The Altar (Ezek 43:15)

Another tenuous but noteworthy connection can be made in regard to the altar. In Ezekiel 43:13–17, Ezekiel described an altar upon which sacrifices would be offered in his temple. In verse 15, the prophet termed the altar hearth an αριηλ/הַרְאֵל.[359] In the OT, הַרְאֵל is rare, being used

354. Hurowitz, "YHWH's Exalted House," 79. Cf. Lev 8:6; 16:4; Exod 29:4.

355. Beale, *Book of Revelation*, 1042–43; Hurowitz, "YHWH's Exalted House," 80; Levenson, "Jerusalem Temple," 51; Mathewson, *New Heaven*, 65; Smith, "Like Deities, Like Temples," 6; Stevens, *Revelation*, 527; Sweet, *Revelation*, 297.

356. Patton, "Ezekiel's Blueprint for the Temple," 165.

357. Hurowitz, "YHWH's Exalted House," 80–81.

358. See Revelation 12:17—13:1; 17:1, 15; 20:13. Beale, *Book of Revelation*, 1042–43; Boring, *Revelation*, 216–17; Mathewson, *New Heaven*, 65.

359. Patton, "Ezekiel's Blueprint for the Temple," 164. Cf. Levenson, "Jerusalem Temple," 32–61.

only as a personal name and an appellation for Jerusalem.[360] The manner in which Ezekiel used הַרְאֵל is unattested otherwise. Various suggestions have been put forth for the etymology of the word, but הַרְאֵל most likely is comprised of a compound of אֲרִי and אֵל, which can be translated literally as "hearth of God."[361]

Although no holocaust altar is present in Revelation, a connection with Ezekiel still might exist.[362] Several features of the altar must be explicated to illuminate the potential connection. First, Ezekiel's altar is the centermost point of the temple complex, a position occupied by the holy of holies in Solomon's Temple.[363] One would expect the divine throne room, the holy of holies, to be the center of the complex, but instead the altar is at the center.[364] Further, the altar itself is square, just like the holy of holies. Second, Ezekiel provided the height of the altar, a dimension that is unspecified otherwise in the temple plan (Ezek 43:13–16).[365] The attention given to the dimensions of the altar indicates that the structure held a prominent place in the overall design of the complex.[366] Correspondingly, the altar sat upon the uppermost peak of the temple complex (Ezek 43:17), which represents the point of contact between God and his people. That sacred areas typically were elevated corroborates the idea

360. Personal name: 2 Sam 23:20; 1 Chr 11:22; Ezra 8:16; name of Jerusalem: Isa 29:1–2, 7.

361. William Albright suggested that הַרְאֵל originates from the Akkadian *arralû*, which can signify either the underworld or the mountain of God (Albright, "Babylonian Temple-Tower," 137–42). Similarly, André Parrot proposed that the הַרְאֵל is related to the Babylonian ziggurat (Parrot, *Babylon and the Old Testament*, 29). William Rosenau suggested הַרְאֵל was connected to אֲרִי, "lion" (Rosenau, "Harel und Ha-Ariel," 350–56). Cf. *DBL* § 789; BDB 72; Blenkinsopp, *Ezekiel*, 214; Block, *Book of Ezekiel: Chapters 25–48*, 600.

362. The altar in Revelation 6:9–11; 8:3; 9:13; 14:18; and 16:7 is the heavenly counterpart of the incense altar in the earthly temple (Briggs, *Jewish Temple Imagery*, 78–79).

363. As in Solomon's Temple and the tabernacle, Ezekiel's temple also contained a second altar, corresponding to the altar of incense (Exod 30:1–3; 1 Chr 28:17; Ezek 41:22). Incidentally, unlike the previous golden altars, Ezekiel's description of a *wooden* table serving as an altar for burning incense seems impractical (Boyle, "Holiness has a Shape," 10–11; Milgrom and Block, *Ezekiel's Hope*, 48–49; Patton, "Ezekiel's Blueprint for the Temple," 156).

364. Block, *Beyond the River Chebar*, 189.

365. Boyle, "Holiness has a Shape," 12–13.

366. Block, *Beyond the River Chebar*, 189; Block, *Book of Ezekiel: Chapters 25–48*, 596.

that the altar has taken the place of the holy of holies.[367] Third, "the altar was massive," allowing for continuous worship on a grand scale.[368] Thus, Ezekiel's altar "takes the place of the holy of holies in the Solomonic Temple as the *locus classicus* of divine presence."[369]

With such foundations in place, the possible connection with Revelation can be elucidated. For Ezekiel, the altar of sacrifice represented the locus of God's presence, and for John, the throne represented the locus of God's presence. Thus, the Lamb, formerly the slaughtered Lamb (Rev 5:6), occupies the same position as Ezekiel's altar of sacrifice.[370] Both the altar of the temple (Ezek 43:17) and the Lamb (Rev 21:22) represent the point of contact between God and sinful people.[371] An allusion cannot be substantiated, but the idea bears consideration.

The River (Rev 22:1–2; Ezek 47:1–12)

Just as most elements of John's vision symbolize relational concepts, the water of Revelation 22:1–2 is not simply a river. "The divine origin of this river of living water is made clear in that it flows from the very throne of God and the Lamb . . . It is their salvific gift to all those who believe in and offer faithful witness to them."[372] Further, the water represents eternal fellowship with God, as sealed by the Holy Spirit.[373] Similarly, the description of the water as "bright as crystal" represents purifying properties, so that sinners may enter God's presence cleansed of their former iniquities (Rev 22:3–5).[374] Through the medium of the water, grace is disbursed throughout the entire population.[375]

That the river flows through the central street of the city indicates that all who inhabit the city have access.[376] "The picture of the nations advancing on the city's main street may imply that they wade in the life-

---

367. Barker, *Gate of Heaven*, 12, 25; Boyle, "Holiness has a Shape," 15.

368. Boyle, "Holiness has a Shape," 11. Cf. Block, *Beyond the River Chebar*, 189.

369. Boyle, "Holiness has a Shape," 15.

370. Cf. Heb 13:10.

371. Block, *Beyond the River Chebar*, 189.

372. Thomas and Macchia, *Revelation*, 387.

373. See 2 Cor 1:21–22; 5:5; Eph 1:13; 4:30. Swete, *Apocalypse of St. John*, 298.

374. Beale, *Book of Revelation*, 1104.

375. Levenson, *Theology of the Program*, 13.

376. Thomas and Macchia, *Revelation*, 387.

giving waters as they walk, just as the prophet waded the closer he was to the cultic source of the water in Ezek 47:3–4."[377] Nonetheless, the flow of the river diverges from Ezekiel to Revelation. In Ezekiel, the water flows from the temple and city to water the surrounding terrain. By contrast, John's river flows only within the city. As Mathewson explained, "Because life is found only within the confines of the city wall in John's vision (cf. 21.27; 22.15), the author has adapted the picture to suit his own vision, since there is no need of a river watering anything outside the boundaries of the new Jerusalem."[378]

Yet, perhaps the divergence has even greater significance. In keeping with Israel's destiny to be a light to all nations, the river that flows from Ezekiel's temple fructifies the entire sea, and by extension the entire world (Ezek 47:8–9).[379] In Revelation, Israel's ministry is complete, as the people of God are joined by the nations in the new Jerusalem.

On the whole, Ezekiel 47:1–12 and Revelation 22:1–2 bear heavy conceptual and linguistic parallels and comprise a clear allusion. Both prophets described an eschatological river that symbolizes the transformed waters of chaos, and hence, the absence of evil. The water is a soteriological gift from the Lord that brings life to the eschatological creation. Most prominently, the water of life furthers the depiction of a restored Eden, in which the saints enjoy eternal sinless fellowship with the Lord. Thus, the allusion can be categorized as another instance of literary prototyping, as both John and Ezekiel portray the fulfillment of the pervasive biblical hope of a return to unhindered fellowship with God, as was enjoyed in Eden.

The Tree of Life (Rev 22:2; Ezek 47:7, 12)

The function of the tree of life in Revelation 22:2 is similar to that of the water, as John continued to draw upon Ezekiel 47:1–12.[380] The trees of Ezekiel are nourished by the water from the temple, and the trees of Revelation are nourished by water from the throne of God and the Lamb.[381]

377. Beale, *Book of Revelation*, 1104.

378. Mathewson, *New Heaven*, 189.

379. Gen 18:19; 22:18; Isa 49:6. Eichrodt, *Ezekiel*, 585–86.

380. Aune, *Revelation 17–22*, 1177–78; Bauckham, *Climax of Prophecy*, 316; Boxall, *Revelation*, 310; Thomas and Macchia, *Revelation*, 387.

381. Cf. 1QH XIV, 14–18.

Grammatically, John seemed to describe a singular tree. However, the ξύλον in Revelation may be a collective term implying many trees:

> A collective interpretation is consistent with Ezekiel's picture of trees growing on both sides of the river bank, and it is in line with the logic of the picture in Rev. 22:1–2 (how could one tree grow on either side of the river?). The absence of the article may point further to a collective meaning. The one tree of life in the first garden has become many trees of life in the escalated paradisal state of the second garden.[382]

To the contrary, Mathewson argued, "Despite the common tendency to understand ξύλον in Rev. 22.2 in a collective sense ('trees') as in Ezek. 47.7, 12, the allusion to Gen. 2.9 suggests a single tree, however much difficulty this may create in conceptualizing John's vision."[383] Further, as has been established already, John's spatial language is not to be taken literally. More important is the symbolic content of the imagery.[384] Regardless of whether John described one tree or many, the more relevant concern is the point John intended to convey with the allusions to Ezekiel 47:1–12 and Genesis 2:9–10.[385]

Boxall interpreted the tree as the cross of Christ.[386] Ξύλον typically is used to describe wood or anything made from wood and in the NT often designates the cross.[387] Δένδρον is the more common term for an actual tree.[388] Resultantly, Boxall wrote, "It is unlikely that the allusion [to the cross] would have been lost on early generations of Christians."[389] To the contrary, ξύλον often is used for "tree" in the LXX, as in Ezekiel 47:12 and Genesis 2:9.[390] So although it is possible that John included

382. Beale, *Book of Revelation*, 1106. Cf. Aune, *Revelation 17–22*, 1177; Ford, *Revelation*, 346; Swete, *Apocalypse of St. John*, 299.

383. Mathewson, *New Heaven*, 189. Cf. Koester, *Revelation*, 823; Mounce, *Revelation*, 387; Stevens, *Revelation*, 543; Smalley, *Revelation to John*, 563; Vanhoye, "L'utilization du livre d'Ezéchiel," 460; Vogelgesang, "Interpretation of Ezekiel," 108.

384. Mathewson, *Revelation*, 300; Smalley, *Revelation to John*, 562.

385. Stevens, *Revelation*, 543; Vogelgesang, "Interpretation of Ezekiel," 108.

386. Boxall, *Revelation*, 311. Cf. Spatafora, *From the "Temple of God,"* 113.

387. Acts 5:30; 10:39; 13:29; Gal 3:13; 1 Pet 2:24. Schneider, "ξύλον," 39.

388. Mathewson, *New Heaven*, 198.

389. Boxall, *Revelation*, 311.

390. Cf. Gen 1:11–12; Exod 10:5; Lev 19:23; Deut 29:19–20; 1 Chr 16:32; Ps 1:3.

a subtle reference to the cross, his primary emphasis appears to derive from Genesis 2 and Ezekiel 47, in which the new Jerusalem represents Eden restored.[391]

Fruit and Leaves (Rev 21:2; Ezek 47:12)

Both John and Ezekiel described fruit and leaves, which are produced by the tree(s). Although the phraseology is similar, the only parallel lexeme in Greek is καρπός, or "fruit." Yet John appears to have been referencing the Hebrew text for his imagery here.[392] Ezekiel's trees bear fruit every month, which is a detail not included expressly in Revelation 22:2. However, John's "twelve fruits" transfer naturally from Ezekiel's לָחֳדָשָׁיו, or "monthly."[393]

John omitted that the fruit is for food, but he also added that the leaves are for "the healing of the nations." The omission is not surprising, as John consistently abridged Ezekiel's vision. His addition is more noteworthy. "John's change from the more restrictive perspective of Ezekiel to a more inclusive one coheres with his concern to extend the benefits of the new Jerusalem to all the nations."[394]

The nature of the healing effected by the leaves has been interpreted in a number of ways. (1) The healing equates to the evangelism of the nations as yet outside the new Jerusalem in the period of the millennium.[395] (2) The leaves heal those martyred for their faith.[396] (3) The leaves promote enjoyment of the new era. They do not heal sin or other ills, since such problems no longer exist.[397] (4) The healing represents physical and spiritual salvation.[398]

391. Mathewson, *New Heaven*, 199.

392. "Bearing twelve kinds of fruit, producing its fruit each month; and the leaves of the tree were for healing of the nations" (Rev 22:2b). Some manuscripts omit "of the nations" possibly to conform to Ezekiel 47:17. Cf. Beale, *Book of Revelation*, 1108; Mathewson, *New Heaven*, 301.

393. In the LXX, Ezekiel did not mention fruit being produced each month, but rather "first-fruits" (Charles, *Critical and Exegetical Commentary*, 176–77; Mathewson, *New Heaven*, 190).

394. Mathewson, *New Heaven*, 190.

395. Charles, *Critical and Exegetical Commentary*, 177; Ford, *Revelation*, 339.

396. Kiddle, *Revelation of St. John*, 443.

397. Morris, *Book of Revelation*, 249.

398. Beale, *Book of Revelation*, 1108; Koester, *Revelation*, 824; Thomas and

Most likely, a combination of the various interpretations comes closest to John's intent. The frequent references to "the nations" through-out Revelation indicates that John intended his readers to understand that individuals formerly opposed to God can experience salvation. Additionally, "Given the context of 'life' (Rev 22:1), it is likely that the reader of Rev. 22:2 should understand the healing, not as a reference to a specific malady, but more broadly as life and as freedom from the effects of sin which plague the old order (cf. 21:4)."[399] Further, the healing of the nations is explained through connection to the death of the Messiah in Revelation 5:9, indicating that the fruit should be associated with salvation.[400]

Additionally, John may have exploited Ezekiel's distinction between the fruit and the leaves. As with the gates and foundation stones that combine the apostles and the tribes, John seemed to combine the twelve tribes (twelve fruits) with the nations (leaves for healing).[401] So again John described the consummation of God's covenant promises by extending salvation to all nations through Israel.

Whether Ezekiel envisioned the eschatological blessings as reserved for Israel or whether he extended the promises to other nations is a matter of dispute. Vogelgesang contended that John expanded upon Ezekiel's particularistic understanding to portray salvation being extended to all nations.[402] Eichrodt argued to the contrary:

> The river of paradise and the marvelous effects brought by it signify the transformation of this world into the garden of para-dise, whence not only the hosts of earthly diseases, but also sin and guilt have been banished, and God's good pleasure in his creation comes to full effect and works a complete inward and outward transformation of the whole shape of human life.[403]

With such edenic echoes, Ezekiel portrayed the extension of eschatological and soteriological blessings that would begin with Israel and spread throughout creation.

Macchia, *Revelation*, 388.

399. Mathewson, "Destiny of the Nations," 39. Cf. Bauckham, *Climax of Prophecy*, 317.

400. Beale, *Book of Revelation*, 1107–8; Mounce, *Revelation*, 387.

401. Mathewson, *New Heaven*, 190.

402. Vogelgesang, "Interpretation of Ezekiel." Cf. Mathewson, *New Heaven*, 190; Pfisterer Darr, "Wall around Paradise."

403. Eichrodt, *Ezekiel*, 585.

To conclude, the linguistic parallels in the botanical imagery of Ezekiel 47:1–12 and Revelation 22:1–2 are somewhat weaker than with the
water. Yet similar phraseology does exist in two parallel lexemes: ξύλον
and καρπός. Similarities with the Hebrew text are present as well.

The verses also exhibit heavy conceptual parallels. The trees, along
with their leaves and fruit, fill out the vision of Eden restored and symbolize eschatological salvation. Whereas the river represents the absence
of sin, evil, and chaos, the trees symbolize the blessings that come with
restoration to God's presence. Thus, based on similar terminology, strong
contextual affinities, and a clear allusion with respect to the water imagery, the allusion will be categorized as clear.

The contextual function is the same as that of the river. Both John
and Ezekiel portrayed a return to paradise along with the idea of eternal
life in God's presence. That the two authors described a similar reality
indicates that John's usage functions as a literary prototype. Yet a fulfillment usage is implicit as well. John exploits Ezekiel's imagery to depict
the salvation of both the Jewish people and the gentiles. Just as with the
tribes and apostles on the gates and foundation stones, so also the leaves
and fruits represent the salvation of all peoples.

No More Curse (Rev 22:3)

The presence of the tree of life in Revelation 22:3 points to the removal
of the curse in Genesis 3:14–19, and indeed, John stated explicitly that
the curse is no more. The edenic overtones underscore the restoration of
fellowship that was lost in the garden, "again making clear the immediate
and direct access the overcomers have to God, for this tree is a sign that
the previous separation and enmity between God and humankind is now
completely removed."[404]

As is typical for John, the curse of Revelation 22:3 hearkens from
several passages. The most obvious intertext is Genesis 3:14–19. However, the Greek terms are different. The translator of Genesis 3:17 rendered
the curse as ἐπικατάρατος, and in Revelation 22:3, John rendered the
curse as κατάθεμα. The Greek of Zechariah 14:11 is closer. In describing
the eschatological Jerusalem, the verse reads, "People will live in it and
there will never again be a curse. Then Jerusalem will dwell in security."

---

404. Thomas and Macchia, *Revelation*, 388. Cf. du Rand, "New Jerusalem as Pinnacle," 298; Sweet, *Revelation*, 311.

Here, "curse" (חֵרֶם) is rendered ἀνάθεμα, which is a step closer to John's κατάθεμα.[405]

The passage in Zechariah refers to healing that takes place after the destruction by Babylon in 586 BCE. In the context of holy war, κατάθεμα/ חֵרֶם is used to describe nations or groups whom God has decreed for destruction. The term even applies to Israel in certain circumstances in association with the withdrawal of God's presence.[406] Indeed, in Zechariah 14, the ban is that which is applied to Israel and executed by Babylon. In alluding to Zechariah 14, John suggested that "not only the nations, but all those who enjoy eschatological life in the new Jerusalem need not fear destruction and will dwell there in perpetual security."[407]

Ezekiel used none of the terms for "curse" directly. The prophet only implied that the curse was gone with the description of desalinized sea water and lush trees whose leaves do not wither. However, Mathewson proposed that in Revelation 22:3, John departed from Ezekiel 47 and relied instead on Ezekiel 43. "A striking parallel to Rev. 22.3 which John was probably aware of is found in Ezekiel, where, according to Ezek. 43.7, the throne of God is situated in the midst of the new temple where God will reside with Israel forever. John, however, has it situated in the midst of the new Jerusalem."[408] In short, the removal of sin and defilement (Ezek 43:7–9) makes possible the placement of God's throne, indicative of his presence in the new Jerusalem.

In typical form, John appeared to conflate his sources, drawing from Genesis 3, Zechariah 14, Ezekiel 43, and Ezekiel 47. However, Ezekiel is not a major source of imagery for the curse removal. Linguistic affinities are completely absent, and conceptual affinities are implied only. Thus, the allusion can be classified as possible, if not probable. Based on the similar language and concepts between Ezekiel and Revelation, the function is a literary prototype.

405. Aune noted that the difference between the two terms is unclear (Aune, *Revelation 17–22*, 1179).

406. See Josh 7:12.

407. Mathewson, *New Heaven*, 202. Cf. Aune, *Revelation 17–22*, 1179.

408. Mathewson, *New Heaven*, 204.

The New Name (Rev 22:4; Ezek 48:35)

In Revelation 2:17, John specified that the saints will receive a new name, and in Revelation 22:4, the inhabitants of the new Jerusalem receive God's name upon their foreheads. The mark of God functions as the inverse of the beast's mark, indicating that those who bear God's name profess allegiance to him.[409] Being marked with God's name also recalls Ezekiel 9:4, in which those who mourn over the idolatry in Jerusalem receive a mark on the forehead and are spared the outpouring of God's wrath.[410] Similarly, in Revelation, individuals who are marked by the Lord receive his protection (Rev 7:1–3).[411] The naming thus represents the security of the saints and "the idea of the eternal residence of God with his people."[412] Such is the case in Revelation 22:4, and also Ezekiel 48:35, wherein Ezekiel's city receives the name יְהוָה שָׁמָּה, or "the Lord is there."

Biblically, a name encapsulates the essence of a person. To know someone's name is to discern his or her character.[413] "When God chooses to reveal himself he does so by revealing his name (cf. Gen 17,1; Exod 3,14; 6,2). In so doing, he reveals more than simply that by which he is called. He discloses a part of himself, of who he is."[414] For saints to bear God's name indicates that they understand something of his nature and correspondingly reflect his character.[415]

In the OT cultic system, the name of God was written on the foreheads of priests.[416] The significance of the inscription was that those who bore the mark served as representatives of the Lord.[417] The inscription of God's name in Revelation 22:4 thus reinforces the priestly character of the inhabitants of the new Jerusalem.[418] Bauckham succinctly explained, "They are priests who worship him and kings who reign with him."[419]

---

409. Mark of God: Rev 3:12; 7:1–5; 9:4; 14:1; mark of the beast: Rev 13:17; 14:11; 16:2; 19:20.

410. Beale, *Book of Revelation*, 1114.

411. Mathewson, *New Heaven*, 208.

412. Cooper, *Ezekiel*, 425. Cf. Tuell, *Ezekiel*, 342.

413. Spatafora, From the *"Temple of God,"* 139.

414. Spatafora, From the *"Temple of God,"* 137–38.

415. Beale, *Book of Revelation*, 1114; Witherington, *Revelation*, 273.

416. Exod 28:36–38.

417. Mathewson, *New Heaven*, 208–9.

418. Beale, *Book of Revelation*, 1114; Sweet, *Revelation*, 312.

419. Bauckham, *Theology of the Book*, 142. Cf. Sweet, *Revelation*, 312; Thomas and

As in Ezekiel and Revelation, several passages in Isaiah indicate that the people of God will receive a new name.[420] These verses may be in the background of Revelation 22:4.[421] However, the inscription of the name on the forehead, as well as the overarching literary prototyping of Revelation 21:1—22:5 on Ezekiel 40–48, indicates that the Ezekielian referents are primary. Further, the author of the Isaian passages did not indicate that the new name was the name of God, as did John and Ezekiel.

Strong conceptual affinities exist between Revelation 22:4 and Ezekiel 48:35. In both passages, those who are marked with God's name (1) reflect God's character, (2) receive God's protection, and (3) enjoy God's presence. Lexical affinities, however, are vague. Although both Revelation 22:4 and Ezekiel 48:35 utilize ὄνομα, or "name," the term is too common to imply dependence. The literary contexts of Ezekiel 48:35 and Revelation 22:4 likewise do not align. In Ezekiel 48, the prophet dealt with land allotments, while in Revelation 22:1–5, John described the renewed heaven and earth. In Ezekiel, the name applies to the city, and in Revelation the name applies to the people. Yet in Revelation, the people are the city, so the parallel remains conceptually similar.

A structural parallel can be identified as well. The naming of the saints is found at the end of the visions in both Revelation 21:1—22:5 and Ezekiel 40–48. Bearing in mind John's tendency to conflate and condense, he may have combined the new name of Ezekiel 48:35 with the mark of God in Ezekiel 9:4 as he iterated the name of the city-saints in Revelation 22:4. In sum, the parallel will be regarded as probable due to the presence of strong structural and conceptual affinities. The function of the intertext is most likely thematic.

Evaluation

Potential parallels between the final visions of Ezekiel and John have been examined in the current chapter. Of the topics surveyed, most were regarded as clear allusions, three were identified as probable, and five were identified as possible. Yet, as stated in the introduction, precisely *how* John utilized his prophetic predecessor is under scrutiny as well. More

---

Macchia, *Revelation*, 390.

420. Isa 56:5; 62:2; 65:15.

421. Beale, *Book of Revelation*, 1114.

specifically, if John wished to dispense with the temple, why did he draw upon Ezekiel's *temple* vision?

Some scholars have suggested that John primarily used Ezekiel's language and imagery to construct his own vision.[422] However, John did not simply reuse OT snippets to create a patchwork quilt. By drawing upon the introductory formulas in Ezekiel 40:1–2 and Ezekiel 43:5, John implied that his entire vision served as a retelling of Ezekiel's. John also concluded his vision in the same manner as Ezekiel, by closing with the name of God characterizing the city-saints. Indeed, John intended his own vision to serve as a lens through which his readers viewed OT prophecy.[423] Most often John was overt as he alluded to his OT predecessors, utilizing Ezekiel 40–48, in particular, as a literary prototype. Yet, in other instances, he wove a variety of OT passages into his own distinct vision. As the successor to the OT prophets, John iterated similar themes and expressed similar hopes as his forerunners.

In order to convey his vision of eschatological fulfillment, John distilled Ezekiel 40–48 to the essence of the prophecy—God's presence with his people. Through frequent allusions to Ezekiel's temple vision, John presented Revelation 21–22 as a clarification of Ezekiel 40–48 based on the advent of the Messiah. Accordingly, passages in which John seemed to diverge from the OT context can be explained by developments in salvation history. John articulated a distinctive Christian ideology as he evoked the eschatological vision of God dwelling with his people without a physical sanctuary.

Considering the pervasive use of Ezekiel 40–48 throughout Revelation 21–22, the omission of the temple cannot be accidental. John intentionally generated the dissonance between his own vision and Ezekiel's to draw attention to essential points. When the heavenly city descends, the saints should know that their eschatological hopes are being fulfilled. God's presence will be available to all people as heaven and earth unite. When walls and gates are not really walls and gates, the saints are to understand that they, themselves, embody the new Jerusalem. When the centerpiece of the vision, the temple, is absent, hearers are expected to understand that the Messiah embodies all that the temple represented.

---

422. Decock, "Scriptures in the Book," 373–410; Moyise, "Ezekiel and the Book," 45–57; Schüssler Fiorenza, *Book of Revelation*, 135.

423. Beale, "Revelation," 318–36; Bauckham, *Climax of Prophecy*, x–xi; Briggs, *Jewish Temple Imagery*, 104–7; Kiddle, *Revelation of St. John*, 443; Mathewson, *New Heaven*, 32.

Though the new Jerusalem does not house an architectural temple, the presence of God and the Lamb takes priority over the physical temple and embodies the very essence of the sanctuary.

7.

Conclusion

THE CURRENT RESEARCH BEGAN with the thesis that in Revelation 21:1—22:2, John portrayed the Messiah as the fulfillment of Ezekiel 40–48. The analysis proceeded along three avenues. First, intertextual models were surveyed and evaluated. The analogical model was determined to be best suited for a faithful historical-critical interpretation of *both* testaments. The unique message and authority of the OT are retained, while Jesus Christ is recognized as the culmination of revelation.[1] According to the analogical model, prophetic texts contain an objective element that was understood by the original author, even if the complete symbolic content of the element was not grasped. When NT authors drew upon such passages, the true meaning and substance of the original prophecy were retained. Accordingly, the timeless theological core of Ezekiel's temple vision was sought in order to determine whether John's utilization of Ezekiel 40–48 conveyed similar theological principles.

Interpretations of Ezekiel 40–48 fall broadly into two categories: literal and figurative. The literal interpretations were distilled into three complementary ideas. First, the fulfillment of God's promises is depicted in Ezekiel 40–48. Second, structures that ensure proper worship are established. Third, the eventual fulfillment of prophetic promises will make the presence of Yahweh available to all people. Undergirding each strand of thought is the idea of a restored relationship between God and humanity. The rebuilt temple serves as a place where God and his people can meet for fellowship and worship.

1. Weir, "Analogous Fulfillment," 65–76.

Figurative interpretations of Ezekiel 40–48 likewise were distilled into three principles. First, the perfection of God's plan is expressed symbolically through highly ordered legislation and architecture. Second, the holiness of God is emphasized through the design and symmetry of the temple and surrounding precincts. Third, all elements of the vision work together to safeguard the perpetual presence of God with his people. True worship can take place because the perfection of the temple creates an inviolable penitence in the people. The renewed individuals are free to commune with God absent any of the former barriers to fellowship.

Finally, the analysis revealed that the foundational emphases of the figurative interpretations do not differ greatly from those of the literal interpretations. Regardless of the hermeneutical standpoints of individual interpreters, the presence of God with his people is of central importance to Ezekiel's message. The timeless theological principle, therefore, is God dwelling with his people in perfect communion.

The second portion of the research was comprised of a diachronic analysis of Second Temple period literature. Various literary works were examined, with particular attention given to the temple and the messiah. Reflective of the diversity in Second Temple Judaism, conceptions of the temple and the messiah are, likewise, diverse.

Although ancient authors did not draw a stark contrast between material and spiritual realities, the results of the investigation can be categorized roughly as follows. First, the expectation for a literal temple was identified in Tobit, Sibylline Oracle 3, and the Mishnah's tractate Middoth. The authors of such works were explicit in their anticipation of an architectural temple in the eschaton. Second, the idea of a heavenly temple that would be established in the eschaton is attested also, as found in Jubilees, Pseudo-Philo, Sibylline Oracle 5, and portions of the Book of Watchers (1 En. 14–25). Third, the Qumran sectarians seem to have embraced all approaches to the temple. While anticipating a restored Jerusalem temple, they also regarded their community as a spiritual sanctuary. At the same time, they worshipped as part of the heavenly temple that God would establish on earth in the future.

In such literature of the Second Temple period, the heavenly Jerusalem often appears on the earth in the eschatological age. Likewise, the author of Revelation 21:2 described the new Jerusalem coming down from heaven. That John implied that his temple-city is the same as Ezekiel's may indicate that John, like other Second Temple period authors, understood Ezekiel's city as some form of the heavenly sanctuary.[2] His depiction of the city's descent thus represents the consummation of Ezekiel's vision. God's heavenly dwelling was being established on earth.

Further, considering the absence or demotion of the temple in much of the literature surveyed, John's omission of a temple may not have been surprising to his readers. The portrayal of the messiah at the center of the heavenly city and as the embodiment of the temple is fully at home in the literary and theological milieu of the time.

Often, the messiah is the focal point of eschatological expectations. In the Testaments of the Twelve Patriarchs, the Similitudes, and possibly 4 Ezra, the messiah seems to take the place of the temple in the eschaton. Similarly, in Sibylline Oracles 1–2 and 2 Baruch, the messiah and community of the saints are described in terms typically reserved for the temple. As in Revelation, people and groups embody what the temple represented.

Thus, while John's own vision is highly innovative, he drew upon traditions that were established already and utilized Ezekiel's temple vision in a manner that was familiar to his first-century audience. Although the mind-set of the audience is not a determining factor in how John utilized Ezekiel's vision, the attestation of similar traditions increases the likelihood that John was intentional in (1) his appropriation of Ezekiel's visionary material, (2) his application of architectural imagery to people and groups, and (3) his replacement of the temple with the Messiah.

The third and final section of the research consisted of a synchronic analysis of John's use of Ezekiel. Broad parallels for the entirety of Revelation and Ezekiel were identified in order to provide a foundation for the exegesis of Ezekiel 40–48 in Revelation 21:1—22:5, which indicated that John overtly drew upon Ezekiel in his portrayal of the end-time city of God. John utilized Ezekiel 40–48 as a literary prototype in order to draw attention to points at which he departed from his source material. Three primary adjustments are present. First, the descent of the city renders the presence of God even more accessible than in the original vision. Second, the city overtly represents the people of God. Third, the temple at the center of the city is the sacrificed Lamb—Jesus Christ. All three concepts can be identified in Ezekiel, albeit in nuce.

John did not intend to modify his source material, but rather to clarify Ezekiel's original vision. Just as the Jewish people could recognize

---

2. Regardless of whether John personally viewed Ezekiel's sanctuary as the heavenly one, he may have drawn upon such traditions in his literary composition.

their deficiencies in the light of the temple's perfection, so also NT believers can see their own inadequacy in the light of Christ. Just as Ezekiel's temple was a source of hope in the midst of defeat and exile, John sought to comfort believers facing persecution. Just as the temple was the place where God's people could experience his presence, so also the Messiah is the point of contact between God and humanity.

Throughout Revelation, John drew upon Ezekiel, consistently progressing toward his final vision of the new Jerusalem. In Revelation 21, John's allusions to Ezekiel became even more pronounced, as John in a sense accelerated toward the theological climax. As such, the absence of an architectural temple in Revelation 21:22 serves as the relational, spatial, and literary core of the vision. With the affirmation that God and the Lamb *are* the temple, John revealed that the Messiah epitomized every ideal that the temple signified less fully: unadulterated access to God's presence, freedom from oppression, and eternal security.

Selected Bibliography

Aichele, George, and Gary A. Philips, eds. *Semeia 69/70: Intertextuality and the Bible*. Atlanta: Society of Biblical Literature, 1995.

Aland, Kurt, et al., eds. *Novum Testamentum Graece*. 28th ed. Stuttgart: Deutsche Bibelgesellschaft, 2012.

Albright, William F. "The Babylonian Temple-Tower and the Altar of Burnt-Offering." *JBL* 39 (1920) 137–42.

Alexander, Ralph H. *Ezekiel*. Chicago: Moody, 1976.

———. "Ezekiel." In *The Expositor's Bible Commentary*, edited by Tremper Longman III and David E. Garland, 641–924. Grand Rapids: Zondervan, 2010.

Alexander, T. Desmond, and Simon Gathercole, eds. *Heaven on Earth: The Temple in Biblical Theology*. Carlisle, UK: Paternoster, 2004.

Allegro, John M. *The Dead Sea Scrolls and the Origins of Christianity*. New York: Criterion, 1957.

———. "Fragments of a Qumran Scroll of Eschatological Midrāšîm." *JBL* 77 (1958) 50–54.

———. "Further Messianic References in Qumran Literature." *JBL* 75 (1956) 174–87.

Allen, Graham. *Intertextuality*. 2nd ed. New York: Routledge, 2011.

Allen, Leslie C. *Ezekiel 1–19*. WBC 28. Dallas: Word, 1994.

———. *Ezekiel 20–48*. WBC 29. Dallas: Word, 1990.

Andersen, Francis I. "2 (Slavonic Apocalypse of) Enoch." In *OTPA* 91–221.

Aune, David E. "The Apocalypse of John and Palestinian Jewish Apocalyptic." *Neot* 40 (2006) 1–33.

———. "The Apocalypse of John and the Problem of Genre." *Semeia* (1988) 65–96.

———. *The Cultic Setting of Realized Eschatology in Early Christianity*. SNT 28. Leiden: Brill, 1972.

———. "Intertextuality and the Genre of the Apocalypse." SBLSP 30 (1991) 142–60.

———. *Revelation 1–5*. WBC 52. Dallas: Word, 1997.

———. *Revelation 6–16*. WBC 52B. Dallas: Word, 1998.

———. *Revelation 17–22*. WBC 52C. Dallas: Word, 1998.

Avi-Yonah, Michael. "The Facade of Herod's Temple." In *Religions in Antiquity: Essays in Memory of Erwin Ramsdell Goodenough*, edited by Jacob Neusner, 327–35. Leiden: Brill, 1968.

Bakhtin, Mikhail. *The Dialogic Imagination: Four Essays*. Edited by Michael Holquist. Translated by Caryl Emerson and Michael Holquist. Austin: University of Texas Press, 1981.

Barker, Margaret. *The Gate of Heaven: The History and Symbolism of the Temple in Jerusalem*. Sheffield, UK: Sheffield Phoenix, 2008.

———. *On Earth as It Is in Heaven: Temple Symbolism in the New Testament*. Edinburgh: T. & T. Clark, 1995.

Barr, David L. "The Apocalypse as a Symbolic Transformation of the World: A Literary Analysis." *Int* 38 (1984) 39–50.

Barthes, Roland. "The Death of the Author." In *Image, Music, Text*, translated by Stephen Heath, 142–48. New York: Hill & Wang, 1977.

Bauckham, Richard. *The Climax of Prophecy: Studies on the Book of Revelation*. London: T. & T. Clark, 1993.

———. "Early Jewish Visions of Hell." *JTS* 41 (1990) 355–85.

———. *The Theology of the Book of Revelation*. NTT. Cambridge: Cambridge University Press, 1993.

Baumgarten, Joseph M. "Sacrifice and Worship among the Jewish Sectarians of the Dead Sea (Qumran) Scrolls." *HTR* 46 (1953) 141–59.

Bautch, Kelley Coblentz. *A Study of the Geography of 1 Enoch 17–79: 'No One Has Seen What I Have Seen.'* Leiden: Brill, 2003.

Beale, Gregory K. *The Book of Revelation*. NIGTC. Grand Rapids: Eerdmans, 1999.

———. "Eden, the Temple, and the Church's Mission in the New Creation." *JETS* 48 (2005) 5–31.

———. *Handbook on the New Testament Use of the Old Testament: Exegesis and Interpretation*. Grand Rapids: Baker Academic, 2012.

———. *John's Use of the Old Testament in Revelation*. JSNTSupp 166. London: Bloomsbury, 1998.

———. "The Millennium in Revelation 20:1–10: An Amillennial Perspective." *CTR* 11 (2013) 29–62.

———. *A New Testament Biblical Theology: The Unfolding of the Old Testament in the New*. Grand Rapids: Baker Academic, 2011.

———. "The Purpose of Symbolism in the Book of Revelation." *CTJ* 31 (2006) 53–66.

———. "Questions of Authorial Intent, Epistemology, and Presuppositions and Their Bearing on the Study of the Old Testament in the New: A Rejoinder to Steve Moyise." *IBS* 21 (1999) 151–80.

———. "Revelation." In *It Is Written: Scripture Citing Scripture: Essays in Honor of Barnabus Lindars*, edited by Donald A. Carson and Hugh G. M. Williamson, 318–36. Cambridge: Cambridge University Press, 1988.

———. *The Temple and the Church's Mission: A Biblical Theology of the Dwelling Place of God*. Downers Grove, IL: InterVarsity, 2004.

———. *The Use of Daniel in Jewish Apocalyptic Literature and in the Revelation of St. John*. Lanham, NY: University of America Press, 1984.

———. "The Use of the Old Testament in Revelation." In *The Right Doctrine from the Wrong Texts?: Essays on the Use of the Old Testament in the New*, edited by Gregory K. Beale, 257–76. Grand Rapids: Baker, 1994.

Beale, Gregory K., ed. *The Right Doctrine from the Wrong Texts?: Essays on the Use of the Old Testament in the New*. Grand Rapids: Baker, 1994.

Beasley-Murray, George R. *The Book of Revelation*. Grand Rapids: Eerdmans, 1974.

Berding, Kenneth, and Jonathan Lunde, eds. *Three Views on the New Testament Use of the Old Testament*. Grand Rapids: Zondervan, 2003.

Bergey, Ronald. "The Song of Moses (Deuteronomy 32.1–43) and Isaianic Prophecies: A Case of Early Intertextuality?" *JSOT* 28 (2003) 33–54.

Bertholet, Alfred. *Der Verfassungsentwurf des Hesekiel.* Freiburg, Germany: Mohr, 1896.

Beyer, Hermann Wolfgang. "ἐπισκέπτομαι, ἐπισκοπέω, ἐπισκοπή, ἐπίσκοπος, ἀλλοτριεπίσκοπος." In *TDNT* 2:599–622.

Biblia Hebraica Stuttgartensia: With Westminster Hebrew Morphology. Stuttgart: Deutsche Bibelgesellschaft, 1997.

Bittell, Kurt. "Hittite Temples and High Places in Anatolia and North Syria." In *Temples and High Places in Biblical Times: Proceedings of the Colloquium in Honor of the Centennial of the Hebrew Union College-Jewish Institute of Religion*, edited by Avraham Biran, 63–72. Jerusalem: Nelson Glueck School of Biblical Archaeology of Hebrew Union College-Jewish Institute of Religion, 1981.

Black, Matthew. *The Book of Enoch or 1 Enoch: A New English Edition with Commentary and Textual Notes.* SVTP 7. Leiden: Brill, 1985.

———. "The Eschatology of the Similitudes of Enoch." *JTS* 3 (1952) 1–10.

Blenkinsopp, Joseph. *Ezekiel.* IBC. Louisville: John Knox, 1990.

Block, Daniel I. "Beyond the Grave: Ezekiel's Vision of Death and the Afterlife." *BBR* 2 (1992) 113–41.

———. *Beyond the River Chebar: Studies in Kingship and Eschatology in the Book of Ezekiel.* Eugene, OR: Cascade, 2013.

———. *The Book of Ezekiel: Chapters 1–24.* NICOT. Grand Rapids: Eerdmans, 1997.

———. *The Book of Ezekiel: Chapters 25–48.* NICOT. Grand Rapids: Eerdmans, 1998.

———. "Gog and the Pouring out of the Spirit: Reflections on Ezekiel 39:21–29." *VT* 37 (1987) 257–70.

———. "Gog in Prophetic Tradition: A New Look at Ezekiel 38:17." *VT* 42 (1992) 154–72.

Boccaccini, Gabriele. "Finding a Place for the Parables of Enoch within Second Temple Jewish Literature." In *Enoch and the Messiah Son of Man: Revisiting the Book of Parables*, edited by Gabriele Boccaccini, 263–90. Grand Rapids: Eerdmans, 2007.

Boccaccini, Gabriele, ed. *Enoch and the Messiah Son of Man: Revisiting the Book of Parables.* Grand Rapids: Eerdmans, 2007.

Bock, Darrell L. "Part 1: Evangelicals and the Use of the Old Testament in the New." *BSac* 142 (1985) 209–23.

———. "Part 2: Evangelicals and the Use of the Old Testament in the New." *BSac* 142 (1985) 306–19.

———. "Single Meaning, Multiple Contexts and Referents." In *Three Views on the New Testament Use of the Old Testament*, edited by Kenneth Berding et al., 105–51. Grand Rapids: Zondervan, 2008.

Bøe, Sverre. *Gog and Magog: Ezekiel 38–39 as Pre-text for Revelation 19,17–21 and 20,7–10.* WUNT 2R 135. Tübingen: Mohr Siebeck, 2001.

Bonar, Horatius. *The Coming and Kingdom of the Lord Jesus Christ.* London: Nisbet, 1889.

Boring, M. Eugene. *Revelation.* IBC. Louisville: John Knox, 1989.

Box, George H. *The Apocalypse of Abraham: Edited, with a Translation from the Slavonic Text and Notes.* London: Society for Promoting Christian Knowledge, 1918.

Boxall, Ian K. "Exile, Prophet, Visionary: Ezekiel's Influence on the Book of Revelation." In *The Book of Ezekiel and Its Influence*, edited by Henk Jan de Jonge and Johannes Tromp, 147–64. London: Routledge, 2007.

————. *Revelation: Vision and Insight*. London: SPCK, 2002.

Boyle, Brian. "The Figure of the *NA*[set macron over A]ŚἸ' in Ezekiel's Vision of the New Temple (Ezekiel 40-48)." *ABR* 58 (2010) 1–16.

————. "'Holiness has a Shape': The Place of the Altar in Ezekiel's Visionary Plan of Sacral Space (Ezekiel 43:1–12, 13–17, 18–27)." *ABR* 57 (2009) 1–21.

Breuer, Joseph. *The Book of Yechzkel: Translation and Commmentary*. Translated by Gertrude Hirshler. New York: Feldheim, 1993.

Briggs, Robert A. *Jewish Temple Imagery in the Book of Revelation*. StBibLit 10. New York: Peter Lang, 1999.

Buitenwerf, Rieuwerd. *Book III of the Sibylline Oracles and Its Social Setting*. SVTP. Leiden: Brill, 2003.

————. "The Gog and Magog Tradition in Revelation 20:8." In *The Book of Ezekiel and Its Influence*, edited by Henk Jan de Jonge and Henk Tromp, 165–81. London: Routledge, 2007.

Bullock, C. Hassell. *An Introduction to the Old Testament Prophetic Books*. Chicago: Moody, 2007.

Burke, David G. *The Poetry of Baruch: A Reconstruction and Analysis of the Original Hebrew Text of Baruch 3:9–5:9*. Chico, CA: Scholars, 1982.

Caird, George B. *The Revelation of Saint John*. Peabody, MA: Hendrickson, 1966.

Campbell, J. Y. "The Origin and Meaning of the Term 'Son of Man.'" *JTS* 48 (1947) 145–55.

Carson, Donald A. "The Lord Is There: Ezekiel 40–48." In *Coming Home: Essays on the New Heaven and the New Earth*, edited by Donald A. Carson and Jeff Robinson Sr., 43–62. Wheaton, IL: Crossway, 2017.

Chae, Young S. *Jesus as the Eschatological Davidic Shepherd: Studies in the Old Testament, Second Temple Judaism, and in the Gospel of Matthew*. WUNT 2R 216. Tübingen: Mohr Siebeck, 2006.

Charles, Robert H. *The Apocrypha and Pseudepigrapha of the Old Testament in English*. 2 vols. Oxford: Clarendon, 1913.

————. *The Book of Enoch: Translated from Dillman's Ethiopic Text, Emended and Revised in Accordance with Hitherto Uncollated Ethiopic Mss. and with the Gizeh and Other Greek and Latin Fragments*. Oxford: Clarendon, 1893.

————. *The Book of Jubilees*. London: Black, 1902.

————. *A Critical and Exegetical Commentary on the Revelation of St. John*. ICC. Edinburgh: T. & T. Clark, 1920.

————. "The Date and Place of Writing of the Slavonic Enoch." *JTS* 22 (1921) 161–64.

————. *The Testaments of the Twelve Patriarchs: Translated from the Editor's Greek Text and Edited, with Introduction, Notes, and Indices*. London: Black, 1908.

Charlesworth, James H. *Jesus and Temple: Textual and Archaeological Explorations*. Minneapolis: Fortress, 2014.

————. *The Old Testament Pseudepigrapha and the New Testament: Prolegomena for the Study of Christian Origins*. Cambridge: Cambridge University Press, 1985.

————. *The Pseudepigrapha and Modern Research with a Supplement*. SCS 7S. Chico, CA: Scholars, 1981.

Churgin, Pinkhos. *Targum Jonathan to the Prophets*. New Haven, CT: Yale University Press, 1907.

Chyutin, Michael. "The New Jerusalem: Ideal City." *DSD* 1 (1994) 71–97.

————. *The New Jerusalem Scroll from Qumran: A Comprehensive Reconstruction.* JSPSup 25. Sheffield, UK: Sheffield Academic, 1997.

Clements, Ronald E. *Ezekiel.* WBC. Louisville: Westminster John Knox, 1996.

————. *God and Temple.* Oxford: Basil Blackwell, 1965.

Clifford, Richard J. *The Cosmic Mountain in Canaan and the Old Testament.* Cambridge: Harvard University Press, 1972.

————. "The Temple and the Holy Mountain." In *The Temple in Antiquity: Ancient Records and Modern Perspectives,* edited by Truman G. Madsen, 107–24. RSMS 9. Salt Lake City: Bookcraft, 1987.

Clorfene, Chaim. *The Messianic Temple: Understanding Ezekiel's Prophecy.* Jerusalem: Chaim Clorfene, 2005.

Clowney, Edmund P. "The Final Temple." *WTJ* 35 (1973) 156–89.

Collins, Adela Yarbro. *The Apocalypse.* NTM. Wilmington, DE: Glazier, 1979.

————. *The Combat Myth in the Book of Revelation.* HDR 9. Missoula, MT: Scholars, 1976.

————. "The History-of-Religions Approach to Apocalypticism and 'The Angel of the Waters' (Rev 16:4–7)." *CBQ* 39 (1977) 367–81.

Collins, John J. *Apocalypse: The Morphology of a Genre.* Semeia 14. Missoula, MT: Scholars, 1979.

————. *The Apocalyptic Imagination: An Introduction to Jewish Apocalyptic Literature.* 2nd ed. BRS. Grand Rapids: Eerdmans, 1998.

————. "Apocalypticism and Literary Genre in the Dead Sea Scrolls." In *The Dead Sea Scrolls after Fifty Years: A Comprehensive Assessment,* edited by Peter W. Flint and James C. VanderKam, 2:403–30. Leiden: Brill, 1999.

————. "Sibylline Oracles." In *OTPA* 317–472.

————. "The Sibylline Oracles." In *Jewish Writings of the Second Temple Period: Apocrypha, Pseudepigrapha, Qumran Sectarian Writings, Philo, Josephus,* edited by Michael Edward Stone, 357–82. Philadelphia: Fortress, 1984.

————. *The Sibylline Oracles of Egyptian Judaism.* SBLDS 13. Missoula, MT: Scholars, 1972.

————. "Was the Dead Sea Sect an Apocalyptic Movement?" In *Archaeology and History in the Dead Sea Scrolls,* edited by Lawrence H. Schiffman, 25–51. Sheffield, UK: JSOT, 1990.

Coloe, Mary L. *God Dwells with Us: Temple Symbolism in the Fourth Gospel.* Collegeville, MN: Liturgical, 2001.

————. "Temple Imagery in John." *Int* 63 (2009) 368–81.

Comblin, José. "La Liturgie de la Nouvelle Jérusalem (Apoc., XXI, 1–XXII, 5)." *ETL* 29 (1953) 5–40.

Cook, Stephen L. "Ezekiel's God Incarnate! The God That the Temple Blueprint Creates." In *The God Ezekiel Creates,* edited by Claudia V. Camp and Andrew Mein, 132–49. LHBOTS 607. London: Bloomsbury, 2015.

Cook, Stephen L., and Corrine L. Patton. "Introduction: Hierarchal Thinking and Theology in Ezekiel's Book." In *Ezekiel's Hierarchal World: Wrestling with a Tiered Reality,* edited by Stephen L. Cook and Corrine L. Patton, 1–23. Atlanta: Society of Biblical Literature, 2004.

Cooke, George A. *A Critical and Exegetical Commentary on the Book of Ezekiel.* ICC. Edinburgh: T. & T. Clark, 1936.

Cooper, Lamar Eugene, Sr. *Ezekiel.* NAC 17. Nashville: Broadman & Holman, 1994.

Craghan, John. *Esther, Judith, Tobit, Jonah, Ruth*. OTM 16. Wilmington, DE: Glazier, 1982.

Crawford, Sidnie White. *The Temple Scroll and Related Texts*. Sheffield, UK: Sheffield Academic, 2000.

Cross, Frank Moore, Jr. *The Ancient Library of Qumran and Modern Biblical Studies*. Rev. ed. Grand Rapids: Baker, 1980.

Damsma, Alinda. "The Merkabah as a Substitute for Messianism in Targum Ezekiel." *VT* 62 (2012) 515–33.

Davies, Philip R. "The Ideology of the Temple in the Damascus Document." *JJS* 33 (1982) 287–301.

———. *1QM, the War Scroll from Qumran: Its Structure and History*. BibOr 32. Rome: Biblical Institute, 1977.

———. "Qumran and Apocalyptic or *Obscurum per Obscuris*." *JNES* 49 (1990) 127–34.

Davila, James R. "The Macrocosmic Temple, Scriptural Exegesis, and the Songs of the Sabbath Sacrifice." *DSD* 9 (2002) 1–19.

Davis, Ellen F. *Swallowing the Scroll: Textuality and the Dynamics of Discourse in Ezekiel's Prophecy*. JSOTSupp 21. Sheffield, UK: Almond, 1989.

Decock, Paul B. "The Scriptures in the Book of Revelation." *Neot* 33 (1999) 373–410.

Deere, Jack S. "Premillennialism in Revelation 20:4–6." *BSac* 135 (1978) 58–73.

Deutsch, Celia. "Transformation of Symbols: The New Jerusalem in Rv 21:1–22:5." *ZNW* 78 (1987) 106–26.

Dimant, Devorah. "The Apocalyptic Interpretation of Ezekiel at Qumran." In *Messiah and Christos: Studies in the Jewish Origins of Christianity, Presented to David Flusser on the Occasion of His Seventy-Fifth Birthday*, edited by Ithamar Gruenwald et al., 31–51. Tübingen: Mohr Siebeck, 1992.

———. "4QFlorilegium and the Idea of the Community as Temple." In *Hellenica et Judaica: Hommage à Valentin Nikiprowetzky*, edited by André Caquot et al., 165–89. Leuven: Editions Peeters, 1986.

———. *Qumran Cave 4, XXI Parabiblical Texts, Part 4: Pseudo-Prophetic Texts*. DJD 30. Oxford: Clarendon, 2001.

Dimant, Devorah, and John Strugnell. "The Merkabah Vision in *Second Ezekiel* (*4Q385 4*)." *RQ* 14 (1990) 331–48.

Dodd, Charles H. *According to the Scriptures: The Sub-Structure of New Testament Theology*. London: Nisbet, 1952.

———. *The Old Testament in the New*. FBBS 3. Philadelphia: Fortress, 1963.

Duguid, Iain. *Ezekiel and the Leaders of Israel*. Leiden: Brill, 1994.

Dumbrell, William J. *The End of the Beginning: Revelation 21–22 and the Old Testament*. Grand Rapids: Baker, 1985.

Dunnett, Walter. *The Interpretation of Scripture*. Nashville: Nelson, 1984.

Efird, James M., ed. *The Use of the Old Testament in the New and Other Essays: Studies in Honor of William Franklin Stinespring*. Durham, NC: Duke University Press, 1972.

Ehrman, Arnost Zvi. "Middot." In *EncJud* 14:180–81.

Eichrodt, Walther. *Ezekiel: A Commentary*. Philadelphia: Westminster, 1970.

Eliade, Mircea. *The Myth of the Eternal Return*. Translated by Willard R. Trask. New York: Pantheon, 1954.

Ellis, Earle E. "How the New Testament Uses the Old." In *New Testament Interpretation: Essays on Principles and Methods*, edited by I. Howard Marshall, 199–219. Grand Rapids: Eerdmans, 1977.

———. *Paul's Use of the Old Testament*. Grand Rapids: Baker, 1957.

Endres, John C. "The Watchers Traditions in the *Book of Jubilees*." In *The Watchers in Jewish and Christian Traditions*, edited by Angela Kim Harkins et al., 121–35. Minneapolis: Fortress, 2014.

Fekkes, Jan, III. "'The Bride has Prepared Herself': Revelation 19–21 and Isaian Nuptual Imagery." *JBL* 109 (1990) 269–87.

———. *Isaiah and Prophetic Traditions in the Book of Revelation: Visionary Antecedents and Their Development*. JSNTSupp 93. Sheffield, UK: Sheffield Academic, 1994.

Felder, Stephen. "What Is *The Fifth Sibylline Oracle*?" *JSJ* 33 (2002) 363–85.

Fishbane, Michael. *Biblical Interpretation in Ancient Israel*. Oxford: Clarendon, 1985.

Fitzmyer, Joseph A. *Tobit*. CEJL. Berlin: de Gruyter, 2003.

———. "The Use of Explicit Old Testament Quotations in Qumran and in the New Testament." *NTS* 7 (1961) 297–333.

Fohrer, Georg, and Kurt Galling. *Ezechiel*. HAT 13. Tübingen: Mohr, 1955.

Ford, J. Massyngberde. *Revelation: Introduction, Translation, and Commentary*. AB 38. New York: Doubleday, 1975.

France, Richard T. *Jesus and the Old Testament: His Application of Old Testament Passages to Himself and His Mission*. London: Tyndale, 1971.

Gaebelein, Arno C. *The Prophet Ezekiel*. New York: Our Hope, 1918.

Galambush, Julie. "Jerusalem in the Book of Ezekiel: The City as Yahweh's Wife." PhD diss., Emory University, 1991.

Gangemi, A. "L'utilizzazione del Deutero-Isaia nell' Apocalisse di Giovanni." *ED* 27 (1974) 311–39.

Ganzel, Tova. "The Defilement and Desecration of the Temple in Ezekiel." *Bib* 89 (2008) 369–79.

———. "The Descriptions of the Restoration of Israel in Ezekiel." *VT* (2010) 197–211.

Ganzel, Tova, and Shalom E. Holtz. "Ezekiel's Temple in Babylonian Context." *VT* 64 (2014) 211–26.

Gardiner, Frederic. *The Old and New Testaments and Their Mutual Relations*. New York: James Pott, 1885.

Gärtner, Bertil. *The Temple and the Community in Qumran and the New Testament: A Comparative Study in the Temple Symbolism of the Qumran Texts and the New Testament*. SNTSMS 1. Cambridge: Cambridge University Press, 1965.

Gaylord, Harry E., Jr. "3 (Greek Apocalypse of) Baruch." In *OTPA* 653–79.

Geffken, Johann. *Komposition und Entstehungszeit der Oracula Sibyllina*. Leipzig: Hinrichs, 1902.

Gentry, Kenneth L., Jr. *He Shall Have Dominion: A Postmillennial Eschatology*. 2nd ed. Tyler, TX: Institute for Christian Economics, 1997.

Gese, Hartmut. *Der Verfassungsentwurf des Ezechiel (Kap. 40–48)*. BHT 25. Tübingen: Mohr Siebeck, 1957.

Giblin, Charles. "Recapitulation and the Literary Coherence of John's Apocalypse." *CBQ* 56 (1994) 81–96.

Ginzberg, Louis. "Apocalypse of Abraham." In *JE* 1:91–92.

———. "The Greek Apocalypse of Baruch." In *JE* 2:549–51.

Glasson, Thomas F. "Order of Jewels in Revelation 21:19–20: A Theory Eliminated." *JTS* 26 (1975) 95–100.

———. *The Revelation of John*. CBC. Cambridge: Cambridge University Press, 1965.

———. "What Is Apocalyptic." *NTS* 27 (1980) 98–105.

Goodman, Martin. "The Temple in First Century CE Judaism." In *Temple and Worship in Biblical Israel*, edited by John Day, 459–68. LHBOTS 422. London: T. & T. Clark, 2005.

Goulder, Michael Douglas. "The Apocalypse as an Annual Cycle of Prophecies." *NTS* 27 (1981) 342–67.

Gray, James M. *Christian Workers' Commentary*. New York: Revell, 1915.

Green, William S. "Doing the Text's Work for It: Richard Hays and Paul's Use of Scripture." In *Paul and the Scriptures of Israel*, edited by Craig A. Evans and James A. Sanders, 58–63. JSNTSupp 83. Sheffield, UK: JSOT Press, 1993.

Greenberg, Moshe. "The Design and Themes of Ezekiel's Program of Restoration." *Int* 38 (1984) 181–208.

———. *Ezekiel 1–20: A New Translation with Introduction and Commentary*. AB 22. Garden City, NY: Doubleday, 1983.

———. *Ezekiel 21–37: A New Translation with Introduction and Commentary*. AB 22A. Garden City, NY: Doubleday, 1997.

———. "Idealism and Practicality in Numbers 35:4–5 and Ezekiel 48." *JAOS* 88 (1968) 59–66.

———. "What are Valid Criteria for Determining Inauthentic Matter in Ezekiel?" In *Ezekiel and His Book: Textual and Literary Criticism and Their Interrelation*, edited by Johan Lust, 123–35. Leuven: Leuven University Press, 1986.

Greene, Thomas. *The Light in Troy: Imitation and Discovery in Renaissance Poetry*. New Haven, CT: Yale University Press, 1982.

Griffin, Patrick J. "The Theology and Function of Prayer in the Book of Tobit." PhD diss., Catholic University of America, 1984.

Gross, Heinrich. *Tobit, Judit*. Würzburg, Germany: Echter Verlag, 1987.

Gundry, Robert H. "The New Jerusalem: People as Place, Not Place for People." *NovT* 3 (1987) 254–64.

———. *The Use of the Old Testament in St. Matthew's Gospel: With Special Reference to Messianic Hope*. SNT 18. Leiden: Brill, 1967.

Haik, Peter R. "The Holiness of God in the Thought of Ezekiel." PhD diss., New Orleans Baptist Theological Seminary, 1980.

Hals, Ronald M. *Ezekiel*. FOTL 19. Grand Rapids: Eerdmans, 1989.

Hamerton-Kelly, Robert G. "The Temple and the Origins of Jewish Apocalyptic." *VT* 20 (1970) 1–15.

Hanson, Paul D. *The Dawn of Apocalyptic: The Historical and Sociological Roots of Jewish Apocalyptic Eschatology*. Philadelphia: Fortress, 1975.

———. "Old Testament Apocalyptic Reexamined." *Int* 25 (1971) 454–79.

———. "Rebellion in Heaven, Azazel, and Euhemeristic Heroes in 1 Enoch 6–11." *JBL* 96 (1977) 195–233.

———. "Zechariah 9 and the Recapitulation of an Ancient Ritual Pattern." *JBL* 92 (1973) 37–59.

Hanson, Paul D., ed. *Visionaries and Their Apocalypses*. IRT 4. Philadelphia: Fortress, 1983.

Haran, Menahem. "The Law-Code of Ezekiel XL–XLVIII and Its Relation to the Priestly School." *HUCA* 50 (1979) 45–71.

Harlow, Daniel C. *The Greek Apocalypse of Baruch (3 Baruch) in Hellenistic Judaism and Early Christianity*. SVTP. Leiden: Brill, 1996.

Harrington, Daniel J. "Pseudo-Philo." In *OTPE* 297–377.

Hays, J. Daniel. *The Temple and the Tabernacle: A Study of God's Dwelling Places from Genesis to Revelation*. Grand Rapids: Baker, 2016.

Hays, Richard B. *Echoes of Scripture in the Gospels*. Waco, TX: Baylor University Press, 2016.

———. *Echoes of Scripture in the Letters of Paul*. New Haven, CT: Yale University Press, 1989.

———. *Reading Backwards: Figural Christology and the Fourfold Gospel Witness*. Waco, TX: Baylor University Press, 2014.

Helyer, Larry R. *Exploring Jewish Literature of the Second Temple Period: A Guide for New Testament Students*. Downers Grove, IL: InterVarsity, 2002.

Himmelfarb, Martha. "Apocalyptic Ascent and the Heavenly Temple." SBLSP 26 (1987) 210–17.

———. *Ascent to Heaven in Jewish and Christian Apocalypses*. New York: Oxford University Press, 1993.

———. "From Prophecy to Apocalypse: The 'Book of the Watchers' and Tours of Heaven." In *Jewish Spirituality: From the Bible through the Middle Ages*, edited by Arthur Green, 145–65. New York: Crossroad, 1986.

———. "Heavenly Ascent and the Relationship of the Apocalypses and the *Hekhalot* Literature." *HUCA* 59 (1988) 73–100.

Hitchcock, Mark L. "A Critique of the Preterist View of the Temple in Revelation 11:1–2." *BSac* 164 (2007) 219–36.

Hitzig, Ferdinand. *Der Prophet Ezechiel*. Leipzig: Weidmann'sche Buchandlung, 1847.

Hollander, Harm W., and Marinus de Jonge. *The Testaments of the Twelve Patriarchs: A Commentary*. Leiden: Brill, 1985.

Hollis, Frederick J. *The Archaeology of Herod's Temple with a Commentary on the Tractate 'Middoth.'* London: J. M. Dent and Sons, 1934.

Hoskins, Paul M. *Jesus as the Fulfillment of the Temple in the Gospel of John*. Eugene, OR: Wipf & Stock, 2007.

Howie, Carl G. *The Date and Composition of Ezekiel*. Philadelphia: Society of Biblical Literature, 1950.

———. "The East Gate of Ezekiel's Temple Enclosure and the Solomonic Gateway of Megiddo." *BASOR* 117 (1950) 13–19.

Hughes, Julie A. *Scriptural Allusions and Exegesis in the Hodayot*. STDJ 59. Leiden: Brill, 2006.

Hultberg, Alan. "Messianic Exegesis in the Apocalypse: The Significance of the Old Testament for the Christology of Revelation." PhD diss., Trinity Evangelical Divinity School, 2001.

Hurowitz, Victor. *I Have Built You an Exalted House: Temple Building in the Bible in the Light of Mesopotamian and North-West Semitic Writings*. JSOTSupp 115. Sheffield, UK: JSOT Press, 1992.

———. "YHWH's Exalted House—Aspects of the Design and Symbolism of Solomon's Temple." In *Temple and Worship in Biblical Israel*, edited by John Day, 63–110. LHBOTS 422. London: T. & T. Clark, 2005.

Isaac, Ephraim. "1 (Ethiopic Apocalypse of) Enoch." In *OTPA* 5–89.

Jackson, Jeffrey Glen, ed. *New Testament Use of the Old Testament*. Bellingham, WA: Faithlife, 2015.

Jacobson, Howard. *A Commentary on Pseudo-Philo's Liber Antiquitatum Biblicarum with Latin Text and English Translation*. AGJU 31. Leiden: Brill, 1996.

James, Montague Rhodes. "The Apocalypse of Baruch." In *Apocrypha Anecdota II*, edited by J. Aarmitage Robinson, li–lxxi. Cambridge: Cambridge University Press, 1897.

Jenkins, Ferrell. *The Old Testament in the Book of Revelation*. Marion, IN: Cogdill Foundation, 1972.

Jenson, Robert W. *Ezekiel*. Grand Rapids: Brazos, 2009.

Johnson, Elliott E. "Author's Intention and Biblical Interpretation." In *Hermeneutics, Inerrancy and the Bible*, edited by Earl D. Radmacher and Robert D. Preus, 409–29. Grand Rapids: Academic Books, 1984.

Johnson, S. Lewis. *The Old Testament in the New: An Argument for Biblical Inspiration*. Grand Rapids: Zondervan, 1980.

de Jonge, Marinus. *Jewish Eschatology, Early Christian Christology and the Testaments of the Twelve Patriarchs: Collected Essays of Marinus de Jonge*. Leiden: Brill, 1991.

———. "Notes on Testament of Levi II–VII." In *Studies on the Testaments of the Twelve Partiarchs: Text and Interpretation*, edited by Marinus de Jonge, 247–60. SVTP 3. Leiden: Brill, 1975.

———. *The Testaments of the Twelve Patriarchs: A Critical Edition of the Greek Text*. PVTG. Leiden: Brill, 1978.

———. *The Testaments of the Twelve Patriarchs: A Study of Their Text, Composition and Origin*. Assen, the Netherlands: Van Gorcum, 1953.

Josephus, Flavius. *The Jewish War: Books 1–7*. Edited by Jeffrey Henderson, et al. LCL 186. Cambridge: Harvard University Press, 1927–28.

———. *Josephus: The Complete Works*. Nashville: Thomas Nelson, 1998.

Joyce, Paul M. *Ezekiel: A Commentary*. LHBOTS 482. New York: T. & T. Clark, 2007.

———. "Ezekiel 40–42: The Earliest 'Heavenly Ascent' Narrative." In *The Book of Ezekiel and Its Influence*, edited by Henk Jan de Jonge and Johannes Tromp, 17–41. London: Routledge, 2007.

———. "Temple and Worship in Ezekiel 40–48." In *Temple and Worship in Biblical Israel*, edited by John Day, 145–63. LHBOTS 422. London: T. & T. Clark, 2005.

Joyce, Paul M., and Andrew Mein, eds. *After Ezekiel: Essays on the Reception of a Difficult Prophet*. LHBOTS 535. New York: T. & T. Clark, 2011.

Joyce, Paul M., and Dalit Rom-Shiloni, eds. *The God Ezekiel Creates*. LHBOTS 607. London: Bloomsbury, 2015.

Kaiser, Walter C., Jr. *The Messiah in the Old Testament*. Grand Rapids: Zondervan, 1995.

———. *The Uses of the Old Testament in the New*. Eugene, OR: Wipf & Stock, 1985.

Kasher, Rimmon. "Anthropomorphism, Holiness and Cult: A New Look at Ezekiel 40–48." *ZAW* 110 (1998) 192–208.

Kee, Howard C. "Testaments of the Twelve Patriarchs." In *OTPA* 775–828.

Keulers, Joseph. *Die eschatologische Lehre des vierten Esrabuches*. BibS(F) 20. Freiburg, Germany: Herder, 1922.

Kiddle, Martin. *The Revelation of St. John*. New York: Harper & Row, 1940.

Kirschner, Robert. "Apocalyptic and Rabbinic Responses to the Destruction of 70." *HTR* 78 (1985) 27–46.

Kistemaker, Simon J. "The Temple in the Apocalypse." *JETS* 43 (2000) 433–41.

Kittel, Bonnie P. *The Hymns of Qumran: Translation and Commentary*. SBLDS 22. Chico, CA: Scholars, 1981.

Klawans, Jonathan. *Purity, Sacrifice, and the Temple: Symbolism and Supersessionism in the Study of Ancient Judaism*. Oxford: Oxford University Press, 2006.

Klijn, Albertus F. J. "2 (Syriac Apocalypse of) Baruch." In *OTPA* 615–52.

Knibb, Michael A. "Eschatology and Messianism in the Dead Sea Scrolls." In *The Dead Sea Scrolls after Fifty Years: A Comprehensive Assessment*, edited by Peter W. Flint and James C. VanderKam, 2:379–402. Leiden: Brill, 1999.

———. *Essays on the Book of Enoch and Other Early Jewish Texts and Traditions.* Leiden: Brill, 2009.

———. "Temple and Cult in Apocryphal and Pseudepigraphal Writings from Before the Common Era." In *Temple and Worship in Biblical Israel*, edited by John Day, 401–16. LHBOTS 422. London: T. & T. Clark, 2005.

Koch, Klaus. "What is Apocalyptic? An Attempt at a Preliminary Definition." In *Visionaries and Their Apocalypses*, edited by Paul D. Hanson, 16–36. IRT 4. Philadelphia: Fortress, 1983.

Koester, Craig R. *Revelation: A New Translation with Introduction and Commentary.* AB 38A. New Haven, CT: Yale University Press, 2014.

Kolenkow, Anita. "An Introduction to II Bar. 53, 56–74: Structure and Substance." PhD diss., Harvard University, 1971.

Köstenberger, Andreas. "John." In *Commentary on the New Testament Use of the Old Testament*, edited by Gregory K. Beale and Donald A. Carson, 415–512. Grand Rapids: Baker Academic, 2007.

———. "The Use of Scripture in the Pastoral and General Epistles and the Book of Revelation." In *Hearing the Old Testament in the New Testament*, edited by Stanley E. Porter, 230–54. Grand Rapids: Eerdmans, 2006.

Kraft, Heinrich. *Die Offenbarung des Johannes.* HNT 16a. Tübingen: Mohr Seibeck, 1974.

Kristeva, Julia. *Desire in Language: A Semiotic Approach to Literature and Art.* Edited by Leon S. Roudiez. Translated by Thomas Gora, et al. New York: Columbia University Press, 1980.

Krodel, Gerhard A. *Revelation.* ACNT. Minneapolis: Augsburg, 1989.

Kurfess, Alfons. "Oracula Sibyllina I/II." *ZNW* 40 (1941) 151–65.

Kutsko, John F. *Between Heaven and Earth: Divine Presence and Absence in the Book of Ezekiel.* Winona Lake, IN: Eisenbrauns, 2000.

Kvanig, Helge S. "The Son of Man in the Parables of Enoch." In *Enoch and the Messiah Son of Man: Revisiting the Book of Parables*, edited by Gabriele Boccaccini, 179–215. Grand Rapids: Eerdmans, 2007.

Lancellottie, Angelo. "L'Antico Testmanto nell'Apocallise." *RivB* 14 (1966) 369–84.

LaSor, William Sanford. *The Dead Sea Scrolls and the New Testament.* Grand Rapids: Eerdmans, 1972.

Lee, Pilchan. *The New Jerusalem in the Book of Revelation: A Study of Revelation 21–22 in the Light of Its Background in Jewish Tradition.* WUNT 2R. Tübingen: Mohr Siebeck, 2001.

Leonard, Jeffery. "Identifying Inner-Biblical Allusions: Psalm 78 as a Test Case." *JBL* 127 (2008) 241–65.

Levenson, Jon Douglas. "The Bible: Unexamined Commitments of Criticism." *FT* 30 (1993) 24–33

———. "The Jerusalem Temple in Devotional and Visionary Experience." In *Jewish Spirituality: From the Bible through the Middle Ages*, edited by Arthur Green, 32–61. WS 13. New York: Crossroad, 1986.

———. *Theology of the Program of Restoration.* Missoula, MT: Scholars, 1976.

Levey, Samson H. "Date of Targum Jonathan to the Prophets." *VT* 21 (1971) 186–96.

———. *The Targum of Ezekiel: Translated with a Critical Introduction, Apparatus, and Notes.* Wilmington, DE: Glazier, 1987.

———. "The Targum to Ezekiel." *HUCA* 46 (1975) 139–58.

Levine, Lee I. *Jerusalem: Portrait of the City in the Second Temple Period (538 BCE–70 CE).* Philadelphia: Jewish Publication Society of America, 2002.

———. "Josephus' Description of the Jerusalem Temple." In *Josephus and the History of the Greco-Roman Period: Essays in Memory of Morton Smith,* edited by Fausto Parente and Joseph Sievers, 233–46. StPB 41. Leiden: Brill, 1994.

Lilly, Ingrid E. "Textual Parallels between Ezekiel and the War Scroll." Paper presented at Society of Biblical Literature Annual Meeting. Atlanta, GA, November 2015.

Liss, Hanna. "'Describe the Temple to the House of Israel': Preliminary Remarks on the Temple Vision in the Book of Ezekiel and the Question of Fictionality in Priestly Literatures." In *Utopia and Dystopia in Prophetic Texts,* edited by Ehud Ben Zvi and Michael Floyd, 122–43. Helsinki: Finnish Exegetical Society/University of Helsinki, 2006.

Longenecker, Richard. *Biblical Exegesis in the Apostolic Period.* 2nd ed. Grand Rapids: Eerdmans, 1999.

Lundquist, John M. "The Common Temple Ideology of the Ancient Near East." In *The Temple in Antiquity: Ancient Records and Modern Perspectives,* edited by Truman G. Madsen, 53–76. RSMS 9. Salt Lake City: Bookcraft, 1984.

———. "Temple, Covenant, and Law in the Ancient Near East and in the Old Testament." In *Israel's Apostasy and Restoration,* edited by Avraham Gileadi, 293–305. Grand Rapids: Baker, 1988.

———. "What Is a Temple? A Preliminary Typology." In *The Quest for the Kingdom of God: Studies in Honor of George E. Mendenhall,* edited by H. B. Huffman, et al., 205–19. Winona Lake, IN: Eisenbrauns, 1983.

Lust, Johan. "Ezekiel 36–40 in the Oldest Greek Manuscript." *CBQ* 43 (1981) 517–33.

———. "The Order of Final Events in Revelation and in Ezekiel." In *L'Apocalypse Johannique et L'Apocalyptique dans le Noveau Testament,* edited by Jan Lambrecht, 179–83. BETL 53. Leuven: Leuven University Press, 1980.

Maier, Johann. "The Architectural History of the Temple in Jerusalem in the Light of the Temple Scroll." In *Temple Scroll Studies,* edited by George J. Brooke, 23–62. Sheffield, UK: Sheffield Academic, 1985.

Manning, Gary T., Jr. *Echoes of a Prophet: The Use of Ezekiel in the Gospel of John and in Literature of the Second Temple Period.* LNTS. London: T. & T. Clark, 2004.

Mansoor, Menahem. *The Dead Sea Scrolls.* Grand Rapids: Baker, 1983.

———. *The Thanksgiving Hymns: Translated and Annotated with an Introduction.* STDJ 3. Grand Rapids: Eerdmans, 1961.

Marshall, I. Howard. "Church and Temple in the New Testament." *TynBul* 40 (1989) 203–22.

Martínez, F. García. "The Apocalyptic Interpretation of Ezekiel in the Dead Sea Scrolls." In *Interpreting Translation: Studies on the LXX and Ezekiel in Honour of Johan Lust,* edited by F. García Martínez and M. Vervenne, 163–76. Leuven: Leuven University Press, 2005.

Mathewson, David. "Assessing Old Testament Allusions in the Book of Revelation." *EvQ* 75 (2003) 311–26.

———. "The Destiny of the Nations in Revelation 21:1—22:5." *TynBul* 53 (2002) 121–42.

———. *A New Heaven and a New Earth: The Meaning and Function of the Old Testament in Revelation 21.1—22.5.* JSNTSupp 238. Sheffield, UK: Sheffield Academic, 2003.

———. "A Note on the Foundation Stones in Revelation 21.14, 19–20." *JSNT* 25 (2003) 487–98.

———. "A Re-examination of the Millennium in Rev 20:1–6: Consummation and Recapitulation." *JETS* 44 (2001) 237–51.

———. *Revelation: A Handbook on the Greek Text.* Waco, TX: Baylor University Press, 2016.

———. "Revelation in Recent Genre Criticism: Some Implications for Interpretation." *TJ* 13 (1992) 193–213.

Maunder, Annie S. D. "The Date and Place of Writing of the Slavonic Book of Enoch." *The Observatory* 41 (1918) 309–16.

McCaffrey, James. *The House with Many Rooms: The Temple Theme of Jn. 14:2–3.* AnBib 114. Rome: Pontifical Biblical Institute, 1988.

McCall, Robin C. "The Body and Being of God in Ezekiel." *RevExp* 111 (2014) 376–89.

McKelvey, R. J. *The New Temple: The Church in the New Testament.* Oxford: Oxford University Press, 1969.

McNicol, Allan J. "Eschatological Temple in the Qumran Pesher of 4QFlorilegium 1:1–7." *OJRS* 5 (1977) 133–41.

Mealy, J. Webb. *After the Thousand Years: Resurrection and Judgment in Revelation 20.* JSNTSupp 70. Sheffield, UK: JSOT Press, 1992.

Metzger, Bruce. "The Fourth Book of Ezra." In *OTPA* 517–59.

———. *An Introduction to the Apocrypha.* New York: Oxford University Press, 1957.

———. *A Textual Commentary on the Greek New Testament.* 2nd ed. Stuttgart: United Bible Societies, 1994.

Meyers, Carol L. "Temple, Jerusalem." In *Anchor Bible Dictionary*, edited by David Noel Freedman, 6:350–69. 6 vols. New York: Doubleday.

Michel, Otto. "οἶκος." In *TDNT* 5:119–31.

Mickelson, A. Berkeley. *Interpreting the Bible.* Grand Rapids: Eerdmans, 1963.

Milgrom, Jacob. "New Temple Festivals in the Temple Scroll." In *The Temple in Antiquity: Ancient Records and Modern Perspectives*, edited by Truman G. Madsen, 125–34. RSMS 9. Salt Lake City: Bookcraft, 1984.

Milgrom, Jacob, and Daniel I. Block. *Ezekiel's Hope: A Commentary on Ezekiel 38–48.* Eugene, OR: Cascade, 2012.

Milik, Józef Tadeusz. *The Books of Enoch: Aramaic Fragments from Qumran Cave 4.* Oxford: Clarendon, 1976.

Miller, Geoffrey D. "Intertextuality in Old Testament Research." *CBR* 9 (2010) 283–309.

Moore, Carey A. *Tobit: A New Translation and Commentary.* AB 40A. New York: Doubleday, 1996.

Morris, Leon. *The Book of Revelation: An Introduction and Commentary.* TNTC 20. Grand Rapids: Eerdmans, 1987.

Moule, Charles F. D. *The Birth of the New Testament.* New York: Harper & Row, 1962.

Mounce, Robert H. *The Book of Revelation.* Rev. ed. Grand Rapids: Eerdmans, 1998.

Moyise, Steve. "Does the Author of Revelation Misappropriate the Scriptures?" *AUSS* 40 (2002) 3–21.

———. "Ezekiel and the Book of Revelation." In *After Ezekiel: Essays on the Reception of a Difficult Prophet*, edited by Paul M. Joyce and Andrew Mein, 45–57. LHBOTS 535. New York: T. & T. Clark, 2011.

———. "Intertextuality and the Book of Revelation." *ExpTim* 104 (1993) 295–98.

———. "Intertextuality and the Use of Scripture in the Book of Revelation?" *Scriptura* 84 (2003) 391–401.

———. *Jesus and Scripture: Studying the New Testament Use of the Old Testament.* Grand Rapids: Baker Academic, 2011.

———. "The Language of the Old Testament in the Apocalypse." *JSNT* 76 (1999) 97–113.

———. *The Later New Testament Writings and Scripture: The Old Testament in Acts, Hebrews, the Catholic Epistles and Revelation.* Grand Rapids: Baker Academic, 2012.

———. *The Old Testament in the Book of Revelation.* JSNTSup 115. Sheffield, UK: T. & T. Clark, 1995.

———. *The Old Testament in the New: An Introduction.* London: Continuum, 2001.

Moyise, Steve, and B. J. Oropeza, eds. *Exploring Intertextuality: Diverse Strategies for New Testament Interpretation of Texts.* Eugene, OR: Cascade, 2016.

Mueller, James R. *The Five Fragments of the Apocryphon of Ezekiel: A Critical Study.* JSPSupp 5. Sheffield, UK: Sheffield Academic, 1994.

Murphy, Frederick James. *Pseudo-Philo: Rewriting the Bible.* New York: Oxford University Press, 1993.

———. "Retelling the Bible: Idolatry in Pseudo-Philo." *JBL* 107 (1988) 275–87.

———. *The Structure and Meaning of Second Baruch.* Atlanta: Scholars, 1985.

———. "The Temple in the *Syriac Apocalypse* of Baruch." *JBL* 106 (1987) 671–83.

Neusner, Jacob. *A History of the Mishnaic Law of Holy Things.* 6 vols. SJLA. Leiden: Brill, 1980.

———. *The Mishnah: A New Translation.* New Haven, CT: Yale University Press, 1988.

———. *The Mishnah: Introduction and Reader.* Philadelphia: Trinity Press International, 1992.

———. *The Mishnah: Religious Perspectives.* Leiden: Brill, 1999.

———. *The Talmud of Babylonia, An American Translation: Tractate Sukkah.* BJS 74. Chico, CA: Scholars, 1984.

———. *The Talmud of Babylonia, An American Translation: Yoma Chapters Six through Eight.* BJS 296. Atlanta: Scholars, 1994.

———. *Transformations in Ancient Judaism: Textual Evidence for Creative Responses to Crisis.* Peabody, MA: Hendrickson, 2004.

Newsom, Carol. "Merkabah Exegesis in the Qumran Sabbath Shirot." *JJS* 38 (1987) 11–30.

———. *Songs of the Sabbath Sacrifice: A Critical Edition.* HSS 27. Atlanta: Scholars, 1985.

Newsom, Carol, and Yigael Yadin. "The Masada Fragment of the Qumran Songs of the Sabbath Sacrifice." *IEJ* 34 (1984) 77–88.

Nibley, Hugh W. "What Is a Temple?" In *The Temple in Antiquity: Ancient Records and Modern Perspectives*, edited by Truman G. Madsen, 19–38. RSMS 9. Salt Lake City: Bookcraft, 1984.

Nickelsburg, George W. E. *Ancient Judaism and Christian Origins: Diversity, Continuity, and Transformation.* Minneapolis: Fortress, 2003.

―――. "Enoch, Levi, and Peter: Recipients of Revelation in Upper Galilee." *JBL* 100 (1981) 575–600.

―――. *1 Enoch 1: A Commentary on the Book of Enoch, Chapters 1–36; 81–108.* Hermeneia. Philadelphia: Fortress, 2001.

―――. *Jewish Literature between the Bible and the Mishnah: A Historical and Literary Introduction.* 2nd ed. Minneapolis: Fortress, 2005.

Nickelsburg, George W. E., and James C. VanderKam. *1 Enoch 2: A Commentary on the Book of 1 Enoch, Chapters 37–82.* Hermeneia. Minneapolis: Fortress, 2012.

Niditch, Susan. "Ezekiel 40–48 in a Visionary Context." *CBQ* 48 (1986) 208–24.

Nielsen, Kirsten. "Ezekiel's Visionary Call as Prologue: From Complexity and Changeability to Order and Stability?" *JSOT* 33 (2008) 99–114.

Nir, Rivka. *The Destruction of Jerusalem and the Idea of Redemption in the Syriac Apocalypse of Baruch.* EJL 20. Atlanta: Society of Biblical Literature, 2003.

Nogalski, James D. *Interpreting Prophetic Literature: Historical and Exegetical Tools for Reading the Prophets.* Louisville: Westminster John Knox, 2015.

Nolland, John. "*Sib. Or.* III. 265–94, An Early Maccabean Messianic Oracle." *JTS* 30 (1979) 158–66.

Nurmela, Risto. "The Growth of the Book of Isaiah Illustrated by Allusions in Zechariah." In *Bringing Out the Treasure: Inner Biblical Allusion in Zechariah 9–14*, edited by Michael Floyd and Mark Boda, 245–59. JSOTSupp 370. London: Sheffield Academic, 2003.

Odell, Margaret S. "The City of Hamonah in Ezekiel 39:11–16: The Tumultuous City of Jerusalem." *CBQ* 56 (1994) 479–90.

―――. "'The Wall Is No More': Temple Reform in Ezekiel 43:7–9." In *From the Foundations to the Crenellations: Essays on Temple Building in the Ancient Near East and Hebrew Bible*, edited by Mark J. Boda and Jamie Novotny, 339–56. AOAT. Münster: Ugarit-Verlag, 2010.

Oesterley, William O. E. *An Introduction to the Books of the Apocrypha.* London: Society for Promoting Christian Knowledge, 1935.

O'Hare, Daniel M. *"Have You Seen, Son of Man?": A Study in the Translation and Vorlage of LXX Ezekiel 40–48.* SCS 57. Atlanta: Society of Biblical Literature, 2010.

Orlov, Andrei. "Glorification through Fear in *2 Enoch.*" *JSP* 25 (2016) 171–88.

Orr, Mary. *Intertextuality: Debates and Contexts.* Malden, MA: Blackwell, 2003.

Osborne, Grant R. *Revelation.* BECNT. Grand Rapids: Baker Academic, 2002.

Ozanne, Charles Gordon. "The Language of the Apocalypse." *TynBul* 16 (1965) 3–9.

Packer, James. "Biblical Authority, Hermeneutics, and Inerrancy." In *Jerusalem and Athens: Critical Discussions on the Philosophy and Apologetics of Cornelius Van Til*, edited by E. Robert Geehan, 141–53. Philadelphia: Presbyterian and Reformed, 1971.

Palmer, Erin. "Imagining Space in Revelation: The Heavenly Throne Room and New Jerusalem." *JTAK* 39 (2015) 35–47.

Parker, Jim. *The War Scroll: Genre and Origin.* Mountain Home, AR: BorderStone, 2012.

Parrot, André. *Babylon and the Old Testament.* SBA 8. London: SCM, 1958.

Parunak, H. Van Dyke. "The Literary Architecture of Ezekiel's *Mar' ôt ' Ělōhîm.*" *JBL* 99 (1980) 61–74.

Patai, Raphael. *Man and Temple in Ancient Jewish Myth and Ritual.* London: Thomas Nelson, 1947.

Patterson, Paige. *Revelation.* NAC 39. Nashville: B & H, 2012.

Patton, Corrine L. "Ezekiel's Blueprint for the Temple of Jerusalem." PhD diss., Yale University, 1991.

Paulien, Jon. "The Book of Revelation and the Old Testament." *BR* 43 (1998) 61–69.

———. *Decoding Revelation's Trumpets: Literary Allusions and the Interpretation of Revelation 8:7–12.* AUSDDS. Berrien Springs, MI: Andrews University Press, 1987.

———. "Elusive Allusions: The Problematic Use of the Old Testament in Revelation." *BR* 33 (1988) 37–53.

Peterson, Brian Neil. *Ezekiel in Context: Ezekiel's Message Understood in Its Historical Setting of Covenant Curses and Ancient Near Eastern Mythological Motifs.* Eugene, OR: Pickwick, 2012.

Pfeiffer, Robert H. *History of New Testament Times: With an Introdution to the Apocrypha.* New York: Harper, 1949.

———. *Introduction to the Old Testament.* New York: Harper, 1941.

Pfisterer Darr, Katheryn. "The Wall around Paradise." *VT* 37 (1987) 271–79.

Porter, Stanley E. "Allusions and Echoes." In *As It Is Written: Studying Paul's Use of Scripture*, edited by Stanley E. Porter and Christopher D. Stanley, 29–40. Atlanta: SBL, 2008.

———. "Further Comments on the Use of the Old Testament in the New Testament." in *The Intertextuality of the Epistles: Explorations of Theory and Practice*, edited by Thomas L. Brodie et al., 98–110. Sheffield, UK: Sheffield Phoenix, 2006.

———. *Hearing the Old Testament in the New Testament.* Grand Rapids: Eerdmans, 2006.

———. "Introduction: The Use of the Old Testament in the New Testament." In *Hearing the Old Testament in the New Testament*, edited by Stanley E. Porter, 1–8. Grand Rapids: Eerdmans, 2006.

———. *Sacred Tradition in the New Testament: Tracing Old Testament Themes in the Gospels and Epistles.* Grand Rapids: Baker Academic, 2016.

———. "The Use of the Old Testament in the New Testament: A Brief Comment on Method and Terminology." In *Early Christian Interpretation of the Scripture of Israel: Investigations and Proposals*, edited by Craig A. Evans and James A. Sanders, 79–96. JSNTSupp 148. Sheffield, UK: Sheffield Academic, 1997.

Postell, Seth D. *Adam as Israel: Genesis 1–3 as the Introduction to the Torah and Tanakh.* Eugene, OR: Wipf & Stock, 2011.

Presser, Nicolás. "La Escatología Apocalíptica de Ezequiel en la Revelación de Juan." *DavarLogos* 12 (2013) 129–46.

Price, Randall. *The Temple and Bible Prophecy.* Eugene, OR: Harvest House, 2005.

Pritchard, James B. *Ancient Near Eastern Texts Relating to the Old Testament.* 3rd ed. Princeton: Princeton University Press, 1969.

von Rad, Gerhard. *The Message of the Prophets.* Translated by D. M. G. Stalker. New York: Harper & Row, 1972.

———. *Old Testament Theology.* Translated by D. M. G. Stalker. New York: Harper & Row, 1965.

Rahlfs, Alfred, and Robert Hanhart, eds. *Septuaginta: SESB Edition.* Stuttgart: Deutsche Bibelgesellschaft, 2006.

du Rand, Jan. "The New Jerusalem as Pinnacle of Salvation: Text (Rev 21:1—22:5) and Intertext." *Neot* 38 (2004) 275–302.

Reader, William W. "The Twelve Jewels of Revelation 21:19–20: Tradition History and Modern Interpretations." *JBL* 100 (1981) 433–57.

Rissi, Mathias. *The Future of the World: An Exegetical Study of Revelation 19.11–22.15.* SBT 23. London: SCM, 1972.

Robbins, Vernon K. *The Tapestry of Early Christian Discourse: Rhetoric, Society and Ideology.* London: Routledge, 1996.

Roberts, Jimmy J. M. "The Hand of Yahweh." *VT* 21 (1971) 244–51.

Rofé, Alexander. *Introduction to Prophetic Literature.* Translated by Judith H. Seeligmann. Sheffield, UK: Sheffield Academic, 1997.

Rooker, Mark F. "Evidence from Ezekiel." In *The Coming Millennial Kingdom: A Case for Premillennial Interpretation,* edited by Donald K. Campbell and Jeffrey L. Townsend, 119–34. Grand Rapids: Kregel, 1997.

———. *Ezekiel.* Nashville: Holman Reference, 2005.

Rosenau, William. "Harel und Ha-Ariel; Ezechiel 43:15–16." *MGWJ* 65 (1921) 350–56.

Rowland, Christopher. *The Open Heaven: A Study of Apocalyptic in Judaism and Early Christianity.* New York: Crossroad, 1982.

———. "The Temple in the New Testament." In *Temple and Worship in Biblical Israel,* edited by John Day, 469–83. LHBOTS 422. London: T. & T. Clark, 2005.

Royalty, Robert. *The Streets of Heaven: The Ideology of Wealth in the Apocalypse of John.* Macon, GA: Mercer University Press, 1998.

Rubinkiewicz, Ryszard. "Apocalypse of Abraham." In *OTPA* 681–705.

Ruiz, Jean-Pierre. *Ezekiel in the Apocalypse: The Transformation of Prophetic Language in Revelation 16,17–19,10.* Frankfurt am Main: Peter Lang, 1989.

Sacchi, Paolo. *Jewish Apocalyptic and Its History.* JSPSupp 20. Sheffield, UK: Sheffield Academic, 1990.

Sanders, Ed P. *Judaism: Practice and Belief, 63 BCE–66 CE.* London: SCM, 1992.

Sandmel, Samuel. "Parallelomania." *JBL* 81 (1962) 1–13.

Saussure, Ferdinand. *Course in General Linguistics.* Edited by Charles Bally and Albert Sechehaye. Translated by Wade Baskin. New York: Philosophical Library, 1959.

Sawyer, John F. A. "Ezekiel in the History of Christianity." In *After Ezekiel: Essays on the Reception of a Difficult Prophet,* edited by Paul M. Joyce and Andrew Mein, 1–9. LHBOTS. New York: T. & T. Clark, 2011.

Schiffman, Lawrence H. *Qumran and Jerusalem: Studies in the Dead Sea Scrolls and the History of Judaism.* Grand Rapids: Eerdmans, 2010.

———. *Sectarian Law in the Dead Sea Scrolls: Courts, Testimony, and the Penal Code.* BJS 33. Chico, CA: Scholars, 1983.

———. "The Temple Scroll between the Bible and the Mishnah." Paper presented at Society of Biblical Literature International Meeting. St. Andrews, Scotland, July 2013.

———. "The Theology of the Temple Scroll." *JQR* 85 (1994) 109–23.

Schlatter, Adolf. *Alte Testament in der johanneischen Apokalypse.* BFCT 6. Gütersloh, Germany: Bertelsmann, 1912.

Schneider, J. "ξύλον." In *TDNT* 5:37–41.

Scholem, Gershom G. *Major Trends in Jewish Mysticism.* New York: Schocken, 1941.

Schuller, Eileen. "A Hymn from a Cave Four *Hodayot* Manuscript: 4Q427 7 i+ii." *JBL* 112 (1993) 605–28.

———. "Some Contributions of the Cave Four Manuscripts (4Q427–432) to the Study of the *Hodayot*." *DSD* 8 (2001) 278–87.

Schüssler Fiorenza, Elizabeth. *The Book of Revelation: Justice and Judgment.* Minneapolis: Fortress, 1998.

———. "Cultic Language in Qumran and in the NT." *CBQ* 38 (1976) 159–77.

———. *Revelation: Vision of a Just World.* Minneapolis: Fortress, 1991.

Schwartz, Daniel R. "The Three Temples of 4QFlorilegium." *RQ* 10 (1979) 83–91.

Scofield, Cyrus I., ed. *The Scofield Reference Bible: Holy Bible: Authorized King James Version with Introduction, Annotations, Subject Chain References and Such Word Changes in the Text as Will Help the Reader.* New York: Oxford University Press, 1967.

Silva, Moisés. *Biblical Words and Their Meaning: An Introduction to Lexical Semantics.* Rev. ed. Grand Rapids: Zondervan, 1983.

Sim, Unyong. *Das himmlische Jerusalem in Apk 21,1–22,5 im Kontext biblischjüdischer Tradition und antiken Städtebaus.* BAC 25. Trier, Germany: Wissenschaftlicher Verlag, 1996.

Simon, Bennett. "Ezekiel's Geometric Vision of the Restored Temple: From the Rod of His Wrath to the Reed of His Measuring." *HTR* 102 (2009) 411–38.

Slingerland, H. Dixon. *The Testaments of the Twelve Patriarchs: A Critical History of Research.* SBLMS 21. Missoula, MT: Scholars, 1977.

Smalley, Stephen S. *The Revelation to John: A Commentary on the Greek Text of the Apocalypse.* Downers Grove, IL: InterVarsity, 2005.

Smend, Rudolf. *Der Prophet Ezechiel.* Leipzig: Hirzel, 1880.

Smith, Mark S. "Like Deities, Like Temples (Like People)." In *Temple and Worship in Biblical Israel*, edited by John Day, 3–27. LHBOTS 422. London: T. & T. Clark, 2005.

Sommer, Benjamin D. *A Prophet Reads Scripture: Allusion in Isaiah 40–66.* Contraversions. Stanford, CA: Stanford University Press, 1998.

Son, HaYoung. "The Background of Exodus 15 in Revelation 15: Focusing on the Song of Moses and the Song of the Lamb." PhD diss., New Orleans Baptist Theological Seminary, 2015.

Spatafora, Andrea. *From the "Temple of God" to God as the Temple: A Biblical Theological Study of the Temple in the Book of Revelation.* TGST 27. Rome: Editrice Pontificia Università Gregoriana, 1997.

Stegemann, Hartmut. *The Library of Qumran: On the Essenes, Qumran, John the Baptist, and Jesus.* Grand Rapids: Eerdmans, 1998.

———. "Some Remarks to 1QSa, to 1QSb, and to Qumran Messianism." *RQ* 17 (1996) 479–505.

Stein, Robert H. *Jesus, the Temple and the Coming Son of Man: A Commentary on Mark 13.* Downers Grove, IL: IVP Academic, 2014.

Stendahl, Krister. "Biblical Theology, Contemporary." In *IDB* 1:418–32.

Steudel, Annette. "The Eternal Reign of the People of God—Collective Expectations in Qumran Texts (4Q246 and 1QM)." *RQ* 17 (1996) 507–25.

Stevens, Gerald L. *Revelation: The Past and Future of John's Apocalypse.* Eugene, OR: Pickwick, 2014.

Stevenson, Kalinda Rose. *The Vision of Transformation: The Territorial Rhetoric of Ezekiel 40–48.* Atlanta: Scholars, 1996.

Stone, Michael Edward. "Ancient *Testimonia* to the Existence of an Ezekiel Apocryphon." In *the Apocryphal Ezekiel*, edited by Michael Edward Stone et al., 7–9. EJL 18. Atlanta: Society of Biblical Literature, 2000.

———. "Apocalyptic Literature." In *Jewish Writings of the Second Temple Period*, edited by Michael Edward Stone, 383–41. CRINT 2.2. Assen, the Netherlands: Van Gorcum, 1984.

———. *Features of the Eschatology of IV Ezra*. HSM 35. Atlanta: Scholars, 1989.

———. *Fourth Ezra*. Hermeneia. Minneapolis: Fortress, 1990.

Stone, Michael Edward, ed. *Jewish Writings of the Second Temple Period: Apocrypha, Pseudepigrapha, Qumran Sectarian Writings, Philo, Josephus*. Philadelphia: Fortress, 1984.

Stone, Michael Edward, et al., eds. *The Apocryphal Ezekiel*. EJL 18. Atlanta: Society of Biblical Literature, 2000.

Strine, Casey A., and Carly L. Crouch. "YHWH's Battle against Chaos in Ezekiel: The Transformation of Judahite Mythology for a New Situation." *JBL* 132 (2013) 883–903.

Strugnell, John, and Devorah Dimant. "4Q Second Ezekiel." *RQ* 13 (1988) 45–58.

Stuart, Moses. *Commentary on the Apocalypse*. Andover, MA: Allen, 1845.

Suter, David Winston. *Tradition and Composition in the Parables of Enoch*. SBLDS 47. Missoula, MT: Scholars, 1979.

———. "Weighed in the Balance: The Similitudes of Enoch in Recent Discussion." *RelSRev* 7 (1981) 217–21.

Sweeney, Marvin A. "The Problem of Ezekiel in Talmudic Literature." In *After Ezekiel: Essays on the Reception of a Difficult Prophet*, edited by Paul M. Joyce and Andrew Mein, 11–23. LHBOTS. New York: T. & T. Clark, 2011.

———. *The Prophetic Literature*. Nashville: Abingdon, 2005.

Sweet, John P. M. *Revelation*. WPS. Philadelphia: Westminster, 1979.

Swete, Henry Barclay. *The Apocalypse of St. John: The Greek Text with Introduction Notes and Indices*. 2nd ed. London: Macmillan, 1907.

Talmon, Shemaryahu, and Michael Fishbane. "The Structuring of Biblical Books: Studies in the Book of Ezekiel." *ASTI* 10 (1976) 129–53.

Tanner, J. Paul. "Rethinking Ezekiel's Invasion by Gog." *JETS* 39 (1996) 29–45.

Taylor, John B. *Ezekiel: An Introduction and Commentary*. Downers Grove, IL: Inter-Varsity, 1969.

Thomas, John Christopher, and Frank D. Macchia. *Revelation*. THNTC. Grand Rapids: Eerdmans, 2016.

Tigchelaar, Eibert. *Prophets of Old and the Day of the End: Zechariah, the Book of Watchers and Apocalyptic*. Leiden: Brill, 1996.

Tiller, Patrick A. *A Commentary on the Animal Apocalyse of 1 Enoch*. EJL 4. Atlanta: Scholars, 1993.

Tov, Emanuel. *The Septuagint Translation of Jeremiah and Baruch: A Discussion of an Early Revision of the LXX Jeremiah 29–52 and Baruch 1:1–3:8*. Missoula, MT: Scholars, 1976.

Trudinger, L. Paul. "Some Observations Concerning the Text of the Old Testament in the Book of Revelation." *JTS* 17 (1966) 82–88.

Tuell, Steven Shawn. "Divine Presence and Absence in Ezekiel's Prophecy." In *The Book of Ezekiel: Theological and Anthropological Perspectives*, edited by Margaret S. Odell and John T. Strong, 97–116. Atlanta: Society of Biblical Literature, 2000.

———. *Ezekiel*. Grand Rapids: Baker, 2008.

———. "Ezekiel 40–42 as Verbal Icon." *CBQ* 58 (1996) 649–64.

———. *The Law of the Temple in Ezekiel 40–48*. HSM 49. Atlanta: Scholars, 1992.

———. "Should Ezekiel Go to Rehab? The Method to Ezekiel's 'Madness.'" *PRSt* 36 (2009) 289–302.

———. "The Temple Vision of Ezekiel 40–48: A Program for Restoration?" *Proceedings* 2 (1982) 96–103.

Unger, Merrill F. "Ezekiel's Vision of Israel's Restoration (1)." *BSac* 106 (1949) 312–24.

———. "Ezekiel's Vision of Israel's Restoration (2)." *BSac* 106 (1949) 432–45.

———. "Ezekiel's Vision of Israel's Restoration (3)." *BSac* 107 (1950) 51–63.

———. *Great Neglected Bible Prophecies.* Chicago: Scripture, 1955.

———. "The Temple Vision of Ezekiel (1)." *BSac* 105 (1948) 418–32.

———. "The Temple Vision of Ezekiel (2)." *BSac* 106 (1949) 48–64.

———. "The Temple Vision of Ezekiel (3)." *BSac* 106 (1949) 169–77.

———. *Unger's Commentary on the Old Testament.* Chicago: Moody, 1981.

VanderKam, James C. "Biblical Interpretation in *1 Enoch* and *Jubilees.*" In *The Pseudepigrapha and Early Biblical Interpretation,* edited by James H. Charlesworth and Craig A. Evans, 96–125. JSPSupp 14. Sheffield, UK: Sheffield Academic, 1993.

———. *The Book of Jubilees.* Sheffield, UK: Sheffield Academic, 2001.

———. *The Dead Sea Scrolls Today.* Grand Rapids: Eerdmans, 1994.

———. *Enoch and the Growth of an Apocalyptic Tradition.* CBQMS 16. Washington, DC: Catholic Biblical Association of America, 1984.

———. *Textual and Historical Studies in the Book of Jubilees.* HSM 14. Missoula, MT: Scholars, 1977.

VanderKam, James C., and William Adler, eds. *The Jewish Apocalyptic Heritage in Early Christianity.* Assen, the Netherlands: Van Gorcum, 1996.

VanGemeren, William A. *Interpreting the Prophetic Word: An Introduction to the Prophetic Literature of the Old Testament.* Grand Rapids: Zondervan, 1990.

Vanhoye, Albert. "L'utilization du livre d'Ezéchiel dans l'Apocalypse." *Bib* 43 (1962) 436–76.

Vermes, Geza. *The Complete Dead Sea Scrolls in English.* New York: Penguin, 1997.

Vlach, Michael J. "What Does Christ as 'True Israel' Mean for the Nation Israel?: A Critique of the Non-Dispensational Understanding." *MSJ* 23 (2012) 43–54.

Vogelgesang, Jeffrey M. "The Interpretation of Ezekiel in the Book of Revelation." PhD diss., Harvard University, 1985.

Vorster, Willem S. "'Genre' and the Revelation of John: A Study in Text, Context, and Intertext." *Neot* 22 (1988) 103–23.

Wacholder, Ben Zion. *The Dawn of Qumran: The Sectarian Torah and the Teacher of Righteousness.* Cincinnati: Hebrew Union College Press, 1983.

Walck, Leslie W. "The Son of Man in the Parables of Enoch and the Gospels." In *Enoch and the Messiah Son of Man: Revisiting the Book of Parables,* edited by Gabriele Boccaccini, 299–337. Grand Rapids: Eerdmans, 2007.

Waltke, Bruce K. "A Canonical Approach to the Psalms." In *Tradition and Testament: Essays in Honor of Charles Lee Feinberg,* edited by John S. Feinberg and Paul Feinberg, 3–18. Chicago: Moody, 1981.

Walton, John H. *The Lost World of Genesis One: Ancient Cosmology and the Origins Debate.* Downers Grove, IL: InterVarsity, 2009.

Walvoord, John F. *The Millennial Kingdom.* Grand Rapids: Durham, 1959.

———. "The Millennial Kingdom and the Eternal State." *BSac* 123 (1966) 291–300.

Weir, Jack. "Analogous Fulfillment: The Use of the Old Testament in the New Testament." *PRSt* 9 (1982) 65–76.

West, Nathaniel. *The Thousand Years in Both Testaments*. New York: Revell, 1880.

Wevers, John W. *Ezekiel*. Grand Rapids: Eerdmans, 1976.

Wintermute, Orval S. "Jubilees." In *OTPE* 35–142.

Wise, Michael O. "*4QFlorilegium* and the Temple of Adam." *RQ* 15 (1991) 103–32.

———. "The Temple Scroll: Its Composition, Date, Purpose and Provenance." PhD diss., University of Chicago, 1988.

Wise, Michael O., et al. *The Dead Sea Scrolls: A New Translation*. San Francisco: HarperSanFrancisco, 2005.

Witherington, Ben, III. *Revelation*. Cambridge: Cambridge University Press, 2003.

Wolff, Hans Walter. "The Hermeneutics of the Old Testament." In *Essays on Old Testament Hermeneutics*, edited by Claus Westermann, 169–99. Richmond, VA: John Knox, 1963.

Xeravits, Géza, and Józef Zsengellér, eds. *The Book of Tobit: Text, Tradition, Theology*. JSJSupp 98. Leiden: Brill, 2005.

Yadin, Yigael. *The Scroll of the War of the Sons of Light against the Sons of Darkness: Edited with an Introduction, Emendations and a Commentary*. Jerusalem: Bialik Institute, 1957.

———. *The Temple Scroll*. 3 vols. Jerusalem: Israel Exploration Society, 1983.

Yoon, David I. "The Ideological Inception of Intertextuality and Its Dissonance in Current Biblical Studies." *CBR* (2012) 58–76.

Zimmer, Robert G. "The Temple of God." *JETS* 18 (1975) 41–46.

Zimmerli, Walther. *Ezekiel 1: A Commentary on the Book of the Prophet Ezekiel, Chapters 1–24*. Hermeneia. Philadelphia: Fortress, 1979.

———. *Ezekiel 2: A Commentary on the Book of the Prophet Ezekiel, Chapters 25–48*. Hermeneia. Philadelphia: Fortress, 1983.

———. *I Am Yahweh*. Translated by Douglas W. Stott. Atlanta: John Knox, 1982.

———. "The Message of the Prophet Ezekiel." *Int* 23 (1969) 131–57.

———. "Planungen für die Wiederaufbau nach der Katastrophe von 587." *VT* 18 (1968) 229–55.

Made in United States
North Haven, CT
26 November 2021

11517944R00128